THE GREAT AMERICAN
Baby Almanac

THE GREAT AMERICAN
Baby Almanac

IRENA CHALMERS
and Friends

An Irena Chalmers Book

VIKING
STUDIO
BOOKS

MANAGING EDITOR: Carlotta Kerwin

TEXT EDITOR: Jean Atcheson

ART DIRECTION AND DESIGN: Helene Berinsky

PICTURE EDITOR: Lisa Sorensen

COPY EDITORS: Linda Stern, Nancy Bauer

WRITERS: Richard Atcheson, Laura Bross, Carolyn T. Chubet,
Mary Goodbody, Christine Gross, Ann Hornaday, Pamela Mitchell,
Lisa Napell, L. Edward Purcell

PRODUCT/RESOURCE GUIDE: Hilary Kirshman

ASSISTANT TO THE MANAGING EDITOR: David Chestnut

ASSISTANT TO THE ART DIRECTOR: Barbara Zapatka

RIGHTS AND PERMISSIONS: Nancy Kipper

The author and editors extend their particular appreciation to Michael
Fragnito, Vice President and Editorial Director, Studio Books, and to
Barbara Williams, Editor, Studio Books, at Viking Penguin, Inc. for their
many contributions to the making of this book.

VIKING STUDIO BOOKS
Published by the Penguin Group
Viking Penguin Inc., 40 West 23rd Street,
New York, New York 10010, U.S.A.
Penguin Books Ltd, 27 Wrights Lane,
London W8 5TZ, England
Penguin Books Australia Ltd, Ringwood,
Victoria, Australia
Penguin Books Canada Ltd, 2801 John Street,
Markham, Ontario, Canada L3R 1B4
Penguin Books (N.Z.) Ltd, 182–190 Wairau Road,
Auckland 10, New Zealand

Penguin Books Ltd, Registered Offices:
Harmondsworth, Middlesex, England

First published in 1989 by Viking Penguin Inc.
Published simultaneously in Canada

Copyright © Irena Chalmers, 1989
All rights reserved

Pages 250–251 constitute an extension of this
copyright page.

LIBRARY OF CONGRESS CATALOGING IN PUBLICATION DATA

Chalmers, Irena.
   The great American baby almanac.

   Includes index.
   1. Infants—Care—Popular works.   I. Title.
PJ61.C445   1989   649'.122   88-40393
ISBN 0-670-82058-X

Printed in Singapore

Set in Bauer Bodoni with University Bold

Typeset by Pica Graphics, Monsey, New York

For Hilary and Philip—
and all the babies
we each recall
with love

CONTENTS

INTRODUCTION

———— ✳ ————

The excitement and jubilation and vast sense of relief that greet the arrival of the newborn baby are universal to us all. The act of bringing a new life into being has to be the most profound and also the most exuberant of human experiences. With the passage of time, the memory seems, oddly, to become heightened, rather than diminished, and we are able to conjure up the minutest details of the birth. As we recapture the rapture of that instant, it is as though in our mind's eye we had become isolated in a moment of time.

The delicious pleasures of watching over and caring for our own child are so private that the recounting of them is diminished in the attempt to tell. Only a parent can know so much joy from first looking into the baby's eyes, the first conscious reaching out of the baby to touch the mother, the first laughter, the first steps, the first acknowledgment of father. Though, of course, everyone will say that all babies do all the same things, it is not at all the same when our baby achieves and rapidly passes the next step in his or her unique development.

In our almanac, we have tried to encompass the celebration of having a baby. We have attempted to include everyone: grandfathers and grandmothers, brothers and sisters, the cat, the dog, and the canary. We wanted the book to convey reality, and if in the process we have idealized the baby, that is appropriate, too. This is the time of satisfaction and gladness when you know, with absolute and total assurance, that yours is the most perfect of infants that ever has been.

Our intent is to inform, amuse, and bring you pleasure, whether you are awaiting the birth of your baby or the child you love is already tucked into the crib. We hope that the resource guide at the back of the book will save you some time and energy. We would like our words and pictures to make you smile, just as the discovery and placement of each painting, photograph, illustration, or essay pleased the happy band which has taken such delight in assembling The Great American Baby Almanac.

IRENA CHALMERS

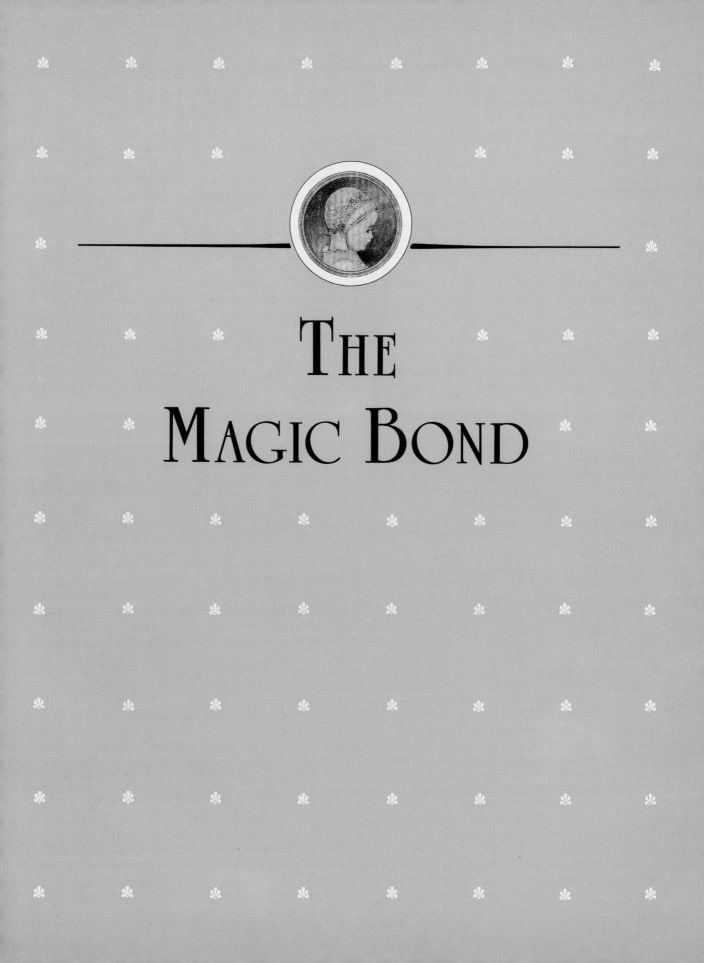

THE
MAGIC BOND

THAT SPECIAL SMILE

———— ❊ ————

When a baby is born, parents experience emotions unlike any others. Nothing is more intense, nothing is more indelible, nothing alters life and personality in quite the same way.

As the wrinkled, wriggling infant emerges into the world, a bond springs up spontaneously. Initially nature's way of providing protection and care for the helpless newborn, a relationship gradually takes shape that will become the most enduring of human ties. People choose and discard mates, but the bond between parent and child is permanent and immutable. Exploring it is the business of life.

Cuddling her sleeping baby close, a mother confirms the deep physical link between parent and child.

Yes, all the potential of humanity is wrapped up in a tiny blanket.

Every Parent Is a Dreamer

The first glimpse of a newborn packs an emotional wallop almost physical in its intensity—a blow to the chest that simultaneously takes away the breath and expands the consciousness.

The baby is no longer an anticipated event—a baby is a *person*.

In a flash, parents see the years unrolling. All the potential of the human race seems tied up in a newborn baby. Hopes and fears well up, and with them an overwhelming sense of responsibility.

All this seems to occur naturally as part of the developing relationship between parent and child. Intense, even frightening, it is only the beginning. As T. Berry Brazelton writes, "bonding *is* instinctive, but it is not instant and automatic."

A Job with Immense Rewards

The first months of the parent-baby relationship often seem to be one-sided, revolving around mind-numbing labor. Dave Barry expresses it well: "Taking care of a newborn baby means devoting yourself, body and soul, twenty-four hours a day, seven days a week, to the welfare of someone whose major response, in the way of positive reinforcement, is to throw up on you."

While the baby learns such elemental functions as successful digestion, parents learn how to relate to this stunning new presence in their lives. It is not always easy, but if it were too hard for most people to bear, the human race would have vanished eons ago.

A complex, two-way communication is soon in place. Parents learn to deal with a range of distressing baby behavior, such as crying through the night for no apparent reason, but they also learn the immense rewards of baby smiles and baby play. This is the give-and-take that forms the basis for the first important personal and social task: developing affection between parents and child.

A baby creates the most ancient and lasting of human groups: a family.

Just swinging in the garden in the sunshine, the new arrival lights up the parents' whole world.

A 1920s MODEL FATHER

"My son takes a despondent view of life. He seldom smiles. But there is no doubt of his ability to register grief, pain, dismay, disappointment, and displeasure. He does it by the hour at the top of his lungs.

"I repeatedly remind my son that after all he is only seven weeks old, and that until he has a wider experience on which to base his opinion, it would be well for him to suspend judgment on the world. I cannot make him understand how enviable is the lot of one who has nothing to do all day but sleep and drink.

"But I suppose the experience is good for me. I am becoming a model father. My training has been arduous. Many a dawn has found me engaged in light practice.

"We become model fathers perforce; we have greatness thrust upon us."

Frederick L. Allen, excerpted from *Harper's*

Perfect understanding.

Babies know just how to get parents to play up.

Learning to Be a Parent

Sometime during the first year, a baby seems to change, as one parent put it, "from a one-man band to a three-ring circus."

By the age of one, babies have ceased to be bundles of physical responses and have developed a strong sense of their own identity. They have learned to distinguish between themselves and the world; they also have an idea how the world (principally their parents) will react to actions and behavior. Everything is more focused. Anger is more intense, but so are expressions of love.

The consequence of this increasing maturity for the relationship between parents and children is to produce more sensitive emotional responses on both sides. The complexity of communication is heightened by the beginnings of speech, at which point babies naturally try to manipulate the world to their own ends. They are now much more than extensions of their parents, and a new phase of the relationship begins.

Experts on child development stress that despite the romantic mythology that surrounds mothering and fathering, learning to be a parent is likely to be a complex process for most people. "Each role is a demanding one," says Brazelton, "and each role requires a kind of dedication for which we have been shaped."

Each role is a demanding one, but one for which we were meant.

As the months pass, expressions of emotion between parents and babies deepen and focus ever more clearly.

Watching and learning, a new relationship evolves as babies grow and mature.

Expanding Horizons

Paradoxically, a bond is never stronger than when it is allowed to loosen.

The bond between parent and child can become complete only when it no longer requires constant, minute-by-minute attention and presence. By the end of a baby's second year, the lifelong process of learning to live as an individual in the context of a family structure is usually well on its way to fulfillment.

As children grow physically toward their second birthdays, they grow also in independence. They have usually mastered speech and know how to manipulate symbols, even to create their own, and they begin to form significant relationships outside the immediate sphere of their parents. This is a period during which they begin to show more fully the developing uniqueness of their own characters. Nurtured by loving parents, they approach the time when they are babies no more.

Yet the magic bond cannot be dissolved. As one close observer says, "The family that a child creates almost never dies."

The long pathway of life beckons (opposite), but the magic bond is unbreakable.

A 1920s MODEL SON

"A little over a year ago I wrote a lament . . . a portrait of a seven-weeks-old son who looked upon the world and found it not to his liking. Thirteen months have passed since then, and justice demands a new report.

"Be it recorded, then, that my son, upon more mature reflection, thinks that things are looking up. Thirteen months ago he could hardly be induced to consume even four ounces of milk and barley water; now his diet is limited only by the size of his mouth.

"Thirteen months ago my son lay on his back and wailed. Now that he is old enough to strut about and see the world more broadly, his attitude has changed. It has become nothing less than boisterous.

"He waddles around the room; flattens his nose against the French windows . . . inspects the appointments of the dining room . . . and waddles out again to the screened porch and his box of playthings, perfectly content.

"For a gentleman of leisure such as he, the day holds a wide variety of entertainment. There is your rattle . . . there are blocks to pick up and drop on the floor . . . and, finally, there is the curved shining bell of an ancient dismembered alarm clock, which you cannot only suck but smite upon the wall.

"But my son knows what is really most amusing. It is to put your head down on the floor, look between your legs, and see your father and mother upside down. . . . The person who can laugh so hard that he loses his balance and falls down is your truly right-minded person."

Frederick L. Allen, excerpted from *Harper's*

LITTLE FOOTNOTES

SALUT!

Philadelphia was the first city to celebrate Mother's Day, on May 10, 1908. In 1914, Congress established the second Sunday in May as Mother's Day and President Woodrow Wilson proclaimed the date a national holiday. It was celebrated throughout the nation for the first time on May 10, 1914.

Father's Day was first observed in Spokane, Washington, on June 19, 1910. Fathers are now honored across the country on the third Sunday in June.

Famous First Facts

"The newborn child should be seen as a 'spiritual embryo'—a spirit enclosed in flesh in order to come into the world."

Maria Montessori

————

"Where did you come from, baby dear?
Out of the everywhere into the here."

George Macdonald, *At the Back of the North Wind*

THE NEW FATHERHOOD

American Baby *magazine recently reported findings of a survey of fathers showing how fatherhood has changed:*

- *80 percent of fathers assisted in the birth in 1984, compared to only 27 percent a decade earlier*
- *35 percent change diapers as often as their wives*
- *81 percent said they are taking a larger role in child care than their fathers did*
- *65 percent said they spend more time with their children than their fathers did*
- *88 percent thought a man should help if the woman works outside the home*

ANOTHER LITTLE PIGGY . . .

"Let us go to the wood," says this pig.
"What to do there?" says that pig.
"To look for my mammy," says this pig.
"What to do with her?" says that pig.
"To kiss her, to kiss her, to kiss her!" says that pig.

WOW!

Even the slightest new accomplishments during a baby's first months can fuel parental pride. One mother recalled for writer Joelle Sander how thrilled she was when her daughter finished her first piece of American cheese by herself. Mom called five friends to tell them the news. "I was convinced it was a miracle," she says.

————

God could not be everywhere and therefore he made mothers.

Jewish proverb

————

"You don't have to deserve your mother's love. You have to deserve your father's. He's more particular."

Robert Frost

"When you're drawing up your list of life's miracles, you might place near the top the first moment your baby smiles at you."

Bob Greene

FAMOUS INFANTS

You Must Have Been a Beautiful Baby

Everyone was somebody's baby, even though with some people one can hardly credit it. All the more fun, then, to look at baby pictures and catch glimpses of the adult enshrined in the yellowing, dog-eared print, to imagine the movie star's smile above that tiny, dimpled chin, the weightlifter's magnificent muscles beneath the profusion of goffered petticoats, the cares of the presidency borne within that downy head. It is a preview of what is to come—from the days when we were all innocents together and the most exciting experience of life was the discovery of our own toes.

Fate would take two-year-old Donna Reed (left) from an Iowa farm to Hollywood stardom. For Franklin Delano Roosevelt (right), a very different path would lead from Hyde Park to the White House.

Engineering 101

When BUCKMINSTER FULLER was given some toothpicks and dried peas to play with as a tot, he promptly fashioned a tetrahedonal octet truss.

Alden Hatch, *Buckminster Fuller At Home in the Universe*

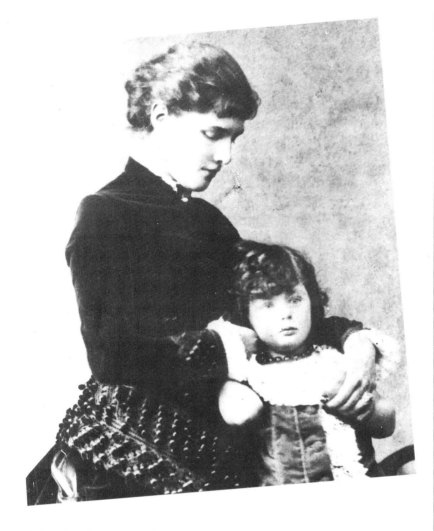

That protective young mother (left) and curly-headed baby are American Jennie Jerome Churchill and her English son, Winston, who would become one of the world's greatest leaders.

Held up for the camera at nine months (below) is a Swedish wonder, Ingrid Bergman, whose touching beauty would later enchant movie audiences the world over.

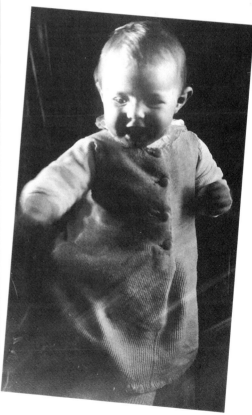

Thanks, Grand-Dad

Upon INDIRA GANDHI's birth the Scottish doctor announced to her grandfather, "It's a bonnie lassie, Sir." "Oh," her grandmother blurted out, "but it should have been a boy!" The old man reportedly snapped back at her, "This daughter of Jawahar, for all you know, may prove better than a thousand sons."

Zareer Majani, *A Biography of Indira Gandhi*

Diva Inspiration

MARIA CALLAS has inspired her share of romantic childhood tales, from her birth—when the doctor reportedly predicted that she would break many hearts—to her late infancy, when we see Maria "crouched under the Pianola, pressing the pedals with her hands and, her little mouth half open, listening ecstatically to the first music she ever made."

Ariana Stassinopoulos, *Maria Callas: The Woman Behind the Legend*

Civil Rites

When their father, a Baptist pastor, enjoined his congregation to pledge their support to the church, MARTIN LUTHER KING, JR.'s sister, Christine, wasted no time in skipping up to the pulpit. Her little brother promptly ran after her to get there first. Thus, his spiritual initiation came not out of "dynamic conviction," he later admitted, but out of "a childhood desire to keep up with my sister."

Stephen B. Oates, *Let the Trumpet Sound: The Life of Martin Luther King, Jr.*

Presages of future movie heroics: His hand protectively on his mother's shoulder, Robert Taylor (above left) strikes a manly pose at the age of two. Standing tall at mother's side, in what looks like a military outfit, is Cesar Romero, aged exactly one year.

"My Father's Such a Bore"

DICK CAVETT's mother kept a series of journals—called "Scribble-In Books"—recording the events of her son's childhood:

"*At four months:* Laughed out loud. Has developed recently a great aptitude for showing off . . . rears out chest and snorts, then awaits laughs. . . . Shows disappointment if the proper appreciation isn't shown.

"*At eighteen months:* Talks in paragraphs rather than sentences. . . . Plays with a Jim Cavett, product of imagination. I hope nothing prophetic. Recites nursery rhymes: 'I am a little boy, not very big/ My father's such a bore, I could have been a pig.'"

Tuli Kupferberg and Sylvia Topp, *First Glance*

Times of the Tenor

PAVAROTTI's mother swears that when Luciano was born the doctor exclaimed, above the boy's screams, "*Mama mia, che acuti!* (What high notes!)."

Luciano Pavarotti with William Wright, *Pavarotti: My Own Story*

"Piz, Piz"

PABLO PICASSO was consumed with "one passion above all others" when he was a baby. "His mother was fond of telling how the first noise he learned to make, 'piz, piz,' was an imperative demand for 'lapiz,' a pencil. For hours he would sit happily drawing spirals, which he managed to explain were a symbol for a kind of sugar cake called 'torruella,' a word formed from a verb which means to bewilder or entangle. He could draw long before he could speak, and many of his first pictures took their ephemeral shape in the sand where the children played in the plaza de la Merced."

Roland Penrose, *Picasso: His Life and Work*

Sing it—loud! A bouncing Martha Raye (left), even in a high chair, catches the onlooker's fancy, just as she would do in her musical-comedy career to come. Looking out from a baby carriage at the beach is Leonard Bernstein (right), whose prodigious musical abilities would bring him fame both as composer and conductor.

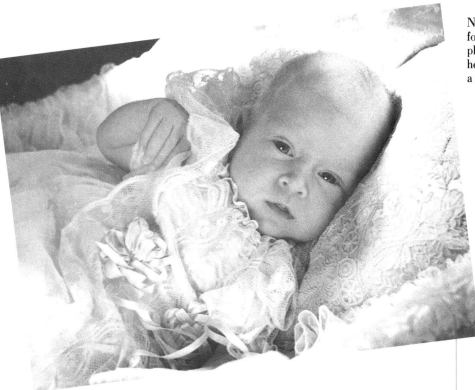

Nestled into a lace-embroidered pillow for the first of many millions of official photographs is Prince Charles (left), heir to the British throne since his birth a few months earlier.

On the Road Again . . . and Again

Wanderlust came naturally to MARGARET MEAD, who estimated that by her teens she had lived in nearly sixty houses and eaten food prepared by 107 cooks. "In a sense," she later recalled, "we were like a family of refugees, always a little at odds with and well in advance of the local customs." Her keen ear was also honed early on: as a toddler, unaware of what she was saying, she would faithfully recite, "My-father-majored-in-economics-and-minored-in-sociology-and-my-mother-majored-in-sociology-and-minored-in-economics."

Jane Howard, *Margaret Mead: A Life*

That's a Blueprint

Even before FRANK LLOYD WRIGHT was born, his mother was determined that he become a great architect. During her pregnancy, she "kept her thoughts on the high things for which she yearned." After her son was born, she hung architectural gravures of old English Cathedrals in his room, and gave him Froebel geometric blocks to play with, which Lloyd Wright would later remark "are in my fingers to this day."

Frank Lloyd Wright, *An Autobiography*; Oligivanna Lloyd Wright, *Frank Lloyd Wright: His Life, His Work, His Words*

Propped against an upholstered armchair, a barefoot Harry Truman (below) faces the camera well before he learned to walk his way out of Independence, Missouri.

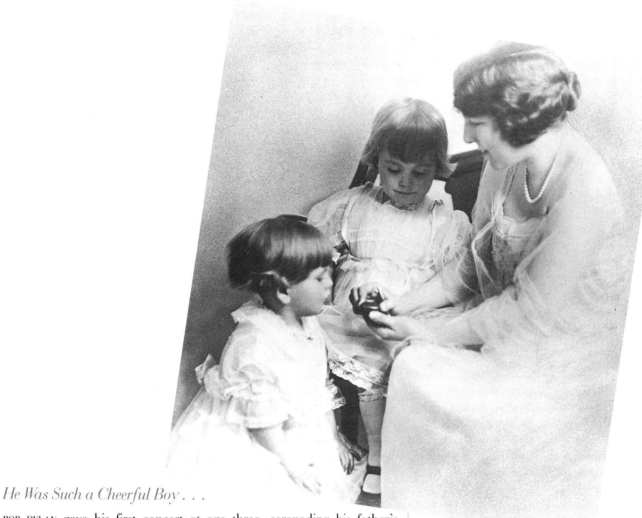

The trio posing here, in the long-ago days when they were still a united family, are Mrs. De Havilland and her two pretty daughters. Four-year-old Olivia (center) would grow up to be a movie star; so would her little sister, though she deliberately chose a different name, Joan Fontaine.

He Was Such a Cheerful Boy . . .

BOB DYLAN gave his first concert at age three, serenading his father's secretaries through an office Dictaphone. Shortly thereafter, he performed at a Mother's Day celebration in Duluth. Bobby Allen Zimmerman, his curly hair in a tousled mop, took the stage and stamped his foot to get the room's attention, opening with "Some Sunday Morning." He encored to thundering applause with "Accentuate the Positive."

Robert Shelton, *No Direction Home*

Guttersnipe

ISAAC ASIMOV started out as a frail child, but "if my body was undersized and weak," he remembers, "my mind didn't seem to be in a bad way." Even as a small child, he would spend hours on the curb, counting cars as they passed. "There weren't very many automobiles then, so that I wasn't forced to strain my counting ability," Asimov writes, "but I've been counting things ever since."

Isaac Asimov, *In Memory Yet Green: The Autobiography of Isaac Asimov*

LITTLE FOOTNOTES

SIR WINSTON CHURCHILL

Once upon a time, a proud new mother reportedly told Churchill that her baby strongly resembled him. "Madam, all babies look like me," the great man replied.

BELA BARTOK

One day, when Baby Bela was a year and a half old, he listened to his mother playing the piano with unusual attention. The next day he led her to the piano and shook his head until she played his favorite.

FREDERICK DOUGLASS

Son of a slave, Douglass was raised by his grandmother and later wrote of his babyhood memories of his mother: "My only recollections of my own mother are of a few hasty visits in the night on foot, after the daily tasks were over . . . these little glimpses, obtained under such circumstances and against such odds, meager as they were, are ineffaceably stamped upon my memory."

KING LOUIS XIV

The Sun King, always renowned for his appetite, was born with two teeth, which wreaked havoc on no fewer than seven wet nurses before doctors found the six-month-old a sturdy peasant woman with sufficient milk and sufficient stamina to become the royal nurse—at a salary of 400 livres a year.

FREDERIC CHOPIN

When only a toddler, he climbed out of his crib at night, managed to get up onto the piano stool, and roused the whole household with his melodic improvisations.

ANDRE AGASSI

When the tennis ace was an infant, his father hung a racquet and a ball on a string over his crib.

JULIUS CAESAR

When his mother was dying in labor with him, the doctors decided on radical surgery—and tiny Julius became the first baby born by what is now known as cesarean section.

BEVERLY SILLS

She sang her first aria in public at the age of three. The place: Tompkins Park, Brooklyn, New York. The occasion: the Most Beautiful Baby of 1932 contest. The song: "The Wedding of Jack and Jill."

NORMAN ROCKWELL

Drawing warships at the time of the Spanish American War gave little Norman, then barely five, his start.

ALBERT EINSTEIN

It seems that the great scientist was very late in talking, so his parents were much relieved when at dinner one night Baby Albert finally spoke some words: "The soup is too hot." Why had he not spoken earlier, they asked? "Because until now, everything was in order," he replied.

WOLFGANG AMADEUS MOZART

When Mozart was no more than two, he was visiting a farm and heard a pig squealing. "G-sharp!" he cried out—and, it turned out, he was right.

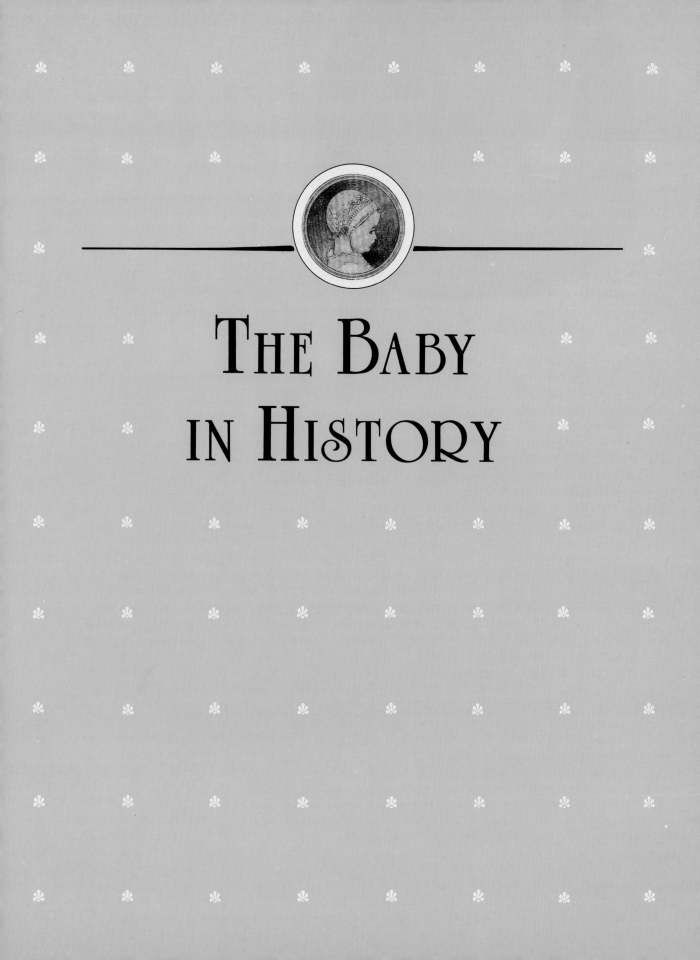

The Baby
in History

"BE FRUITFUL, AND MULTIPLY"

Parents in every civilization have valued their offspring for both practical and spiritual reasons. The treatment of babies, however, has varied dramatically through the ages. Depending on the society (and the baby's gender), a newborn might expect to be sold, exposed, swaddled, blessed, or ignored. Written references to babies are almost nonexistent before the modern era, yet archaeologists continue to unearth clay baby rattles and rush dolls, suggesting that mothers through the ages cherished their infants just as tenderly as we do today.

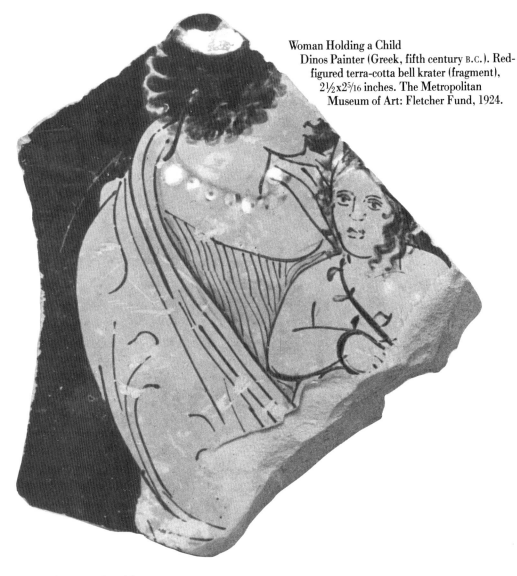

Woman Holding a Child
Dinos Painter (Greek, fifth century B.C.). Red-figured terra-cotta bell krater (fragment), 2½x2⁵/₁₆ inches. The Metropolitan Museum of Art: Fletcher Fund, 1924.

Babies As Art

Babies are rarely the subject of ancient art, and when they do appear, it is usually in an idealized form. This is partly a reflection of the roles played by babies in mythology, and partly because of the fragility of infant life in those harsh days.

The Greeks showed babies chiefly as *putti*—fat, playful cherubs who probably had their origin in Eros, god of love, who like his Roman counterpart, Cupid, was always portrayed as a smiling child. Yet there are glimpses of reality, as in the fragment at left, that reveal a lovingly human bond between mother and baby.

The wealth of depictions of the infant Jesus that show him as a minute, fully clothed adult indicate that such idealization continued into medieval times, when most real babies spent all-too-brief lives tightly swaddled, or tumbling about dirty floors with assorted livestock. As toddlers, the lucky survivors graduated to primitive wooden walkers, like the one shown above in an unusually candid portrait of the baby Jesus in his home.

Madonna and Child
Luca della Robbia, Italian (Florentine),
1399/1400–1482. Glazed terra-cotta relief. The Metropolitan Museum of Art:
Bequest of Susan Dwight Bliss, 1966.

From Ideal to Real

In late medieval times a few real children began to appear in altarpieces,
kneeling with their wealthy parents in descending order of height. But
when the Renaissance burst forth in the fifteenth century, the classical
putti made a spectacular comeback. Winged cupids were soon swarm-
ing through painted heavens, peeping out from foliage in tapestries, and
squeezing dolphins in fountains. Even the infant Jesus began to lose his
clothes and to relate to Mary in a more natural, baby-like way.

Madonna Surrounded by the Holy
Innocents
Peter Paul Rubens, Dutch, 1615. Oil
on canvas, 54x39 inches. The Louvre
Museum, Paris.

The Lacemaker
Nicolaes Maes, Dutch, 1634–1693. Oil on canvas, 17¾x20¾ inches. The Metropolitan Museum of Art: Bequest of Michael Friedsam, 1931, The Friedsam Collection.

Portrait of a Child
Paulus Moreelse, Dutch, 1571–1638. Oil on wood, oval, 23x19⅝ inches. The Metropolitan Museum of Art: Bequest of Alexandrine Sinsheimer, 1958.

Reality Comes to the Home

As the Renaissance spread northward, a newly prosperous middle class was able to provide a safer environment for their offspring. With their babies' survival more assured, parents began to want them included in secular family portraits. It was the great Dutch genre painters who first captured families in a natural setting, where babies clutch teething corals and throw cups and shoes on the floor, just like real babies. But they are still miniature adults externally, wearing tiny versions of adult clothing.

Mrs. Elizabeth Freake and Baby Mary
Unidentified artist, American, c. 1674. Oil on canvas, 42½x36¾ inches. Worcester Art Museum, Worcester, Massachusetts: Gift of Mr. and Mrs. Albert W. Rice.

The Duchess of Devonshire: 1784
Engraving by P. Lightfoot after the oil
painting by Sir Joshua Reynolds.

Bad Baby, Good Baby

No one could accuse America's Puritans of coddling their young. Parents thought of babies as replicas of themselves whose actions reflected directly upon *them;* because all children were born innately sinful, they could be brought to salvation only through strict, if loving, discipline.

In Europe, child-rearing attitudes were moving in the other direction. John Locke, in 1690, urged parents to ban the rod, and by the late eighteenth century, Jean-Jacques Rousseau was maintaining that children were born naturally perfect. "Rural innocence" became a byword among the upper classes, loose clothes replaced stiffly adult garments for children, and spontaneous enjoyment of babies was the latest fashion.

The Hatch Family
Eastman Johnson, American, 1824–1906. Oil on canvas, 48x73⅜ inches. The Metropolitan Museum of Art: Gift of Frederic H. Hatch, 1926.

The Century of the Family

The Victorian age was characterized by the cult of motherhood and *Godey's Lady's Book* extolled wives as "the perfection of womanhood" and "the light of the home." As the steady expansion of the Industrial Revolution galvanized society, Father became preoccupied with business and Mother with home and social life. Meanwhile, babies remained chiefly in the nursery, finding comfort in Nanny's arms and delight in a cupboard filled with building blocks, baby dolls, and toy soldiers.

When families gathered in the parlor, Victorian stiffness prevailed, but a certain sentimentality pervades even this classic family portrait, as well as the idealized vision of childhood mischief in the detail below.

Hide and Seek (detail)
James Jacques Tissot, French, 1836–1902. Oil on wood, 28⅞x21¼ inches. National Gallery of Art, Washington: Chester Dale Collection.

The Boating Party
Mary Cassatt, American, 1844–1926.
Oil on canvas, 35½x46⅛ inches. National Gallery of Art, Washington: Chester Dale Collection.

The Century of the Child

Ushering in the twentieth century, Mary Cassatt, America's noted portrayer of children, captured the essence of a time when babies' needs and wants were becoming their parents' prime considerations.

As a result, theory after theory surfaced on child raising—from Freud, who emphasized the importance of the mother–baby relationship, to Dr. Benjamin Spock, whose baby-care bible outsold every book but the real thing.

The nuclear family, with baby at its heart, has gone into a meltdown, but children still maintain their pre-eminence as society moves into the era of the blended family or "yours, mine, and ours." Will new families be any better than the old ones? Wait a few years; then ask your baby.

Nurse and Child
Mary Cassatt, American, 1844–1926. Pastel on paper,
31½x26¼ inches. The Metropolitan Museum of Art:
Gift of Mrs. Ralph J. Hines, 1960.

Mother Playing with Her Child
Mary Cassatt, American, 1844–1926. Pastel on paper,
25½x31½ inches. The Metropolitan Museum of Art:
Gift of Dr. Ernest B. Stillman, 1922, The Collection of
James Stillman.

LITTLE FOOTNOTES

LIKE FATHER

In his novel Dombey and Son, *Charles Dickens compared a father with his baby:*

"Dombey was about eight-and-forty years of age. Son about eight-and-forty minutes. Dombey was rather bald, rather red, and though a handsome well-made man, too stern and pompous in appearance to be prepossessing. Son was very bald, and very red, and, though (of course) an undeniably fine infant, somewhat crushed and spotty in his general effect, as yet."

CHEAPER BY THE DOZEN

In colonial America, large families were encouraged. The pioneers needed the labor. The Reverend Cotton Mather had fifteen children, and reported other families with as many as twenty-seven.

CAREFUL, NOW!

It was the custom for a Saxon father to place the first morsel of solid food in a baby boy's mouth on the point of his sword, so that the baby would grow up to be a warrior.

BIRD OBEYANCE

John S. C. Abbott, an Evangelical pastor, wrote The Mother at Home; or Principles of Maternal Duty *in 1833. He maintained that children were never too young to be taught to obey, and advanced the following argument:*

"A Frenchman has recently collected a large number of canary birds for a show. He has taught them such implicit obedience to his voice, as to march them in platoons across the room, and directs them to the ready performance of many simple manoeuvers.

"Now, can it be admitted that a child, fifteen months or two years of age, is inferior in understanding to a canary bird?"

TINKER, TAILOR, INDIAN CHIEF

In England, the upper classes thought it charming to dress their children in outfits befitting lower-class occupations. The most popular item of "occupational" clothing was the sailor suit, introduced in 1846.

EARLY ROYAL APPEARANCES

Henry VI of England presided at his first royal council at the age of six months, sitting on his mother's lap.

After the defeat of Charles I, his eighteen-month-old daughter, Henrietta, was smuggled over to France by her nurse, who dressed herself and the child in rags and pretended the baby was a boy. Affronted by this treatment, Henrietta announced to anyone they met that she was "not Pierre, but Princess." Fortunately, she did not speak very clearly, so their disguises went undetected.

NO CAKE OR ICE CREAM

The early Christians observed the anniversary of a child's death, rather than his birth, based on the assumption that things were better in the afterlife.

FIRST AMONG EQUALS

Jimmy Carter was the first of all American presidents to be born in a hospital.

ON BEING A
MOTHER-TO-BE

The Outside/Inside Story

Maternity clothes, the expectant mother's outward cloak, are an invention of this century, the first era when pregnant women continue to lead normal lives, looking good, dressing expertly, exercising regularly, eating wisely . . . and planning almost without cease. The inside story, begun long before, will continue until she feels as big as the new home she has made ready for the baby who has been her roommate for so long. That story, retold so many billions of times, is remarkable both for variety and consistency, yet it is always new—for each woman who undertakes it, every time.

Maternity Moments from the Mists of Time

Imagine a fabulous fashion show, where women from every era have come together, transcending the laws of physics and time to celebrate the ways women of many epochs have found to deal with an eternal dilemma: what to wear when pregnancy makes a slim waist bigger than a breadbox.

Visualize a long ramp leading from the stage and, to its left, a woman behind a podium who is our Mistress of Ceremonies.

"When we become pregnant," she says to the audience, "it suddenly occurs to us that we have nothing to wear. Today we are going to highlight some of our solutions over the centuries. We'll begin near the beginning, with the clothes of ancient Greece.

"Please welcome Lydia," she says, as a young woman walks onto the runway. "Lydia comes to us today from the third century B.C., wearing a *chiton*, your basic unisex house dress–party dress from 1500 B.C. until the first century A.D., entirely adaptable to any conditions. Her *chiton* is in the Doric style, and late in her pregnancies she wore it without a belt. The rectangular linen panels are sewn part way up the sides and secured at each shoulder with a clasp, or *fibula*. The bright geometric pattern at the hem is her own embroidery, and, of course, she wove the linen for the dress herself."

The M.C. smooths her hair and takes a sip of water from the glass she has beside her on the podium.

"The fashion of our Greek sisters had a big influence on the world of our next girl—come on out, honey—this is Flavia; isn't she a darling?

She's only sixteen years old. Flavia is a Roman matron in the second century A.D. This is her second pregnancy and, as you can see, she's wearing a *stola*, a simple straight robe, over an undertunic similar to the *chiton*. Over the whole outfit she throws a *palla*—that's the enwrapping floor-length garment which is the female version of the toga. Thank you, Flavia.

"Now here's Matilda. Matilda comes to us from England in the ninth century A.D. Step up, darling, let them see the blue headrail, as they call it, the scarf; this is a length of linen draping the head and neck, while the red mantle is draped over the shoulders and covers her expanding middle. The green one-piece dress is called a *bliaud*; it's embroidered around the hem and the sleeve openings. Hold your arms up for a minute, honey. The vertical band of embroidery draws the eye away from the belly. Isn't that cute? Under it she wears a white linen chemise. Thank you, dear.

"As the centuries passed, women's dress grew quite a bit more elegant. Our next model is Blanche, from fifteenth-century France, wearing an azure blue silk gown flecked with gold. Crimson velvet trims the bottom of the skirt, the cuffs, and collar. High waists like this one were handy for pregnant ladies, because the waistband could be raised, allowing the flowing skirt to accommodate her growing stomach. An elaborate gold-brocaded stomacher draws attention upward, away from her tummy. So does that stunning *hennin* on her head. Can you believe it? She starched all that muslin veiling herself. *Merci*, Blanche.

"Incidentally, you will recall that during the Middle Ages—which lasted roughly from the fall of the Roman Empire to the middle of the fourteenth century—clothes became increasingly elaborate, and by the

end of the period the fashionable waist was the *slim* waist. Corsetting had taken over."

Amid groans from the audience, the M.C. refills her glass, and continues.

"Along with the spiritual and secular awakening of the Renaissance there came an explosion in fashion, which was influenced strongly by the taste of Queen Elizabeth I. By her time, skirts had spread out into a huge hoop called a farthingale, topped by a starched ruff around the neck. The queen liked a partial ruff that was extremely high in the back and tapered on the sides, allowing her to reveal her decolletage. All ladies of fashion were tightly corseted in this period, so during the latter part of their pregnancies they didn't go out at all.

"Leaping ahead a couple of centuries, and keeping well clear of the French Revolution, during which fashion was entirely out of fashion, we pop up again in Napoleon's day with an entirely new style, which we call Empire, after him. Women abandoned corsets completely and wore simple, 'Roman-style' dresses, usually made of white muslin, which were full over the breasts with very high waists. Ideal for maternity wear.

"By the 1850s corsets were back in fashion and huge crinolines were all the rage in America. Here's Laura, in a faille silk gown with a striped silk skirt over a crinoline, ideal for making afternoon calls. The high waist and stiffness of the 'turkey-back' over-jacket help hide Laura's tummy. Turn around, dear, so we can see the charming cord and tassels on its hood. Thank you.

"What a change in our next two models, a half century later! The youthful lines of Francesca's printed linen dress are quite concealing. The pleated collar echoes the myriad pleats of the dress's loose-fitting first tier, which floats down from an empire waist, tied with easily adjusted satin ribbon. The second tier of the dress ends just above Francesca's ankles. Her tiny cloth hat is adorned with a cloth gardenia. Thank you, Francesca.

"Odette is in her seventh month, yet how elegant she looks in this white silk day-dress and the white straw hat that shaded her on the Côte d'Azur in 1914. Just the same, this is an outfit that harks forward to the 1920s, in my view. The loose, simple lines of the upper part of the dress give ample room to her growing belly, while the wide, smooth band that circles her thighs and descends into four layers of pleated fabric draws the eye naturally downward."

Another quick sip, and the M.C. continues.

"Erté, the French designer whose work graced the covers of *Harper's Bazaar* between 1918 and 1932, never designed actual maternity clothes, but many of his designs were perfect for the purpose . . . Rosemary? Come out, dear . . . As a socialite in New York, Rosemary needed costumes of this kind. She wore this creation in 1930, to the gala for the fiftieth anniversary of the Metropolitan Museum. *Everyone* was there, and not one of them could tell that she was five months pregnant. This piece was intended to be a wrap, but it's made of such rich material

that it doubles as a dress. The gray satin is cut into four rectangles, with their upper corners wrapped over a ruffled collar of gray fox. The sleeves reach to the floor, with geometric embroidery in gold thread around the openings for the hands. The dress drapes from the collar much like Flavia's *stola* and its lower points reach the floor around Rosemary's ankles. With it, she wears a turban of gold-embroidered gray satin.''

Our M.C. pauses dramatically. All eyes are on her.

''And that wraps it up,'' she says, smiling. ''The next step in fashion is the totally modern woman who takes her pregnancy in stride. Her clothes stay chic while accommodating her expanding waistline. But that's the subject of a very different show.''

The audience bursts into applause and cheers, and a large bouquet is brought on stage for the Mistress of Ceremonies, who is persuaded to come out from behind the podium and take a bow. Wouldn't you know—she is wearing a very smart maternity suit.

Our Designer Speaks

Gone are the days when pregnant women wore silly, girlish maternity smocks, or worse still, tried to conceal their condition. Now women can look absolutely terrific right up to the day they deliver, says our Liz Parkinson, maternity clothes designer, illustrator, and mother. First of all, she advises, don't rush out and buy a lot of maternity clothes. During the first five months, a woman's usual clothing will probably do very well, with a few minor adjustments.

For instance, unbuttoning the top button makes trousers more comfortable, especially with an elastic belt and a loose blouse or sweater over them. Pregnant women get bigger on top, too, and it is important to wear blouses and dresses that are wide enough in the shoulders, because everything hangs from there. Adding firm shoulder pads will square up the figure and help minimize the vision of expansion below. Never wear cuffed trousers, which create the impression of short legs. Diagonal stripes are very flattering, as is a large square scarf worn over one shoulder and tied at the hip. As a woman gets bigger, she should wear proportionately bigger earrings and necklaces.

By the fifth month, it is time to go shopping. Ms. Parkinson suggests planning around these considerations:

1. What will the season be during the second and third trimesters? Spring and summer clothes are interchangeable, but a new winter coat may be necessary if the baby is due in March.

2. Be sure each garment works at least three ways with other pieces.

3. Stick to current wardrobe colors. Someone who looks ghastly in green now is not going to look any better in it when twenty pounds heavier. A woman who looks smashing in red, on the other hand, should not be afraid to wear it. Choose a main color and add variety with accessories and less expensive items.

4. Manufacturers size maternity clothes appropriately, so a size eight is still a size eight at eight months.

5. Get rid of bulky shoulder bags. They are no good for anyone's posture, but are especially poor for expectant mothers. Likewise, try to wear flat heels. As a woman's weight changes, so does her center of gravity, and teetering around on high heels could lead to disaster.

Liz Parkinson's designs on this and the following pages are ample evidence that pregnancy is no time for women to look anything but their best.

PANTS ALTERNATIVE
Pants of the same or contrasting fabric will dress this outfit up or down.

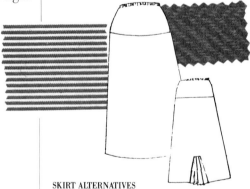

SKIRT ALTERNATIVES
The jacket can be worn over a number of skirts, but be sure they all have a roomy kick pleat.

Career Dressing

This classic two-piece suit—a three-pocket blazer and slim, pleated skirt—serves as the foundation for dressing for the office. Wear the jacket over pants, or the skirt with a big, soft sweater.

BLOUSE ALTERNATIVES

Add some zip with a striped or floral print blouse, with short or long sleeves and either a tailored or elegantly feminine collar.

Casual Wear

Pear-shaped or round, anybody's figure looks slimmest one color from head to toe, like this pants and sweater ensemble that can also be worn with a matching skirt.

BLOUSE ALTERNATIVES

This sporty outfit can be dressed up or down with blouses ranging from plaid to floral. The effect will be most flattering if the blouse patterns are in the same hue as the ensemble.

Evening Wear

A beaded bodice, dramatic back, and billowing skirt of gauzy georgette create a gorgeous evening gown that can be worn year round, pregnant or not.

Mirror, Mirror on the Wall

One of the things that every pregnant woman cares about is how to stay looking attractive at a time when it is all too easy not to. Surprisingly, this information is not easy to come by, so we went directly to Robert Verdi, a long-standing expert on beauty who has contributed to all the major women's fashion magazines, owned his own salon, and currently produces fashion commercials.

Verdi debunks what he calls the old wives' tale that "pregnant women virtually shine with an inner glow or radiance. I think the opposite is true." Most pregnant women undergo certain visible changes, many of which are temporary and will go away in a matter of weeks after the baby is born. While psychologists advise women to accept these signs with patience and a sense of humor, Verdi counsels them to keep up their looks.

The Hair and Now

A pregnant woman's hair is one of the first parts of the body to respond to changes in its chemistry and unfamiliar levels of stress. Common symptoms are dull, dry, or thinning hair, and for some women, even temporary hair loss. Verdi's suggestions:

1. It is best to keep hair clean and preferably cut short. Tailor the cut for an easy, natural look.
2. Long hair should be trimmed regularly and not overly curled or permed because hair becomes brittle during pregnancy.
3. Maintain the coloring in color-treated hair, but test periodically with an inconspicuous patch of hair to be sure that changing internal chemistry will not sabotage the new coloring.
4. If the hair is dry or dull, avoid overusing conditioners.
5. Problems with temporary hair loss are best dealt with by brushing as usual, but more gently, without tugging or pulling the hair, and by massaging the scalp lightly with the fingertips.

Reflecting on Complecting

The texture and tone of a pregnant woman's complexion can change suddenly, often unpredictably. Women who outgrew acne problems years ago sometimes have a fresh outbreak, caused by the stress of early pregnancy, or find themselves developing one of a number of pregnancy-related skin rashes. Verdi is reassuring: "The condition is temporary. Stay calm, and stick to a regular skin maintenance routine that includes cleansing and moisturizing."

His regimen basically involves washing the face twice a day with a mild soap that has no fragance and using a night cream—he particularly recommends the new cell-builder night creams—after removing makeup. As a quick pick-me-up, he suggests applying a mayonnaise treatment to the face and hair.

It is crucial to keep the skin lubricated with moisturizers, he insists. "Use them on the face and any other part of the body that is swelling; the skin is only elastic to a point."

His practical skin-care guidelines:

1. Use only skin and beauty products with natural or pure ingredients, without any fragrances.
2. As an alternative to night creams, use Vaseline as a moisturizer.
3. Avoid situations, such as sunbathing, that tend to dry the skin.
4. Avoid aggravating acne problems with heavy abrasive scrubs. Use a light astringent instead, and if the problem persists, consult a dermatologist.

In Verdi's view, pregnant women look best with a natural look and should keep makeup to a minimum. One of his beauty secrets is to use a dark foundation with a light foundation, to highlight some features while concealing others. Another is to use bronzers as an alternative to makeup, which can give an added boost and an illusion of color, without exposure to the sun.

Hilary Kirshman

Active at Work and Play

Though a modern pregnant woman readjusts her life to some extent, she counts on actively running her household and business affairs almost up to the day she delivers.

In Victorian times, matters were very different. Pregnancy was regarded as the equivalent of an unspeakable illness, and the word itself was never used in polite circles until well into the twentieth century. Women were said to be "in trouble," even if they were married, "increasing," "in an interesting condition," "in the family way," or "expecting a little stranger." They spent much time reclining on couches like invalids, and took walks only at twilight, when no one could observe their embarrassing shape.

Pregnancy has not stopped these women from running a business (far left), keeping up an exercise program, or turning out original art in a creative home workshop (above).

Outstanding Actresses Achieve Prominence in Other Roles Too

If looking fabulous and being pregnant seem like mutually exclusive conditions, just take a look at these women, all stars of the stage and screen and all quite obviously pregnant. Incipient motherhood certainly seems to suit them.

Ordinarily svelte, these three didn't go into embarrassed seclusion the minute they started showing. Far from it—they practically flaunted their bulging bellies as if to say, "I'm a mother! Look at me!"

Even rotund, Pia Zadora (above) looks adorable. A glowing Meryl Streep (right) receives the People's Choice Award with Don Johnson, while Cybill Shepherd (opposite) shows off her twins-in-waiting.

The Power Shower

It used to be just a small party given by well-wishers to celebrate mother and the imminent or just-arrived new baby. No longer. The affluent generation has updated and up-marketed the conventional welcoming of the new baby. Gifts come from a store where the expectant parents are registered, as for a wedding. These days, a child born with a silver spoon in its mouth can expect an entire table setting to go with it. Up to three showers per mother-to-be are not uncommon.

The idea of a shower derived from the notion of bountiful gifts raining down on the promise of new life; the trend toward lavish spending on layettes, bassinets, and strollers has given it fresh meaning. Today's events are co-ed, catered, and classy.

A mother-to-be admires a welcome baby gift as a friend performs the traditional function of recording the name of each giver. ·

Mother and infant can amass quite a stash from a shower of real power—no wonder both are beaming.

SHOWER GIFTS

These are the gifts all mothers really want—loving, helpful contributions to this new life with baby. Showers that follow themes are fun, and some suggestions follow. Another good idea is to organize contributions to one large gift (a stroller, for instance) and have each individual bring a token small gift.

Possible themes or groupings of gifts:

SLEEP

The focus can be something very special when each guest contributes a quilt square in a particular theme and these have been sewn together by one person as a wall hanging or comforter. Other possibilities:

crib sheets
blanket
decorative pillow and pillow
    cases for the carriage
music box
special teddy or other stuffed
    animal
sleepwear

TOYS

Present a toy chest—perhaps personalized in some way—filled with small toys:

rattle
stuffed animal
soft ball
soft blocks

FOOD

Especially appropriate for a mother and/or father who likes to cook:

a mini food processor (the perfect size for baby food)

baby food cookbook
a batch of jars and a recipe for
    really good applesauce
feeding bottles
personalized baby bib

AT YOUR SERVICE

Here's the chance to be generous—guests offer their services to overwhelmed new parents, written up, perhaps, as vouchers for one (or more) day/night of:

babysitting
cooking a meal
housecleaning
doing the laundry

THE SHOWER YESTERDAY

A shower in the 1940s might have included the following party planning:

Perhaps the stork is about to visit your circle of friends for the first time. The coming of a new baby is always a splendid excuse for a party.

Daintiness should characterize the decorations. Bibs and bonnets and baby faces, bunnies and storks and woolly lambs may all help to set the stage. The stork himself is a great favorite. Use bassinets or cradles as table decorations, a large one for the centerpiece to hold favors and small ones for nut cups. Crepe-paper bonnets or bootees laced with ribbon make appropriate nut cups, too. A giant bootee or a bonnet filled with flowers makes a good centerpiece. Bibs cut from organdy or crepe paper can be laid as place mats and used as place cards. Make the invitations in the shape of bibs, or fold them like diapers.

Some party themes:

IN HONOR OF THE STORK:

You are sure of success if you make Mr. Stork himself the guardian spirit of a baby shower.

Yonder flies the stork,
See, against the moon!
He's on his way to _____'s
    house,
And he will be there soon.

So let us help prepare
A nest for the little one
By bringing each a shower gift
And sharing in the fun.

You can make one without too much difficulty [out of crushed newspaper and wire]. Set Mr. Stork in a place of honor at the table. A branch of green pine makes an effective setting for him as he presides over his nest of favors, which is a wicker basket or a shallow cardboard box wound with vines and set upon a mat of green. Wrap favors with plenty of tissue paper until they resemble pink and blue eggs. Little satin sachet balls make very nice favors, and resemble eggs just as they are, without wrapping. Nut cups are smaller nests of Jordan almonds. Stand a cardboard stork beside each cup as a place card.

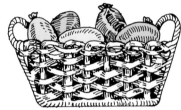

A MOTHER GOOSE SHOWER

Not only our young mother-to-be but all of us will enjoy renewing acquaintance with Old Mother Goose and her family. The invitations should parody one of her rhymes.

Girls, oh, girls, come out to play.
The moon is shining bright as day.
Leave your supper and leave your
    sleep,
And come with us to _____
    Street.
Come with a whoop, come with a
    call,
Come with a good will, or not at all.
For _____ we're giving a
    Mother Goose shower,
We hope you will join us; _____
    is the hour.

*Colorful decorations can be made
easily and inexpensively from dime-
store Mother Goose books. Get the
large ones with gay pictures and separate the pages by removing the staples. These can be mounted on
cardboard mats, but you will probably find them sufficiently heavy just
as they are. Hang them as pictures,
using transparent tape or thumbtacks
to hold them in place upon walls,
windows (or window shades) and
mantels.*

*If you want to do something unusual
for an anticipating friend, convert
your house into Lollipop Lane and
send out the following invitation:*

Let's stroll for an evening in Lollipop
    Lane
    Where the Sugar Plum Tree grows
And the Marshmallow Maidens, so
    plump and plain,
    Live in gingerbread bungalows.
The reason we're taking this sugary
    tone
    Is that _____ awaits (have you
        guessed?)
A sweet little sugar plum all for her
    own,
    And we're going to help make ready
        his nest.

Games for the baby shower:

BABIES' SUPPER RACE

*Give two or more contestants each a
bottle of soda pop which they must
drink through a nipple. They may
have nurses to help them by tipping
up the bottle or patting them on the
back when they choke, as they will.
Removing the nipple or biting holes in
it are, of course, outlawed. The first to
empty her bottle may have another as
a prize and special treat.*

HOW MANY BABIES?

*This provides an amusing interlude of
fortune-telling. With a piece of thread
stretched taut between her hands, just
above the flame of a lighted candle,
the honor guest, or anyone else who
wishes to try her luck, counts aloud
very slowly, since the number counted
before the thread burns in two is said
to foretell the number of children she
will have.*

Helen Emily Webster, excerpted from
Shower Parties for All Occasions

The Inside Story

When a man and a woman decide to have a baby, they set in motion a process that is as marvelous as it is commonplace. On the outside, Mother's breasts start to swell and she feels out of sorts. Father and Mother fret over whether the baby will inherit his oversized ears or her flat feet. Maybe they will begin to discuss names. But while they repeat the time-honored rituals of expectant parents, a sperm and an egg will have joined silently in her womb, ready to undergo a miraculous transformation.

The embryo will soon grow into something that at first is indistinguishable from any other embryo—a platypus, say, or a fish—then, somehow, it will metamorphose into a tiny human being. Every baby's growth in the womb follows a pattern that has been passed on in an unbroken chain from generation to generation. It is a pattern that goes back to the evolutionary roots of the human species, yet the mixture of genes from both parents means that every baby is unique. From a tiny fertilized egg no bigger than the period at the end of this sentence will come a new person, filled with possibilities.

The act of conceiving a baby may seem simple to the two people involved, but inside, conception is the beginning of an arduous journey. Upon their release, up to 200 million sperm beat their tails in a desperate race through the woman's uterus toward her fallopian tubes, where a single fertile egg lies waiting. Only a few hundred will make it to the fallopian tubes, and about a tenth of those will crowd in a wriggling halo around their quarry, eagerly seeking admission. One penetrates, and, instantly, all other suitors are excluded by the egg's special membrane.

De Formato Foetu (On the Formation of the Fetus), 1627
Adriaan van der Spiegel, author, Padua, Italy. Copperplate engraving. The National Library of Medicine, Bethesda, Maryland.

Der Swangern Frauwen und Hebammen Rosengarten (The Rose Garden of Pregnant Women and Midwives), 1522
Eucharius Roeslin, author, Strasbourg, France. Woodcut. The National Library of Medicine, Bethesda, Maryland.

WHY ARE BABIES BORN AT NINE MONTHS?

According to some evolutionary biologists, even babies that are carried to full term are premature when born. The babies of other mammals of comparable weight and size stay in the womb longer and are born larger, but human infants must come out when they do because the human species is caught between opposing evolutionary forces. One force restricts the size of the adult female's pelvis so that she can walk upright. The other force increases the size of the baby's brain. But a human infant's head is already so big, it can barely make it out of the birth canal as it is. As a compromise it is born a bit early, leaving some critical development to occur outside the womb. That is why human infants are so helpless for their first few months of life.

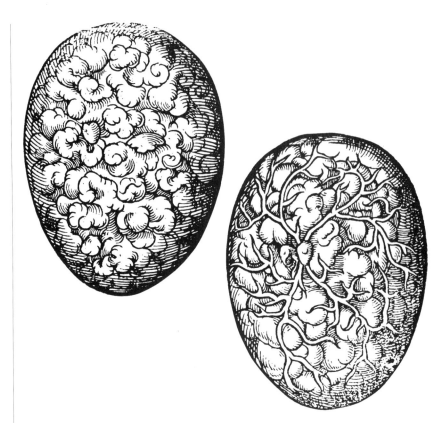

The lucky sperm soon dissolves inside the egg, releasing its precious cargo of DNA, the genetic contribution from the father. Within half an hour, DNA from both parents has mingled and made copies of itself. The single egg divides into two cells and the miracle of life has begun.

The embryo continues to divide on its way down the tube to the thimble-sized uterus, where it will drift about on its own in a watery fluid for three days. Then the minute ball of cells burrows into the uterus's spongy wall which will serve as a lifeline to Mother's body, the embryo's sole source of nourishment for the next nine months.

With a little imagination, a twenty-eight-day embryo vaguely resembles an animal, but not a human being. Though less than half an inch long, the embryo is ten thousand times bigger than the fertilized egg. It has buds where arms and legs will be, a spinal column, and a bulbous head.

At the end of the second month, the embryo almost looks like a miniature person. Two dark eyes appear, and the limb buds sprout fingers and toes. A crude heart begins beating, while liver and kidneys form. A lilliputian brain swells inside its head, which accounts for half its total length. At this stage the embryo is called a fetus; it has all the rudiments of a baby, even whorled ridges of fingerprints—yet it is so small that it could nestle in the shell of a peanut.

In its third month, the fetus still weighs no more than a letter and could fit inside a goose egg, but many fine details are added that make it seem more human. Girls are distinguishable from boys, as sexual organs are molded from virtually identical swellings. Nailbeds appear on fingers and toes and the two little lumps on either side of the head become delicately shaped ears. The fetus moves now, curling its fingers, squinting, frowning, and opening its mouth.

By the second trimester, the fetus begins a pattern of sleep and wakefulness. When awake, it kicks vigorously and turns somersaults inside the fluid in the amniotic sac. Asleep, it assumes a favorite position. The fetus increases its size more than tenfold, so that by the sixth month it weighs just over a pound and has reached fourteen inches in length. It can hear now—Mother's heartbeat, music, Daddy's talking.

In the third trimester, the fetus enters the home stretch. It is considered viable at this stage—meaning that it has a chance of surviving outside the womb—but reaching full term is best. There is weight to be gained—at least a pound in the seventh month and a good four more in the following six weeks. It acquires immunity to a number of diseases, such as measles, colds, and the flu. Mother's immune system sends the baby antibodies, cells that help fight off infection.

By the ninth month, there is no more room in the uterus and the baby settles head down (usually). It is time for this baby to be welcomed into the world.

Shannon Brownlee

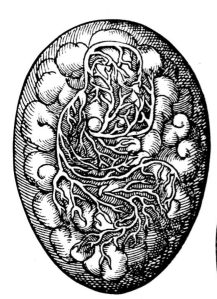

De Conceptu Et Generatione Hominis (On the Conception and Birth of Mankind), 1554
    Jakob Reuff, author, Zurich, Switzerland. Woodcut on vellum. The National Library of Medicine, Bethesda, Maryland.

HISTORICAL IDEAS

Most of us know that storks don't bring babies, but until the late eighteenth century, common notions about where babies come from were just as absurd.

In the second century A.D., the Greek physician Galen proposed the theory that women had intact miniature embryos inside them, like little prefab babies. He thought that semen merely caused an embryo to break out of a shell and increase in size until birth.

When the microscope was perfected in the late 1600s, biologists saw individual sperm for the first time. This discovery spawned a new theory: The prefab embryo was contained not in the woman, but in the head of the sperm.

Not until the nineteenth century did biologists find that embryos are constructed step by step from cells, the building blocks of all living things.

Don't Touch That Dial!

At last, an alternative form of parenting is available to the career-oriented who work seventeen hours a day, yet feel strangely familiar biological clocks ticking internally. No muss, no fuss—an absolutely 1980s-type deal, without any commitment to obstetricians, pediatricians, and a college education. *Video Baby* is the latest brainchild of Creative Programming Inc. in New York (previous successes: *Video Dog* and *Video Cat*). She comes with her own birth certificate, medical records, and child guidance manual; she coos, she gurgles, she crawls, and she has a pair of baby blues that will melt the hardest heart. And best of all, you can switch her OFF.

LITTLE FOOTNOTES

GETTING THE TIMING RIGHT

The story is told of a woman who goes to her doctor to confirm her suspected pregnancy. The busy doctor stamps her belly with a rubber pad dipped in blue ink. Some nine months later, the expectant mother views herself, naked, in the mirror. The writing on the stamp has enlarged with her expanded girth. She can now make out the message:

HURRY, GET TO THE HOSPITAL QUICKLY. YOUR TIME HAS COME.

JOYOUS EQUATION

The German mathematician Peter Dirichlet was renowned for never writing letters, but when his first baby was born he broke silence and wired his father-in-law:

"2 + 1 = 3."

REMEMBER THIS

A reason, provided in perfect candor, for having given birth to thirteen illegitimate children was that their mother had suffered a severe back injury as a child and had been assured by her doctor that she would never be able to marry.

So she never had.

PROLIFIC MOTHERS

According to the 1988 Guinness Book of World Records, *the wife of a Russian peasant, Feodor Vassilyev, holds the record for producing the most babies ever: a total of 69. Feodor himself was born in 1707 and died after an active life about 1782. The name of his laboring wife is unknown and may have ceased to be important in her efforts to keep up with naming the 67 survivor babies, all of whom took their first breaths during the forty years between 1725 and 1765.*

How did she do it? In twenty-seven confinements, she gave birth to sixteen pairs of twins, seven sets of triplets, and four sets of quadruplets. A couple of idle questions:

1. If each of these children had a mere fifteen children apiece, how many descendants unto how many generations might the Vassilyevs have today?
2. If Mrs. Vassilyev had been taking fertility pills, how many children could she have had if she had really been trying?

Among the world's living-at-this-very-moment most prolific mothers must be counted Leonina Albina, resident of San Antonio, Chile, born in 1925. She gave birth to her 55th child at the age of 56. (Her age was 56.)

KNOWING WHAT'S BEST

A pediatrics text written in 1472 by Paolo Bagellardo instructs midwives how to care for newborn babies. After the infant emerges from the womb, the midwife is to wrap the baby in smooth linen and sit him on her lap to make sure he is breathing. The baby is then bathed in warm water, swaddled, and laid in a darkened room with a piece of sugar in his mouth.

SUPERSTITIONS LAST LONG

Some nuggets from A Treasure of American Superstitions:

A mother must expect to lose a tooth for each child she brings into the world.

Indulging a craving for sweets during pregnancy influences the unborn babe to become female.

Babies born to mature parents are more likely to have brilliant minds.

A TRUE TALE

A technician is making an electrocardiogram of the fetal heartbeat. Anxious mother-to-be, observing the stylus tracing a record on graph paper with red ink: "I think we should stop now. I don't think the baby can spare all that blood."

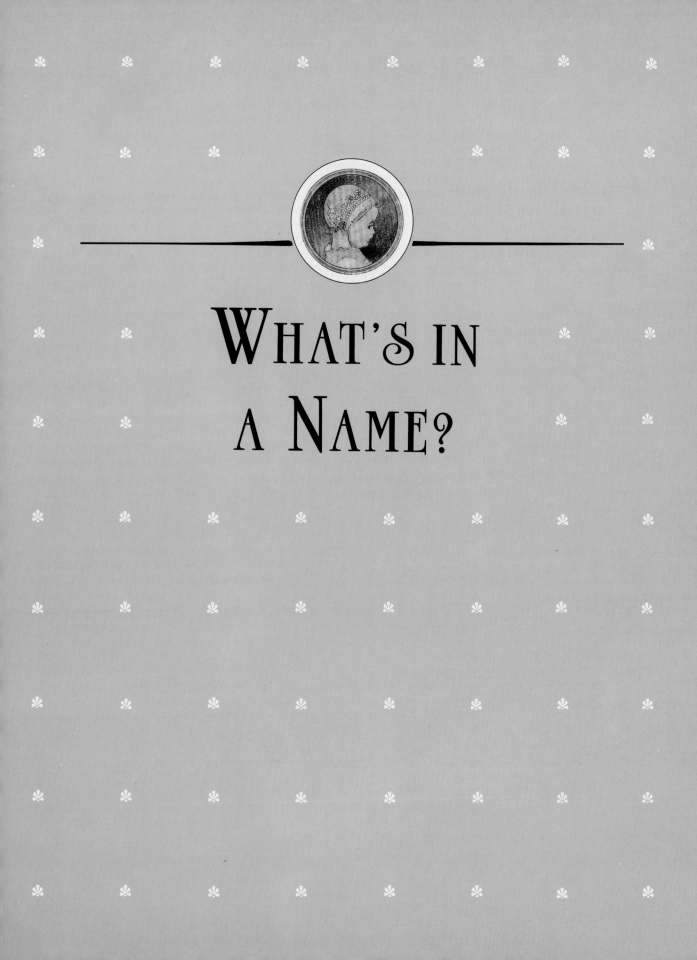

WHAT'S IN A NAME?

THE PERMANENT GIFT

You named your twins Hortense and Herbert? You didn't! Don't you know the old proverb that a good name is worth more than great riches? Unusual family names may do very well as one of several (preferably in second or third position), but remember that your baby's legal name will be the first one. Names you give now will precede your children onto the playground . . . into the classroom . . . over the phone . . . into every new situation for the rest of their lives. A name stays with a child for good, so make it a good one.

Dipping into the Name Pool

When American parents today get down to the important business of naming the new baby, they stand at the edge of an enormous name pool that is as deep as it is wide. It has been estimated that the name pool we share with all English-speaking peoples now contains more than ten thousand names. Most of us take this abundance for granted, and some harried new parents view it as an actual disadvantage. For them, picking just the right names from a pool of thousands of possibilities can sometimes seem to be an impossible task.

But it does not behoove us to complain. Back in the very early, formative days of the English language, there were so few choices available that parents stood on the edge of not a pool but a puddle, and a dammed-up puddle at that. Thousands of children answered to the same few names in every generation. What happened to start the flow that created the name pool we have today?

The ancient Britons, an agrarian people, were Celts. We know very little about the Celtic language or about Celtic names though *Arthur* is one and *Brian* is another—very little that was Celtic has passed down to us today in modern English.

Britain was occupied by Rome in 55 B.C. and thrived as a province under its rule for nearly four hundred years. In A.D. 498, the Romans abandoned this outpost to its own resources, and the Britons were soon invaded and ravaged by successive gangs of barbarians, beginning with the Scots and ending with the Angles and the Saxons, two Germanic tribes that settled down to stay, bringing with them their languages and

REMARKABLE NAMES FOR REAL PEOPLE
(A SELECTION)

Cardinal Sin
Cigar Stubbs
Horsey de Horsey
Ima Hogg
Justin Tune
Katz Meow
Memory Lane
Noble Teat
Shine Soon Sun
Rosetta Stone
Trailing Arbutus Vines

John Train, *Remarkable Names*

their names and creating in Britain the language known today as Anglo-Saxon.

An Anglo-Saxon person used only one name—no surname—and that one was likely to be fairly short. *Wulfa* is the sort of name they liked and used a lot. It was as good for a boy as for a girl, and may or may not have meant "wolf." When the Anglo-Saxons wanted to go for something rather more complicated in a name, they put two of their blunt word-names together to couple, though not necessarily to join or to signify, two ideas. Take their *Aelf-raed*, for example, which has come down to us as *Alfred. Aelf* meant "elf," and *raed* meant "counsel," and what the two thoughts were doing together is anybody's guess today.

Even so, the puddle of possible names stayed very small for nearly five hundred years. New parents had only a limited repertoire of options to choose from, such as *Dene*, *Kragg*, *Fuga*, and *Etheldreda*.

The Norman Conquest in 1066 was calamitous for the Britons as a people, but in the long run it proved to be a very good thing for the emerging English language. The Normans, who were actually of Scandinavian descent, arrived in Britain speaking French and addressing each other by such names as *Harry*, *Emma*, *Richard*, *Matilda* (or *Maud*), *Walter*, *Roger*, and *Hugh*. At first, British parents would rather have died than name their children after these invaders, but after a hundred years or so, their attitude softened and they began to adopt these foreign names, along with a few frenchified phrases and manners. At the same time, the descendants of the invaders began to drop French and take up English, so that in time a common tongue emerged from the mixture.

This was a time of great ascendency for the Roman Catholic church in Britain, and the practice then emerged under ecclesiastical guidance of dipping into the Bible for new names for babies. *Mary* and *Elizabeth* came from this source and enjoyed widespread popularity, as did the names of the apostles—among them *James, Stephen,* and *Thomas*—and of the great evangelists, *Matthew, Mark, Luke,* and *John.* The names of nonbiblical saints and martyrs also came into use, notably *George, Nicholas, Benedict, Katherine, Margaret, Helen,* and *Agnes.* Because of the vast spread of Christianity many of these names were literally outlandish to the English. *George* and *Nicholas* belong to the Greeks, and *Paul, Benedict,* and *Agnes* to the Romans. But they all turned out to live very well in the English climate.

Crazy pattern patchwork crib quilt Arlette Hathaway Howard, Franklin, New Hampshire, 1884. Pieced and embroidered silk, 46x34 inches. The Currier Gallery of Art, Manchester, New Hampshire: Gift of Mrs. Ruth Gilkerson Watts.

Old Testament naming reached its zenith in England during the Puritan ascendancy. However, because the Puritans were a minority in England, the emergence of a few little *Aarons* never overcame the crowds of little *Roberts* and *Richards* and *Hughs* out running around.

In the American colonies, the situation was very much the reverse, and the old Norman names and saints' names practically disappeared. In the Massachusetts Bay Colony, in the period from 1630 to 1670, all the women's names were biblical and half were Old Testament— *Hannah, Abigail, Ruth*, and the like. Great English women's names like *Katherine* and *Agnes* had disappeared without a trace, and only seven *Margarets* were listed.

Now came a time for the invention of meaningful names by American Puritans as expressions of their godliness. If the Hebrew name *Mehetabel* meant "God-is-doing-good," then why not mint new English names in this fashion? *Praise-to-the-Lord*, for example. Allied to this were names given to express the parents' prayer for the child's good character: *Patience, Prudence, Comfort, Thankful, Temperance, Peace, Hope, Submit, Charity*, and *Endurance* are some of these.

German immigrants came in numbers to Pennsylvania in the late seventeenth century, bringing with them the first name–middle name concept, which had not been employed at all by the English but became commonplace in America. *Anna, Emma*, and *Ida* were names the new German-Americans may have helped to popularize. Another name they brought with them, *Frederick*, became prominent in the American name pool. Their usual first name for boys was *Johann*, German for "John." The Scots also made a contribution with *James*, the name of seven of their kings. Other Scots names to make it fairly big on this side of the Atlantic were *Andrew, Alexander, Archibald, Duncan, Donald*, and *Kenneth*.

In the late nineteenth century, adulatory first names—*Washington, Jefferson, Franklin*, for example—came into use. Imbued with mid-century romanticism, such aristocratic English names as *Howard, Percy, Douglas, Sidney*, and *Chester* came to the fore. Tennyson's epic poem *Idylls of the King* inspired the use of such Arthurian names as *Guinevere, Enid, Elaine*, and *Vivien*, while Sir Walter Scott's work glamorized *Bruce, Douglas, Ronald*, and *Roy*; and Shakespeare furnished *Juliet, Rosalind, Olivia*, and *Viola*.

Common nouns now came into play. Among precious stones, we found *Pearl, Ruby, Emerald*, and *Diamond*. Among flowers, the long-established *Rose* was joined by *Lily, Heather, Violet, Hazel*, and *Iris*. Feminizing came very much into fashion. *George* became *Georgina* or *Georgette; Robert* became *Roberta*. And from *Bill*, we arrived at *Billy* for a boy and *Billie* for a girl.

At the same time the people in the South and rural Midwest began to invent extraordinary names for girls, and the craze has continued to the present. Some early examples were *Blandina, Coritha, Dovinda, Keturah, Parnethia, Minuleta, Typhosa, Rodintha, Sula, Isaphene*, and

Woodward Family Register
Ink and watercolor c. 1837, 16x18
inches. New England: Collection of
Bertram K. and Nina Fletcher Little.

Levantia. Newer artificial names include *Gelda, Marette, Xanthe,* and *Zella.* A like fancy in boys' names has not surfaced—fortunately, perhaps.

The most significant flooding of the American name pool took place, of course, during the enormous wave of immigration to this country in the nineteenth century. Many of the traditional names people bore were changed for them at their port of entry. In addition, immigrants themselves often suppressed or converted their names in an effort to become better assimilated into American society. For many generations, *Vasilos* became *William, Harutyoun* answered to *Harry*; and *Mahmoud* called himself *Mike.* Now there is a new pride in the origins of all Americans, and *Vasilos* is back. Today, the name pool that new parents are free to contemplate has become luxurious in its options and perfectly oceanic in its opportunities.

A fifth child, Clarence Darrow had this to say about his name: "When it came my turn to be born and named, my parents had left the Unitarian faith behind and were sailing out on the open sea without rudder or compass, and with no port in sight, and so I could not be named after any prominent Unitarian. Where they found the name to which I have answered so many years I never knew. Perhaps my mother read a story where a minor character was called Clarence, but I fancy I have not turned out to be anything like him. The one satisfaction I have had in connection with this cross was that the boys never could think up any nickname half as inane as the real one my parents adorned me with."

Kevin Tierney, *Darrow: A Biography*

Naming Names

"Over the years I have been astonished at the recklessness with which my friends have appeared outside the delivery room with names beribboned in pink and blue, waiting for their owners' debut. These babies were slipped into names even faster than into their first set of diapers. Why the rush? Why the quick imposition of raw nomenclature on these tiny helpless creatures staring up from their cribs, not yet even able to exercise their proper right of rebuttal and—even more—not yet able to contribute to *your* final choice of a name? Suppose you were the parents of a true Clarissa—and instead you named her Gertrude? or Harriet? or Violet? It boggles the heart; you have misdialed a human soul.

"Babies' names should gestate for months, the way embryos do. No plunging of infants into premature names. Rather, holding off until you've had time to savor all the emanations, vibrations, the cooing and smiling ascending from the bassinet, and only then translating these one-of-a-kind elements into a name that catches the essence of the newcomer.

"Naming our first child, born in 1961 in the Indonesian capital of Jakarta, turned out to be a drama even in a country known for its love of the theatrical. We hovered lovingly over the wicker cradle, searching for possible clues. Several days went by. The nurses clucked at us in Indonesian and English, warning us that we were violating the laws of the archipelago by failing to produce a name.

"I had, by the time the baby arrived, spent several years as a news correspondent in Indonesia, and so I began thinking in terms that provided linkage—our child to the land of her birth. Girls' names au courant in Jakarta at the time included Fatmawati and Sukawati. 'Fatmawati Kalb'? 'Sukawati Kalb'? I could hear her college friends, twenty years hence, calling her things like 'Fat' and 'Suk.' She would never forgive me.

"In the end it was my wife, Phyllis, who had the inspiration; she suggested an Indonesian *word* that would harmonize nicely with the Deborahs, Judiths, and Lisas in the world in which our baby would eventually grow up. 'Tanah,' my wife murmured. The baby, by then, was already nine days old. 'From *tanah air kita*.' Pronounced *tan-nah ayer keeta*, the phrase is Indonesian for 'our country,' *tanah* meaning 'earth,' *air* 'water,' and *kita* 'our.'

"'Tanah Kalb.' I sang the name several times to try it. I hurried to the cradle. 'Tanah Kalb,' I whispered. She smiled. I swear she smiled.

"Even now, more than two decades later, I can still recall the surprise and pleasure that the choice of 'Tanah' generated among our Indonesian friends. . . .

"As for our eldest daughter, the other evening I asked her over a family Chinese dinner how she liked her name.

"'I love it,' Tanah answered firmly. 'It's just me.'"

Bernard Kalb, excerpted from *Esquire*

About Traditions

Christians are united in the belief that no baby shall be given an anti-Christian name—get thee behind me Satan Jones! Otherwise, there are no longer any hard-and-fast rules.

Even the centuries-old Roman Catholic requirement that a baby be given a saint's name has now become a matter of choice.

A boy named after his father becomes *Jr.* unless his father is already a *Jr.* In that case, the new baby becomes the *3d.* If the boy is named after his grandfather, uncle, or cousin, he becomes the *2d.*

Children born into the Jewish faith are usually given both a Hebrew name and a name in the language of the country; the latter name may be a translation of the Hebrew name or merely have assonance with it, or there may be no relationship between the two.

Among Ashkenazic communities of Jews (primarily from Europe), a child is not named after a living relative, but among Sephardic communities (primarily from Spain, Portugal, and Arab countries), it is quite customary to do so. A boy receives his Hebrew name at his circumcision ceremony. Baby girls are given theirs at a service in the family synagogue or at home.

The use of the mother's maiden name as a middle name for both boys and girls has long been a traditional way to keep that name in the family. Now there is an even more direct way: Parents are legally free to select both the given *and* the family name of their offspring. Options include giving the father's surname to one child and the mother's to another, alternating in using the father's and mother's surnames as middle and last names, or giving all the children hyphenated versions of both surnames.

BIRTHSTONES AND FLOWERS
IDEAS FROM ANCIENT LORE

JANUARY	APRIL	JULY	OCTOBER
Garnet (Constancy)	Diamond (Love)	Ruby (Contentment)	Opal (Hope)
Carnation	Sweet Pea	Larkspur	Marigold
FEBRUARY	MAY	AUGUST	NOVEMBER
Amethyst (Sincerity)	Emerald (Success)	Peridot (Happiness)	Topaz (Fidelity)
Violet	Lily of the Valley	Gladiolus	Chrysanthemum
MARCH	JUNE	SEPTEMBER	DECEMBER
Aquamarine (Courage)	Pearl (Health)	Sapphire (Mental Acuity)	Turquoise (Prosperity)
Jonquil	Rose	Aster	Narcissus

In an incredible testimonial to a long-gone photographer's patience, *all* the babies of Gardiner, Maine, class of 1895, are assembled for a group portrait. We will never know their names—but they are just as wonderful without them.

How Do *You* Spell Tom?

How many Peters or Lisas do you know? or Herberts or Samanthas? Back in school, was there always someone else with your name? Chances are more likely than not. Although there are thousands of names to choose from, trends have their way with naming babies as with anything else.

According to a survey of 2,544 new parents conducted by Gerber Products Company, geography seems to be a strong influence in name selection. Currently, the most popular names in the Midwest are *Katherine* and *Ryan*; in the North, *Jennifer* and *Michael*; in the East, *Lauren* and *Gregory*; in the Northeast, *Haley* and *Matthew*; in the West, *Nicole* and *Brandon*; and in the South, *Jessica* and *Robert*.

Nationally, here are the top ten names for girls, chosen from a possible 1,716 names cited in the 1987 poll: *Jessica, Jennifer, Amanda, Sarah, Ashley, Melissa, Nicole, Lauren, Megan,* and *Lindsay*. And for boys: *Matthew, Jonathan, Brian, Michael, Jason, Daniel, Christopher, Joseph, Andrew,* and *Ryan*.

The Announcement

A child's birth may not make newspaper headlines, but parents like to announce the event in style. Such heralding can range all the way from ecstatic (3:00-A.M. phone calls from the maternity ward) to exotic (skywriting above a city's horizon). With modern technological advances, the sex of the baby may no longer be a surprise, but the name and vital statistics of the new arrival still merit some fanfare.

There is no right or wrong way to announce a baby's birth, though traditionally an engraved calling card with the child's name and birthdate is laced with a satin bow (pink or blue) to a bigger card bearing the parents' name and address. Some people fasten party favors, candies, or ribbons curled in fanciful bows to their stationery. Others insert photographs of the newborn, copies of the birth certificate, or even a tiny footprint. Commercial cards range from museum reproductions of nursery-rhyme illustrations to modern stationers' bold graphic designs. One innovative card store sends miniature hobbyhorses in florists' boxes.

Protocol—updated to handle the most "modern" of situations—recommends the following:

- For a woman who keeps her maiden name, a card should be printed with her name, her husband's name, and the baby's *full name*, to avoid last-name confusion.
- Twins can be recognized on the same card, perhaps with mirrored messages of each name and weight.
- A single mother uses her name without a title and the full name of the baby.
- Adoptive parents may announce the "arrival" or "adoption," along with the age and full name of the child.

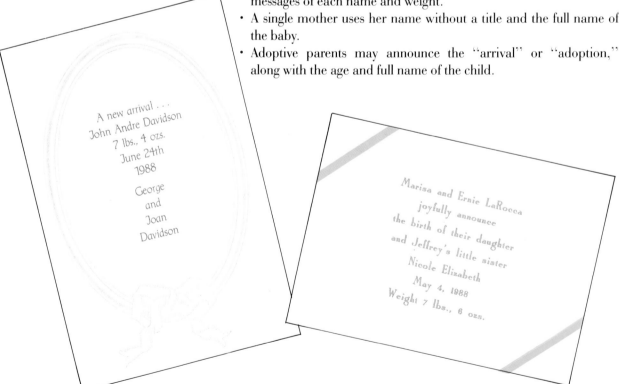

A new arrival . . .
John Andre Davidson
7 lbs., 4 ozs.
June 24th
1988

George
and
Joan
Davidson

Marisa and Ernie LaRocca
joyfully announce
the birth of their daughter
and Jeffrey's little sister
Nicole Elizabeth
May 4, 1988
Weight 7 lbs., 6 ozs.

Sarah Ann

June 12, 1988   8 lbs., 2 ozs.

Carl & Hetty Tegen

JONATHAN RYDEN ANDREWS

EIGHT POUNDS, TWO OUNCES   MARCH 10, 1988

ALICIA AND BENJAMIN ANDREWS

Kaitlin Marie Christianson

Seven pounds, two ounces   May 3, 1988

Mr. and Mrs. Stephen Jacob Christianson

Katherine Davis Tyler

February 2, 1988

Six pounds, twelve ounces

Laura and Adam Tyler

Simon John Lang   ♡   Born August 14 1987

Andrew Ann Lang

LITTLE FOOTNOTES

FAMOUS NAMES NEED NO INTRODUCTION

FDR and JFK, JR and PDQ command instant recognition.

LET US NOW PRAISE FAMOUS MEN

Pious Puritans labored long and hard before selecting a name for a new arrival. One luckless babe was baptized Through-Much-Tribulation-We-Enter-The-Kingdom-Of-Heaven. *Naturally enough, this was soon abbreviated to "Tribby."*

Less fortunate with the selection of a diminutive was the lad named If-Christ-Had-Not-Died-For-Thee-Thou-Hadst-Been-Damned. *His surname was Barebone. Alas, he went through life burdened with the name,* Damned Barebone. *Damned hard luck, we say. Shakespeare, on the other hand, observed in* King John, *"When we were happy we had other names."*

AS LONG AS THERE IS GOOD REASON

A sampling of unique names with even more unique reasons for being, drawn from Alfred J. Kolatch's Dictionary of First Names:

PENNOKY *Wood*
Columbus, Ohio
> *Her father was employed by the* PENN*sylvania, Ohio and Kentucky Railroad.*

NIRA *Lynn Dolan*
Livonia, Michigan
> *Her grandmother named her after the National Industrial Recovery Act.*

MICHONA *E. Hummel*
Phoenix, Arizona
> *Her parents were born in* MICH*igan and she was born in Ari*ZO*NA.*

JOELLE *Moore*
Vacaville, California
> *A television commercial for an aftershave lotion by that name inspired her parents.*

NARDI *Ann Dunn Ferge*
Rawlings, Wyoming
> *Her father was a sportscar buff who admired this Italian model.*

RONEEL *G. Bowden*
Linden, Texas
> *This is a scrambled version of her mother's name, Lorene. Roneel, in turn, named her daughter Eloren.*

STATE YOUR NAME

Wisconsin Illinois and Arizona Dakota were two North Carolina brothers named in honor of the country's westward expansion in the nineteenth century. We are left to conjecture on what the consequences might have been if they had met and married the sisters named Louisiana Purchase and Missouri Compromise.

"What's in a name? that which we call a rose
> *By any other name would smell as sweet."*

Shakespeare, *Romeo and Juliet*

COMMON NAMES

The most frequently given name in the world is Muhammad.

"Fools' names, like fools' faces, Are often seen in public places."

Anonymous

TRADITIONAL
CELEBRATIONS

GOD BLESS

❊

Having a baby prompts us to recognize our connections with the larger society; it is as if in creating a family we fulfill our role in the universal scheme of things. The religious rituals that take place in every society soon after birth reinforce the infant's reception into the inner community of basic blood affiliations with parents and relatives. The blessings and prayers also mark the newborn's first separation from the immediate family and acceptance as an independent member of the larger community, whether it be a tribe, a race, or the family of man.

Presenting the Baby
Artist unidentified, c. 1825–1850. Oil on canvas, 20x14 inches. New York State Historical Association, Cooperstown.

Christening: The Age-Old Ritual of Baptism

The Christian practice of baptizing and naming a newborn child is more familiarly referred to today as a *christening*—making the baby officially a Christian. One explanation of its origin, as stated by St. Augustine in the fourth century, is that all people are born in a state of original sin, and that if an infant were to die before being baptized, it would therefore die in sin. This being so, the high rate of infant mortality caused the church to require that all babies be baptized immediately after they were born.

Today, Protestant babies are generally christened when they are between two and six months old, while Catholic infants are baptized as soon as possible after birth. In some Latin American countries, babies are often christened before leaving the hospital.

The ceremony itself is usually held during or at the end of a regular Sunday church service, with parents, godparents, friends, and relatives in attendance as well as the congregation. While those present stand, the clergyman asks the baby's baptismal name. In the Protestant ceremony, the godmother then passes the infant to the minister and gives the baby's name. In a Catholic ceremony, only the godmother handles the baby over the baptismal font, thus establishing spiritual contact between her and her godchild. Depending on the faith, the minister then blesses the water and anoints the infant with it, by sprinkling or pouring the water over the child's head, or, in some cases, by immersing the baby briefly. Whatever method is used, the sacrament of baptism has now taken place and the child has been accepted as a member of the church.

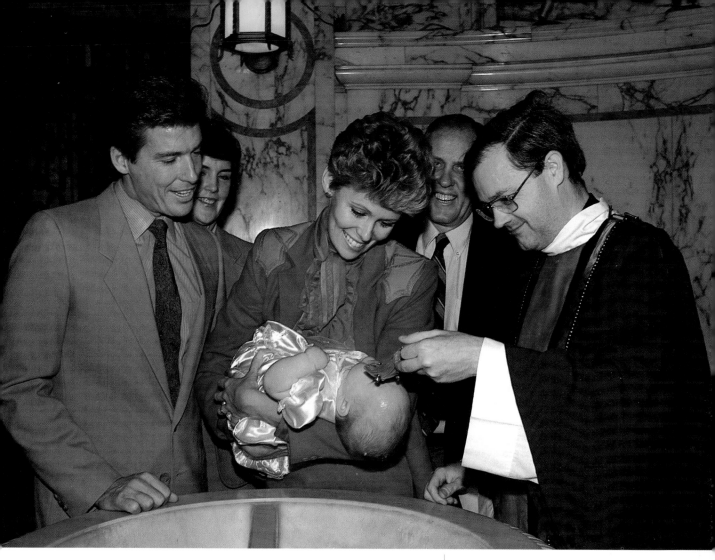

In a time-honored, intimate ritual, parents, godparents, and minister welcome the tiny new Christian.

After the ceremony the baptismal certificate is signed by the clergyman. This is an important document for Catholics, as it is required for First Holy Communion, confirmation, and for eventual marriage in the Catholic church.

There is no set fee for the service and parents give the minister what they can afford (from ten to fifty dollars is usual), and customarily invite him (and his wife, if he has one) to the christening party, if one is being given.

A small reception is frequently held at the home of the baby's parents, at which a luncheon buffet or light refreshments are served, as appropriate, and the baby's health is drunk.

Both christening and celebration are traditionally kept simple, emphasizing that this is a time when the tiny child is welcomed into the family fold with closeness, warmth, and love.

ON RECORD

The first birth registration law in the United States was passed by the State of Georgia on December 19, 1823. The law simply required courts to "enter and register in a permanently bound book" every birth in the state by individual county. The charge was 25 cents for each registration.

The Godparents

It is a great honor to be asked to serve as godparent to a newborn infant. Because it is hoped that the duties of the godparents will not be taken lightly, parents should have particular esteem and regard for each person they ask to fulfill this important role.

- The primary duty of a godparent is to guide the child's religious education, until he or she is an adult.
- Catholic children must have Catholic godparents, although co-godparents may be chosen as well, who need not be Catholic.

The just-christened royal heir held in 1894 by proud great-grandmother Victoria, seated between her son, later Edward VII (left), and *his* son, later George V, would grow up to become Edward VIII.

- Protestant children normally would have godparents of the same denomination, but this is not a set rule.
- There are normally at least two godparents, usually a man and a woman, not necessarily married to one another and not necessarily relatives of the baby. Frequently, there are two of the same sex as the baby and one from the opposite sex.
- Godparents are required to be present at the christening ceremony and a special gift (usually of silver) is given the baby jointly or individually by the godparents.
- It is understood, though quite informally, that godparents will remember their godchildren with a gift at each successive birthday and Christmas until they are grown up.
- It is no longer expected that the godparents will take responsibility for raising the child in the event of the untimely death of both parents. A legal guardian is appointed.
- Ideally, in asking godparents to serve, the parents hope that they will develop a special bond of affection with their godchild that will endure into adulthood, long after all religious duties have been fulfilled.

Porthault's modern christening outfit (left) is as exquisitely detailed as a priceless antique, while Tiffany's silver cup, porringer and rattle will become instant heirlooms.

CHRISTENING GIFTS

Grandparents and godparents delight in giving these classic presents; they will be treasured for years to come, and will gain in appreciation, so to speak, as the baby grows up.

STERLING SILVER, almost inevitably, monogrammed:
- knife, fork and spoon set, or a spoon on its own
- rattle shaped like a barbell
- rattle incorporating a mother-of-pearl teething ring
- porringer
- mug
- brush and comb set
- picture frame
- bracelet
- diaper pins

NURSERY CHINA, usually a bowl, plate and mug depicting characters ranging from Peter Rabbit to the Sesame Street gang.

THE BABY'S LAYETTE, interpreted as generously and specifically as the parents and giver please.

MONEY, in various appealing forms:
- a savings account or trust fund, set up in the baby's name
- stocks
- bonds
- real estate

WAY-OUT GIFT IDEAS:
- a rocking horse, antique or modern
- a year's supply of diapers
- a real or reproduction Edwardian or Victorian christening gown
- a case of port or brandy bottled in the year of the child's birth
- four years' worth of college tuition

And God said to Abraham, Thou shalt keep my covenant, therefore, thou and thy seed after thee in their generations.

This is my covenant, which ye shall keep between me and thee and thy seed after thee; Every man child among you shall be circumcised.

And ye shall circumcise the flesh of your foreskin; and it shall be a token of the covenant betwixt me and you.

And he that is eight days old shall be circumcised among you, every man child in your generations, he that is born in the house, or bought with money of any stranger, which is not of thy seed.

He that is born in thy house, and he that is bought with thy money, must needs be circumcised: and my covenant shall be in your flesh for an everlasting covenant.

And the uncircumcised man child whose flesh of his foreskin is not circumcised, that soul shall be cut off from his people; he hath broken my covenant.

Genesis 17, verses 9–14

Confirming the Covenant with Circumcision and Ceremonies

On the eighth day after birth, the sons of Jewish parents are initiated into the Jewish covenant, or *brit*, between God and man. During this traditional ceremony, the *brit milah*, the child is circumcised and given his Hebrew name. The ceremony usually takes place at home or in the synagogue, though it can also be performed in the hospital in a special room provided for this purpose. Guests consist of relatives and close friends and a small party is customary following the ceremony. A wine toast is made to the baby and his family, and gifts are offered.

All firstborn creatures are considered in the Jewish faith as dedicated to God and hence the property of the priest, but following the instructions in the Book of Numbers, firstborn sons are redeemed at the age of one month in a ceremony known as *pidyon ha-ben*, which is performed on the thirty-first day after birth. The sum of five shekels is offered to the *cohen* or priest, who redeems the child from his obligation and then entrusts him to his father for proper upbringing.

A Jewish daughter is given her name in the synagogue on the first Sabbath after her birth. The father is called to the Torah, where he recites a prayer and states his daughter's Hebrew name. The rabbi gives his blessing and a reception follows the service.

If the family belongs to a Reform synagogue, the congregation states the child's name, whether boy or girl, at the first Sabbath that can be attended by *both* parents after the baby's birth. Prayers are offered by those in attendance and a blessing is given. This ceremony takes place even if the son has been named previously when he was circumcised.

Torah binder
Schmalkalden, Germany, 1762.
Linen, embroidered with silk thread, 7¹/₁₆x137 inches. The Jewish Museum, New York: Gift of Dr. Harry G. Friedman.

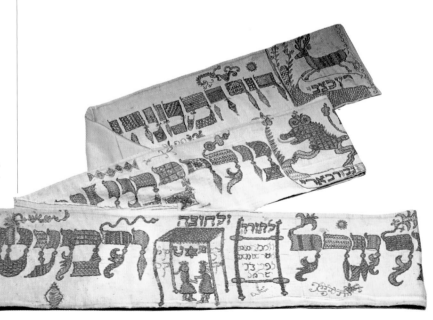

Circumcision set
Holland, 1827 and 1866, Box: 9½x7⅜x4⅛ inches. Box: silver, cast, filigree, and hammered, inlaid with semiprecious stones. Utensils: silver, cast, filigree, and hammered; carved mother-of-pearl. The Jewish Museum, New York: The H. Ephraim and Mordecai Benguit Family Collection.

A RITUAL FILLED WITH MEANINGS

The father is responsible for arranging this important ceremony on the appropriate date, as early in the day as possible, to show zeal. There must be a *minyan* or quorum of at least ten people present for it to be legal. The parents select three people they wish to honor to act as godfather, godmother, and *sandaq*, who will hold the child.

Two candles are lit; everyone stands, except the *sandaq*, who is seated on the "throne of Elijah," a chair named for the prophet regarded as each baby's guardian at the covenant of circumcision.

At the *mohel*'s call, the godmother brings in the baby on a pillow and gives him to the godfather. Those present bid the child welcome. With a prayer, the *mohel* takes the baby and places him on the *sandaq*'s lap. He then recites the blessing and performs the circumcision.

The baby's father says a blessing, and everyone responds: "Just as this child has been entered into the covenant, so may he be entered into the Torah, marriage, and good deeds."

The *mohel* then blesses the wine and prays for the well-being of the baby and his family. The child is named, and a piece of gauze is dipped in the wine and applied to the baby's lips. The parents then drink from the cup, the baby is put back in his mother's arms, and the ritual ends.

Circumcision: The Symbolic Wound

Kiddush cup
Austrian, Augsburg, 1761–63. Silver,
5⅜ x 2¹¹/₁₆ inches. The Jewish Museum,
New York.

The ritual framework for circumcision—still traditional in much of the world despite heated medical controversy—is complicated and varied. But the tradition best known in the United States is the Jewish one, set forth in Genesis.

In the late nineteenth century, circumcision, the surgical removal of the normally present foreskin of the penis, began to be common medical practice in the United States. There arose a culture of confidence in its role in preventing all kinds of ills, real and imagined—from rheumatism and rectal prolapse to enuresis. It is estimated that in 1870 only 5 percent of American men had been circumcised. That figure rose to 25 percent by the turn of the century, and kept on increasing. After a peak of 95 percent in the 1960s, the rate has declined to about 80 percent; yet it remains the most commonly performed operation in the United States today—at a cost of as much as $200 million a year.

Although it is now done quickly and safely within days of birth, it is still a painful procedure. It remains the center of a vigorous debate. Does it prevent penile or cervical carcinoma? Does it at least prevent infection? Or is it simply an instance of medical mythology, a collusion between gullible physicians and their tiny patients' compliant parents—a holdover from a semibarbaric past?

Much lower and declining rates in some countries—30 percent or less in Canada and Australia, 10 in New Zealand, 1 in Great Britain—together with the difficulty of justifying circumcision medically, have led to an "intact baby movement" in which the National Organization of Circumcision Information Resource Centers (No Circ) has figured. Edward Wallerstein, a urologist, and others have argued that physicians should oppose the procedure or even refuse to do it, as was done in the recent past with the once-popular tonsillectomy. Few if any object to ritual circumcision, but some feel, as Wallerstein said in a leading journal, that "routine newborn nonreligious circumcision will soon pass from the scene to join blood-letting and cupping in medical history."

The overwhelming majority of circumcisions are done as a routine modification of normal anatomy. A physician, usually an obstetrician or pediatrician, after obtaining a standard consent from the parents, performs the procedure in minutes. It is almost without risk. The infant certainly feels and shows signs of pain, but these are transient. A recent study in child development showed that behavioral distress such as crying and agitation had passed within two and a half hours, along with a parallel decline of the stress hormone cortisol, released in response to any injury. The infants' equanimity surprised the researchers—psychologists with no professional stake in circumcision—"providing a striking indication of the coping capacity of the healthy human newborn."

It is not surprising that a joint statement of the American Academy of Pediatrics and the American College of Obstetricians and Gynecologists says, "There is no absolute medical indication for the routine circumcision of the newborn." But critics ask why the statement seems indecisive, and why physicians are not actively opposing the procedure. Venality seems an inadequate explanation. Something is at work here psychologically, but no one understands what.

In 1981, when our son was born, his circumcision was performed by a man who was not only a Jewish ritual circumciser, or *mohel*, but also a physician doubly certified—in obstetrics and gynecology as well as in pediatrics. We weren't taking any chances. He said what any good doctor would say: "There is no sufficient medical reason to do this." Like most Jews, we did it for religious, or, in our case, ethnic reasons. Call it pride or stubbornness, but I wanted my son to be physically identified with his past, lest in the chilling words of the biblical injunction, he "be cut off from his people." Thus did a pair of unbelievers keep that most ancient covenant.

Melvin Konner, M.D., excerpted from *The New York Times*

A WIDESPREAD RITUAL

Elsewhere in the article at left, Dr. Konner describes some other cultures' use of circumcision as a rite of passage:

"Circumcision has been done at various times of life for various ritual purposes. Among the Ngatatjara of Australia's Gibson Desert, it was done at puberty, in the setting of an exotic dance around a great bonfire, in homage to the sacred Kangaroo. . . . Among the Nedembu of Zambia, who did it between ages eight and ten, the circumciser was likened to a lion—the ritual dance imitated lions—and his role was to sever the child's dependence on his mother. . . . Among the Merina of Madagascar, it was done between one and two years of age—in a sedate, dignified ritual for which many relatives gathered together. The ceremony emphasized continuity with the ancestors, and insured the infant ultimate sexual potency and fertility."

Seventeenth-century circumcision ceremony.

A Celebrated Seminole Warrior and
His Family
George Catlin, 1796–1872. American
Museum of Natural History, New York.

Honoring the New Being

All over the world, the arrival of a new baby is an event loaded with
significance for both the immediate family and the larger community.
From earliest times, specific rites have celebrated the infant's separation
from the security of the womb and incorporation into the real world
outside, where evil spirits threaten the precious life at every turn.

Ceremonies of purification and cleansing appear in almost every
culture. Primitive Semitic peoples set baptism rituals on the eighth and
fortieth day after birth, at the close of periods when demons were
thought to have power and expulsion rites were especially appropriate.

For the first seven days of life, which are referred to as "the days of
need, danger, or death," nomadic Bedouin tribes still smear newborn
babies all over each day with salt (mixed either with olive oil, buttermilk, or clarified butter, depending on the tribe). During this period the
newborn is called by a general title or disguising name so that evil spirits
will not be able to identify it. After the seventh day a sacrifice is made,
the baby is washed in camel or cow urine (water is too valuable), rubbed
again with salt, and given an individual name.

Severance from the baby's previous environment is represented in many different ways. Sometimes the child is passed through, across, or under a ritual object, in a ceremony to reinforce the separation between baby and mother. Rites that involve cutting, such as the first hair-cut or shaving the head, and rituals of putting on clothes for the first time are generally separation rites, while naming, ritual nursing, ear-piercing, and preserving the first tooth are acts that incorporate the baby into the community—whether they take place among the Yao of East Africa or the Dyaks of North Borneo. Later rites mark further transitions from one stage of development to the next.

An ancient Hindu custom was to fasten a wooden talisman around a ten-day-old baby's neck, while saying, ''Take possession of this charm of immortality. I bring you breath and life; do not go toward the dark shadows; remain safe, go before you toward the light of the living.''

Wherever they took place or still occur, all such ceremonies have the same purpose: to establish beyond doubt that the newcomer is no stranger but safely one of us—for ever and ever.

CARING FOR THE CORD

In most cultures the most common separation rite was the very immediate ceremony of cutting the umbilical cord, and the exact implement used to sever the cord was considered extremely important. Indians in the Punjab, for instance, would cut a male child's cord with a knife belonging to an older male in the family, such as a grandfather or uncle, while a girl child's cord would be severed with a spindle. The Hopi Indians of Arizona used the head of an arrow to cut the cord of a baby boy; if the child was a girl, the cord would be cut with a stick used to put grain into storage jars.

In several cultures, the umbilical cord itself also has significance. It might be entrusted to a relative, or attached to the baby's cradle, or carried in a special bag around the child's neck. Sometimes it was buried under a threshold or in the spot where the child was born. By preserving the cord from falling into unsafe hands, the child's personality was protected from becoming weakened during his lifetime.

Cree shoulder bag
Beads and hide. American Museum of Natural History, New York.

LITTLE FOOTNOTES

RED BRINGS GOOD

In many cultures red is the color of prosperity, and Chinese ceremonies, performed for both boy and girl babies at three days old, included fastening their wrists with a long red cotton string, festooned with coins and silver charms, and hanging a sign on red paper above the door to ward off unfavorable influences.

LET THEM EAT GOAT

Among the Sofwa of West Africa, the birth of a couple's first child requires both grandmothers to brew beer—the first time both families exchange the same gift with each other—and the paternal grandfather to kill a goat which all will eat. The child receives one name from each grandfather's family, and the two sets of in-laws become known as "those who have eaten goat together."

CHEERS FOR THE GROANS

Special fare, traditionally made and served to family and friends celebrating a birth in old England: Groaning Cake, Groaning Cheese, and plenty of Groaning Beer.

PRIMITIVE PANTHEISTS

As far apart as Germany, Africa, and Australia, anthropologists have traced beliefs that the souls of unborn children live in the fields or forests, in the form of trees, bushes, flowers, or even vegetables. Could this be the origin of the myth that babies are found in the cabbage patch?

BEATING THE WITNESS

Because an infant's baptism was an important means of establishing legitimacy in the Middle Ages, the youngest witness, who was deemed likeliest to live the longest, was customarily struck very hard with fists by the other guests, to keep the memory prominent should he be called upon to verify the ceremony at a later date.

"The baby at a christening is both the undisputed center of attention and completely free from social responsibility. (The only other occasion at which the guest of honor has these distinctions comes at the extreme other end of life.)"

Judith Martin, *Miss Manners' Guide to Rearing Perfect Children*

CLASSICAL CUSTOMS

In ancient Greece and Rome a baby's arrival was honored by a ceremony at which the newborn was bathed, named, and recognized by the father as his own child. In both cultures, too, friends would send in small tokens or gifts to the new baby, and five days after the birth, the family held a feast with dancing—and drinking. "Wetting the baby's head" has antique roots, it seems.

BAPTISMAL NOTE

The word baptism *comes from the Greek, meaning to dip in water.*

SOULBUILDING

The Ainu people of Japan believed that a baby acquired its body from the mother during pregnancy and its soul from the father during the first twelve days after birth. During this important period all three would be secluded, with the father spending the first six days in a friend's hut and the remainder in his own. From the twelfth day onward, the baby was regarded as an independent being.

BABY'S WORLDLY GOODS

THE ENCHANTED NURSERY

Since the beginning of time, relatives and friends have delighted in showering the new arrival with the gifts that seemed appropriate. Once it was the children of royalty who slept in superb cradles or whose layettes bore thousands of tiny hand-stitches, but in these affluent days, those who have it, flaunt it for the benefit of the tiny newcomer. Yet the welcome is real, whether it involves the expenditure of thousands of dollars or the hunting of a furry animal and the skillful preparation of its soft, warm skin "to wrap the baby bunting in."

When Too Much Is Not Even Coming Close to Enough

Who was it who declared that all any child needs is three square meals a day, a roof over his head, and a lot of love? Today's pampered babies are benefiting from the laws of supply and demand: Fewer babies born, fewer siblings to share the largesse. We speak, of course, of the offspring of the superachievers who spare nothing to shower their babies with everything.

Among the thirty-something, college-educated, dual-working-parents crowd, having a baby has become the ultimate status symbol, and as such the newborn is not too young for a role in displaying the family's assets. There is certainly one heap of assets to display. Estimates are that next year parents will spend $20 billion on furnishing babies with their basic needs. By the time a just-born kid reaches kindergarten, he will have been nurtured to the tune of $21,000. At this point, the costs begin in earnest with the onset of school fees.

Privileged babies cannot be expected to begin life wearing hand-me-down clothes, sleeping in a secondhand crib, or bathing in a bath that some other baby has previously splashed in. Everything must be top-of-the-line, from the choice of the birthing center to the brand name on the stroller. To hold your own on a first-class flight, you need to be hand-carried in the very best carry-on sleeper, and to attend a tony nursery school, you simply *must* be properly dressed. A visionary company located, not surprisingly, in Los Angeles, offers gold and silver lamé

Exquisite styles for America's youngest set come to *Bon Point* on fashionable Madison Avenue in New York from the shop's headquarters, appropriately located in Paris.

diaper covers for infants. According to one of the owners, "Attitudes have come of age. Those drab terrycloth sleepers and ho-hum rubber pants simply won't do anymore."

Custom decorators are finding a fertile market among those who willingly decorate a nursery for sums that once were sufficient to buy an entire house. An average order is $2,250 at Bellini, a chain of children's furniture stores. A designer fabric crib sheet with a matching pillow sham sells for $200. And manufacturers are falling behind in filling orders for $250 stuffed animals and $750 dolls. There is even a $4,000 miniature Mercedes-Benz that uses real gasoline. Compared with that, a $400 stroller seems like a real bargain.

The Rise and Fall of the Nursery

It doesn't take much to catch the nuance of the word. To even *have* a nursery indicates that a person's means are sufficiently substantial to provide other rooms in addition to it. No one could be pretentious enough to refer to a corner of a one-room apartment as a nursery. There have to be rooms to spare before one of them can be afforded a single-purpose designation.

For a baby to have access to both a day *and* a night nursery implies that the father (seldom is this a single-mother situation) is a man of very considerable consequence, because this is not, by a long chalk, the end of the expense. What is also required, of course, is the staff to keep the operation going. In order to be taken seriously, any proper nursery needs (in addition to the absolute core of the operation—a baby) a nanny who lives in—and has her own day and night accommodations, too—a laundress to take care of the washing and ironing, and a housemaid capable of keeping the place spotlessly clean. A cook is required to be on hand at all times, too.

During the Victorian era when fully staffed nurseries were most frequently to be found, mothers had far too many things to do than to be spending a whole lot of time with their children. For these busy women, the nursery served a most useful purpose. It was here that their young were fed, cleaned, and taught the rudiments of civilized behavior; it was from the nursery that they were brought before their parents, who checked on their progress before returning them to the hands of others who were often better equipped to cope with them.

This fashion has passed. Some would like to bring it back.

Lavish lace and a big silk bow reflect Victorian America's taste in cradles (left). In contrast, simplicity and beauty of line are preserved in this nursery in the Hancock Shaker Village near Pittsfield, Massachusetts (opposite).

OUTFITTING THE NURSERY TODAY

A baby's basic essentials are a consistent place to sleep, somewhere to be changed, and storage for all the paraphernalia: clothes, diapers, linens, and toiletries. Within these parameters, there are countless possibilities:

SLEEPING:

Early alternatives:

- cradle (snug, soothing, but quickly outgrown)
- bassinet (a wicker basket that has a stand, but can also be carried from room to room)
- carrycot (variation of the bassinet, with handles, no stand)

From birth until graduation to a regular bed:

- crib (worth spending time and money for researching safety, durability, and good design)

BEDDING:

- crib mattress (firm, thick , and sized to fit exactly)
- crib sheets (preferably cotton and fitted)
- waterproof pads (flannel-backed rubber sheeting)
- blankets (lightweight cotton or wool, cellular construction)
- bumper pads (to protect baby from the crib sides)

  Note: no pillow

OTHER:

- changing table (with storage beneath)

- storage furniture (drawers, shelves, containers, as appropriate)

Optional:

- bath
- portable infant seat
- rocking chair (can work wonders when nursing colicky infants)

Later possible additions:

- high chair
- safety gates
- playpen
- swings, bouncers
- walkers

Pastel checks and white wicker combine to create everybody's dream nursery, put together by the modern interpreter of traditional charm, Laura Ashley.

Cats Quilt
Artist unknown, Kentucky, c.1930s.
Cotton, feed sacks, and muslin,
82½x66½ inches. Museum of American Folk Art, New York: Gift of Laura Fisher.

In winter I get up at night,
And dress by yellow candle light:
In summer, quite the other way,
I have to go to bed by day;
I have to go to bed and see
The birds still hopping on the tree,
And hear the grown-up people's feet
Still going past me on the street.
And does it not seem hard to you,
That when the sky is clear and blue,
And I should like so much to play,
I have to go to bed by day?

Robert Louis Stevenson,
A Child's Garden of Verses

The Well-Dressed Baby

Right shoe, wrong foot.

Because people worry a lot about clothing babies appropriately, we asked a popular New York pediatrician a few of the questions that most frequently come up. Dr. Katherine Karlsrud teaches pediatrics at Cornell University Medical Center and collaborates on the "Birth to 1 Year" page for *Parents Magazine*.

What is the most common mistake made when dressing a baby?

Overdressing, particularly with newborns. In August I've had kids come in with wool hats on. Often, the first time I see a baby in the office, she comes wrapped in a cloth carrier, which is a very warm place to begin with. And she has a hat on, a T-shirt, *and* a baby outfit. When she comes out of the carrier, she looks as red as a beet.

It is very important not to overdress the baby. A young infant, especially, has very poor temperature regulation. Babies will adapt to whatever environment you put them in, cold or hot. That's another point to remember. They get colder faster, too.

How should you dress your baby?

Generally, I tell parents to dress their baby exactly as they would dress themselves. If you need a jacket, the baby needs a jacket. If you need a sweater, the baby needs one, too. But they *will* need a hat sooner than an adult, because they are either bald, or without a lot of hair. Hats that are meant to protect from the sun need a broad beak, like baseball players wear, to shield the baby from the rays. Most hats you see on baby heads don't have that.

How do you know if a baby is warm enough or too hot?

You have to experiment as a new parent. If after you have been outside for a while and you take the baby home, her hands feel freezing cold, then you probably haven't put enough on. If the baby is too hot, the whole body will feel like a hot potato and look sort of reddish. Then you've put too much on.

Infants do not complain about being overheated, contrary to popular belief, nearly as much as they should. A lot of babies will be content to be bundled up just like they were inside the womb. They simply go to sleep and retain all that heat.

What are some ways to keep cool when it is very hot?

Cool baths or showers help babies *and* their parents. Don't use soap, just cool the baby off. And then dress him in a diaper and T-shirt, or if it is very hot, just a diaper. And keep him hydrated with lots of liquids, milk or water. Milk is 95 percent water.

Little-girl charm is already reflected in this baby's favorite nightgown of flowered flannel edged with lace.

This helpful schedule comes from a 1918 Good Housekeeping:

SCHEDULE

MONDAY—*Wash diapers; wash two shirts, bands, and bootees or stockings.*

TUESDAY (washday)—*Wash diapers and all other soiled clothes, including bed clothes; wash one shirt, band, flannel skirts, and other woolens if necessary.*

WEDNESDAY—*(ironing day).*

THURSDAY—*Wash diapers; wash two shirts, bands, and the bootees or stockings.*

FRIDAY—*(cleaning day).*

SATURDAY—*Wash all soiled clothes, including bed clothes. If wash-day seems too full, the woolens may be washed now instead of on that day. Iron this lot of clothes either on the same day, or on Monday.*

The schedule is arranged so that one semi-weekly washing falls on the regular wash-day, and ironing and cleaning days are left free. If the regular washing is done on Monday, the schedule can be rearranged as necessary. In order to carry out this schedule the mother should provide: 5 dozen diapers, 7 or 8 dresses, 3 or 4 flannel skirts, 3 shirts, 3 bands, 3 pairs of stockings or bootees, 4 nightgowns.

What about protecting those crawling knees?

Generally, you don't have to do much of anything. When the baby starts to rock on his knees and then begins to crawl, the knees toughen up and get a thicker skin. So even if it is hot outside, you don't have to put on long pants, unless, of course, the baby will be crawling outside where it is dirty. But very often babies in diapers crawl nicely—and if it's 85 degrees out, I'd want to be in my diaper, too!

Sizes vary wildly from manufacturer to manufacturer. To ensure a proper fit, bring the baby along.

HOW TO CLOTHE THE BABY

Our climate has not changed that much since 1902 but a baby's basic summer wardrobe certainly has. Herewith a proper layette, according to Harper's Bazaar, which prefaced its recommendation by noting ,"the days of the large and elaborate wardrobe for infants, happily, have gone by."

"For the layette of a baby born in the late spring or early summer months the following is ample: six dresses; six petticoats; six flannel skirts; six shirts; three flannel bands; four night-gowns; two dozen diapers eighteen inches wide by thirty-six inches long; four dozen diapers twenty-two inches wide and forty-four inches long; four flannel or cashmere sacques; four pairs of thin cashmere or woollen stockings; four pairs of bootees or moccasins; two long wraps made of cashmere or light flannel, and one or two soft mull caps.

"The dresses should not be more than twenty-eight or thirty inches long at most and should be made of soft white material, with a tiny band of featherstitching finishing the yoke, and perhaps a narrow frill of very fine hand-embroidery or a bit of fine lace may be used. The hem of the dress should be four or five inches deep, hemmed by hand or hemstitched.

"Next is the flannel petticoat. Make the waist of this garment about half an inch longer than that of the white skirt, so the double row of pleatings do not come one over the other, mak-

Get me out
of this and into
something comfortable!

ing an uncomfortable thickness about the body at this point.

"The night-gowns for summer should be made of fine outing flannel or French flannel. Nightgowns are somewhat of an innovation, the old-fashioned method being to dress the new-born infant in a little muslin slip instead of a dress, putting him to bed in it and letting the child wear it for twenty-four hours before making any change. It is most desirable and much more comfortable and healthful that the child should be regularly un-dressed each night.

"The shirts are the next article in the baby's wardrobe, and these should be composed chiefly of wool. Unfortunately, a very thin woollen shirt cannot be found in the shops, but a mixture of silk or cotton and wool can be found and of fairly light weight.

"I advise stockings long enough to cover the legs of the infant. They should be pinned to the diaper, a piece of tape being sewed to the stocking for this purpose.

"The bootees mentioned are not ab-solutely necessary until short dresses are put on, but if there is the slightest tendency to cold feet they are indis-pensable.

"Sacques made of cashmere, me-rino, or flannel are to be preferred to those made of knitted or crocheted worsted; the latter do not wash well, and baby's fingers are always getting caught or tangled in the coarse meshes.

"The afghans are better in warm weather made of flannel or some light woollen material and can be either bound or scalloped. These are to throw over the child in case of draught or on a cool day.

"It is not necessary to include a cloak in the summer wardrobe; it would probably be outgrown before there was any use for it."

Never too young for a garden-party hat, especially in Newport, Rhode Island.

THE MODERN LAYETTE

According to Consumer Reports *Guide to Baby Products*, these are the basic clothes a baby needs on arrival. Other items, such as receiving blankets, stretchsuits, and disposable diapers, can and will be added.

- 6–8 snap or tie-front T-shirts (6-month size is most useful)
- 3–4 nightgowns (6-month size)
- 2–4 dozen cloth diapers
- 3 pairs booties or socks
- 3–4 pairs waterproof pants
- 2 small sweaters
- knitted tie-on cap (winter) or small tie-on brimmed hat (summer)
- bunting or hooded jacket (winter)

LITTLE FOOTNOTES

HOW DID IT BEGIN?

The custom of dressing boys in blue and girls in pink has its origin in the idea of protecting newborns from evil spirits. Blue, as the color of the heavens, was especially potent in frightening away demons, hence it was allotted to the most important child, the boy. Girls were thought so little of in those early days that there was no point in giving them a particular color; pink was probably a later attempt to balance the color scheme. A European legend is much prettier: baby boys were found under cabbages, which were, well, sort of blue, while a baby girl was born in the heart of a pink rose.

ONCE UPON A TIME

Nursery names for baby toes:

> *Harry Whistle*
> *Tommy Thistle*
> *Harry Whible*
> *Tommy Thible*
> *Oker Bell*

Nursery names for the fingers:

> *Tom Thumbkin*
> *Bess Bumpkin*
> *Will Winkin*
> *Long Linkin*
> *Little Dick*

THE COST OF PRIVILEGE

According to New York *magazine, the first year of life for the child of a "privileged" family (i.e., a child one of whose parents earns $200,000 a year) costs $71,543.*

THE "HEIR CONDITIONER"

One of the most renowned inventions of behavioral psychologist B. F. Skinner was the "air crib" he built for his second child, Deborah, who actually spent much of her first two years living in this air-conditioned, sound-proof device with a sliding window of safety glass. It accommodated a growing baby, for sleep or play, without the need for clothing or bedding, and although laymen tended to think of it as a prison, Skinner's intention was to provide maximum comfort and plenty of stimulation. "It was really just a special sort of crib," he explained in 1946.

DIAPER STATS

Consumer Reports *claims that a baby undergoes 5,000 diaper changes in the first two and a half years.*

CLEAN AND FANCY

In the 1890s, readers wrote to the Ladies' Home Journal *about concerns all could share:*

> *"I wonder if any of the Mothers have tried a creeping skirt for their little ones? Mine is such a saving to me, I should like you all to know about it.*
>
> *It is made like a bag open at both ends, and as long again as the dress, with a band on one end and a wide elastic run in the other end.*
>
> *Button on over all the skirts, then turn the other end having the elastic up under all the clothes. In this way the skirts are all in a bag. All others I have seen allowed the creeper to get pushed up, thus affording no protection to the dress. Of course the elastic must be removed for the wash."*

HELMETS FOR BABIES

From medieval times until the eighteenth century, babies used to wear a "black pudding," a round, thickly wadded cap of black velvet, which was put upon their heads when they started to toddle, to cushion the bumps when—inevitably—they fell down.

Baby's
First Friends

HI THERE!

——— ❋ ———

Baby looks up at all the smiling faces—brother, sister, granny, grandpa. These are the people who are going to be around, who after the parents figure first in a baby's first years and are—if they are willing to be—a baby's first friends. Not all the interactions, especially with siblings, will be peaceful—they were not the ones who invited this little stranger, after all—and family pets need careful introduction as well. But there is a special bond linking the real family in the home, and it will always be there.

The Brighter Side of Siblings

So much has been written about sibling rivalry that it is easy to overlook the positive aspects of the children's interaction. Brothers and sisters have an enduring relationship. A child spends just as much time with siblings as with parents. The siblings will almost certainly outlive the parents, and if the relationship is a good one, they will be there to offer each other companionship throughout their lives.

Brothers and sisters are a baby's first friends. They are wonderful sounding boards and have a marked effect on a child's willingness to share. Although all the experiences a baby has with them may not be pleasant, interaction with siblings instills a healthy sense of competition as well as the ability to stand up for one's rights. Both will be invaluable in the world beyond the home.

Siblings are protective. They serve as a security blanket when a child moves into a new neighborhood or attends the traumatic first day of school.

Siblings act as trailblazers, too. After the parents have been through a conflict with the oldest child, their techniques become more refined. They can be calmer when the problem pops up with the second child. Instead of paging the pediatrician at four in the morning, or delivering frenzied lectures, they just put their feet up on the couch and think: "Oh, *that* again."

Babies and toddlers learn a great deal from their siblings. They imitate the older children, and are more independent and verbal in their company.

The benefits of having brothers and sisters extend beyond the

A small explorer gets a helping hand.

Nearly new siblings share a secret.

immediate family. A boy who grows up with sisters will be more comfortable having female friends, and is likely to have a well-rounded relationship with the woman he eventually marries. A girl who has brothers grows up with more innate understanding of the opposite sex.

Siblings help with communication, too. Parents may not always understand what their toddler is saying, but often an older brother or sister will.

Two children are more work than one, but not always.

"When I just had one, I was busy all the time," says one young mother. "But with two, they entertain each other. They hold tea parties for their stuffed animals, and I have time to read!"

PREPARING FOR THE NEW BABY

- Discuss the pregnancy with your toddler as it comes up in normal conversation.
- Include your older child in preparations for the new baby, such as selecting baby clothes or a car seat.
- If possible, bring your older child along when you tour the birth facilities at the hospital to show where you will be while you are away.
- Try not to create false expectations. Well-meant statements such as "You're just going to love the new baby," or "The baby will be such a good playmate for you," may not turn out to be true.
- Take care not to overdo the preparation. Focus on the older child's immediate activities and interests instead.
- Have a sitter or relative stay with the older child in your home while you are in the hospital, rather than moving the child to another location.
- Reassure your child that you will be coming back after you give birth.

IT WAS JUST A SUGGESTION

The daughter of a pediatrician in Washington was bundling up her three-year-old son, David, to accompany her to a department store.

"Aren't we going to take Jonathan?" he asked, referring to his four-month-old brother.

"Not today," said Mom, zipping his jacket. "He's a little too young to be interested in shopping, and besides, he's taking a nap."

"Oh." David seemed disappointed.

His mother's curiosity was aroused.

"Why do you want to take him to the store?"

He shrugged his shoulders nonchalantly.

"Maybe we could sell him."

I WAS HERE FIRST!

After the birth of his second child, a boy, a father said proudly to his five-year-old little girl, "Well, now we have a son and a daughter." Not about to give up star billing, she politely corrected him. "A daughter and a son," she said.

BRINGING HOME THE NEW BABY

· Get someone else to carry the baby the day you return, so you can have a warm, unhurried reunion with the older child.

· Spend some time alone every day with the older child. Extra attention from father and grandparents is especially welcome now.

· Reassure the older child of your love. One woman used the metaphor of an overflowing fountain. Her love for her children was like the water, continuously flowing, with more than enough for everyone.

· Suggest that close friends and relatives who are bringing the baby a gift consider bringing a gift for the older child as well.

· Point out the privileges of being older. "Well, the baby isn't old enough to eat yet, but you and I can have an ice-cream cone."

· Encourage your older child to help you with the new baby. It will make the child feel important, and special.

· Celebrate the older child's birthday with enthusiasm and fanfare. It's a perfect opportunity to say "You're special!"

INTRODUCING YOUR PET TO YOUR BABY

A cat or dog is accustomed to a certain amount of attention, and may experience jealousy around a new baby. The following tips will help ensure a happy homecoming for all.

- Set up the crib early and allow your pet to become familiar with the baby's belongings.

- Have someone feed your pet just before you arrive with the baby.

- Let your pet sniff the new baby and satisfy his curiosity.

- Your pet may be upset by the baby's crying. After tending to your baby, soothe your pet as well, letting him know the crying is nothing to be frightened of.

- Ask visitors who are friendly with your dog to greet the dog first upon entering the house, then the baby.

Cats, Dogs, and Cradles . . . A Good Combination

Pregnant? Thinking of buying a puppy?

Wait. Now may not be the best time. Just like a baby, a puppy requires love and attention. Caring for two infants can be time-consuming—even if they are from different species!

When the child is a few years older, however, a pet makes a wonderful friend. Kittens and puppies provide endless entertainment. Like children, they have a high energy level, and delight in romping around the house and inventing new games.

A pet becomes the "baby" of the family, giving even the youngest child someone to take care of. Pets respond to children and make them feel important. Always accepting and uncritical, they are only too happy to listen to whatever their young master has to say. And unlike a child's two-legged playmates, pets never talk back.

Having a pet can contribute to a child's emotional well-being. Merely petting or talking to an animal has a calming effect. Studies have linked certain health benefits, such as increased socialization and lowered blood pressure, to owning a pet. Some children's hospitals encourage parents to bring their child's pet for visits, as a boost for the child's morale.

As they grow older, children can assume responsibility for feeding, grooming, and exercising their pet. In return, they receive an affectionate, playful companion who will never betray them. An animal's love is absolute and unconditional.

Fat cat keeps an eye on his snoozing companion.

CHOOSING THE FAMILY DOG

While it is difficult to generalize, the following breeds are noted for being gentle with children:

LARGE DOGS: Labrador, Golden Retriever, Old English Sheepdog, Collie

MEDIUM-SIZED DOGS: Standard Poodle, Schnauzer, Beagle, Basset Hound

Experts do not advise adding very small or "toy" dogs to families with children because they tend to be nervous. They are also delicate, and could be hurt if a child unthinkingly squeezes too hard.

SOME TIPS:

- Every dog has its own temperament, and there can be great variation within the same breed. A reputable dog breeder will recommend the pup best suited to be a family pet.

- When buying a puppy, find out how large it will be as an adult. That cuddly 5-pound pup you see now could develop into a 70-pound dog that could knock over a toddler.

- Does your family have a history of allergies? Select a short-haired or wire-haired breed that sheds as little as possible.

- Both male and female dogs can make good pets, but females are usually easier to handle and more even-tempered.

- The dogs we affectionately call mutts, "Heinz 57s," or mongrels often make better children's pets than purebreds, especially those that are "in fashion," which tend to be susceptible to inherited diseases as a consequence of overbreeding. A good source of mixed breed dogs is the local Humane Society, where the animals are fed, walked, and played with on a regular basis. Staff members are then in a position to screen a potential owner's needs and try to match them with a suitable pet.

My heart leaps up when I behold
    A rainbow in the sky;
So was it when my life began;
So is it now I am a man;
So be it when I shall grow old,
    Or let me die!
The child is father of the man;
And I could wish my days to be
Bound each to each by natural piety.

William Wordsworth

Wisdom and Wonder: The Magic of Grandparents

Grandchildren and grandparents have a unique relationship, founded securely on the bond of kinship and cemented by their mutual affection for the children's parents. But they have something else in common: time.

They are positioned at opposite ends of the life span, on either side of the breadwinning obligations that occupy the middle generation. Before babies are old enough for kindergarten or day care, they can be free agents. More often than not, so can their grandparents, who may either be retired or able to introduce flexibility into their working schedules.

Grandparents today are healthier than ever before. As a result of their increased longevity, they can look forward to establishing lasting relationships with their grandchildren, and to celebrating many of the important events in the children's lives.

They are also more affluent. While Grandmother may still greet her young visitors with a plate of sugar cookies, she is probably baking them between returning from her aerobics class and planning a trip to Tahiti.

Parents are changing, too. With the majority of young mothers and fathers in the work force, grandparents who live near are often called upon for babysitting assistance. Most grandparents welcome the opportunity to see their grandchildren, but appreciate being able to return to the quiet sanctuary of their homes at the end of the day.

As one grandfather puts it, "I can sum up the advantages of being a grandparent in a single word: Good-bye."

Remembering Granny

Her name was Mary Annetta Curtin Williams, but to me she was just Granny. She was a *true* granny, too, of the old school: She wore her white hair pulled back in a bun, she wore starched cotton "wash" dresses every day but Sunday, and she had a very ample bosom where I was always welcome.

I ate my granny's cooking from the time I could gum my mashed potatoes until I was seventeen, and never tasted any food I liked better. When I was a tiny shaver I lived with my grandparents for a couple of years; later, my parents and I went to my grandmother's house for lunch every Sunday. The whole family did. Often, she would come to stay in our house for weeks and weeks in a row. Wherever she was, she did *all* the cooking.

A sprightly modern grandfather tries not
to win the race.

One of my earliest childhood memories, as vivid as a scene from a
movie, is of sitting at Granny's dining-room table for dinner. There was a
very large pan-fried steak, with a "round bone" in the middle, and the
bone was specially cut out by my grandfather so that I could suck the
marrow. I recollect supping it up with great enthusiasm.

When Granny stayed at our house, she always provided a hot
cooked cereal for breakfast, and bacon and fried eggs, and fresh
biscuits. She also packed my lunch for school, in my square tin lunch
pail: usually a meat sandwich, slathered with butter and mayonnaise, a
cookie, a piece of fruit, and a thermos of milk.

Her main personal passion was for the whey from soured milk,
which she called clabber. Her main passion for *me* was regular elimination, and she made a potion of the juice of stewed prunes (and God

The face of an aging grandfather reflects the tranquil, enduring bond that transcends the constraints of time.

This is excerpted from an essay by Robert L. Raymond, which appeared in The Atlantic Monthly in January 1932:

"I have been thrown a good deal with a baby lately, and flatter myself that we have become intimate, and even that she enjoys my society. At any rate, she protests vigorously when nurse, mother, or some other interfering third party comes to take her away for bath, bed—the disciplined routine of life.

"She knows with me there is to be no welfare work, no uplift. It is all plain sailing.

"Our time is short and we get down at once to the business of happiness. Would this be amusing? No! All right—something else, then. How about this? First-rate! And in a moment we are hard at it.

"We are not constrained by any burdensome idea, however, that when we have chosen a diversion we must stick to it through thick and thin. Not at all. The instant before it becomes a bore we switch to something else.

"In this way we avoid ruts and keep ourselves from becoming stale. We are just as keen at the end of our hour as we were in the first joyful moment of being left by ourselves.

"Of course we realize life isn't all beer and skittles. We can be serious enough when we like. Possibly we exchange ideas sedately; but generally we prefer to relax in mere thought. On such occasions the baby is likely to be sitting on the wide sofa before the fireplace, inserting colored pegs in a square board. Every now and then she pauses in her work and looks over at me inquiringly. I nod, she nods back, and thereupon the work is resumed.

"My family and friends, so everyone says, are charming people, and I

knows what else) which she called "Doctor Pepper" and tried to trick me into drinking. She also loved lemonade and iced tea, both made freshly with lots of sugar. She did not believe in carbonated beverages, and as far as she was concerned, the Coca-Cola people could just forget about it.

Granny always said that most folks threw out food enough to feed a Chinese family for a week. When she had fed all her relations off a chicken at one meal, and stretched it out for lunch and dinner a time or two, she would take the carcass into the kitchen and go at those old bones like they were the best meal in the world. And when she found a particularly tasty bit, she would give it to me.

Richard Atcheson

think so myself. They do the best they know how to be entertaining. It is pathetic, though, how uninteresting these good folks are—I mean, compared with the baby. Moreover, I never know what is actually going on in the back of their minds. They say so and so; but what do they really think?

"I am never puzzled about what goes on in the back of the baby's mind. There is no back of her mind. Anything she thinks comes out before it has been sullied by being brooded over.

"It is a pleasure to make anyone happy. All you have to do to make a baby happy is to smile and speak kindly. And for reward you receive a spontaneous and understanding sympathy such as all older people have long ago forgotten how to proffer.

"Another pleasant thing: you can wear your heart on your sleeve with a baby. In fact, she expects it. Her own is defenselessly exposed, so why not yours?

"All these things are obvious and superficial. If you are a close observer, however, a baby can lead you pretty deep into the mystery of life. Until she is, say, three years old, nothing is plainer than that a baby is the mere conduit of a message from another world. It can only be God Himself taking a hand until such time as He may retire and allow the new life to go on without His direct intervention.

"This particular baby looks like an angel. It really would be absurd for a baby to look like anything else."

For an instant, four generations are fused into one (overleaf).

SPECIAL GIFTS FROM GRANDPARENTS

Grandparents often have nursery items that were once used by their children. Polished up or repaired, these can make lovely gifts for a grandchild, provided they meet today's safety standards.

- An old crib can be refinished to bring out the wood's natural beauty. Dressed up with pastel sheets and quilted bumper pads, it makes an excellent beginning for the new nursery.
- Wicker bassinets can be sponged clean, spray-painted, and outfitted with fresh pillows and ruffles.
- Children's furniture makes a charming addition to any household. The craftsmanship that went into the old ladder-back rockers and cane-bottom chairs is almost obsolete. Have them tended to by a professional, then present them gift-wrapped with a bow and a complement of stuffed bears.
- Old silver baby cups, rattles, and teething rings, which may seem dented and tarnished beyond recall, can often be restored to their original condition by a silversmith.
- Beautifully detailed knitted baby bonnets and sweaters can be rewoven in spots by the expert at the local knitting store, and washed gently in Woolite.
- Parents often preserve their children's christening gowns. One woman embroidered her granddaughter's name beneath her daughter's and passed it on to the next generation.
- The old-fashioned dolls with porcelain, bisque, or glazed-china faces are now sold as antiques. One grandmother had her daughter's doll repaired by the man who fixed her china. Then she pieced together a new dress from satin and velvet scraps. Only one problem remained: What to do with the doll's tangled hair?

An hour later the tiny treasure was installed in a chair at the grandmother's hairdresser's.

"Now, Mrs. Smith," said Filippo, raising his scissors, "what kind of look did you have in mind for Dolly?"

Iron-bound painted plaque, Nancy Thomas, 1988.

LITTLE FOOTNOTES

LIFE IN AN ESKIMO FAMILY TENT

"Both babies lived in an aura of love, not just their mothers' love but in the effusive affection of everyone in camp. . . .

"Oched (aged three) and Puglik (five) were encouraged to play with the baby, though Ella kept a careful eye on Oched. Puglik was gentle and affectionate with the baby (her mother had made her a rag doll which she now often carried in the back of her parka). But Oched was a tempestuous little boy who got easily carried away. He either poked the baby with a grubby finger, or smothered it with so much love, the poor thing could barely breathe, and Ella gently intervened."

Fred Bruemmer, *Children of the North*

HONOR THY GRANDPARENTS

In 1979, President Jimmy Carter designated the Sunday after Labor Day as Grandparents' Day, in recognition of their ability to "close the space between generations."

GRANDMA! GRANDPA!

Words with a universal meaning but many variations in sound:

CHINESE	
Zumu	Zufu
FRENCH	
Grand-mère	Grand-père
GERMAN	
Grossmutter	Grossvater
GREEK	
Ghiaghia	Papous
HAWAIIAN	
Kupuna wahine	Kupuna kāne
ITALIAN	
Nonna	Nonno
JAPANESE	
O-bāsan sóbo	Ojüsan sófu
POLISH	
Babka	Dziadek
PORTUGUESE	
Avó	Avô
RUSSIAN	
Babushka	Dyedushka
SPANISH	
Abuela	Abuelo
SWEDISH	
Mormor (maternal)	Morfar (maternal)
Farmor (paternal)	Farfar (paternal)
VIETNAMESE	
Bà	Ông

The Grandparents' Catalogue

PRAYER FOR AN INFANT BROTHER

The Infant's Primer, *published in the 1850s by the American Tract Society, included this prayer for a young sibling to recite:*

Lord, look on little brother dear,
Safe may he sleep when Thou art near;
Preserve his life to know Thy love,
And dwell at last in heaven above.

ADVICE TO THOSE VISITING A BABY

Interview the baby alone if possible. If, however, both parents are present, say, "It looks like its mother." And, as an afterthought, "I think it has its father's elbows."

If uncertain as to the infant's sex, try some such formula as, "He looks like her grandparents," or "She has his aunt's sweet disposition."

. . . If left alone in the room with the baby, throw a sound-proof rug over it and escape.

Christopher Morley, *Mince Pie*

THE
CARETAKERS

LOVING CARE IS EVERYWHERE

The notion that people need help taking care of a new baby is as old as the hills. What is new is the notion of being able to choose exactly what sort of care it will be and what type of person will provide it. Then it becomes a question of finding the appropriate solution for a particular situation—and of affording it. Baby care can be profitable in other ways than financially, however, and some caretakers are volunteers. Some are even the babies' mothers—taking a "sabbatical" from work to pursue an enriching alternative career: motherhood at home.

One of the most familiar of all human gestures: handing a child into mother's arms.

The Options

Sandra Scarr, currently chairman of the Department of Psychology at the University of Virginia and herself a mother of four, believes that "it's healthy for infants to discover that other adults can be trustworthy." And in her authoritative and comprehensive work *Mother Care Other Care*, she defines the options for mutually beneficial baby care as follows:

"Basically, there are four kinds of child care situations: Mother or father at home, babysitter at home, family day care home, and day care center. Although one might assume that being cared for by a parent at home is necessarily the best, such is not the case. The qualities of good child care . . . may or may not be offered by parents. . . . So it is with all child care situations—some are wonderful and some are awful. Choosing the best care for your child means being informed about child development, your own child's characteristics, and what is offered by the setting. Each of the four different settings has its own advantages and disadvantages for different children at different ages.

"Briefly, homes are more informal care settings than centers, and they offer more spontaneous interaction between caregivers and children. The typical family day care home is run by a neighbor or local mother who usually likes children and probably has several of her own. Babysitters are more likely to be older women, who are freer to come to your home to care for your child, or immigrants whose job options are limited. Centers are more likely to offer scheduled activities, a preschool educational program, and other children of the same age to play with.

- 37 percent of preschool children of working parents spend their days in family child-care homes
- 31 percent are cared for in their own homes by relatives, sitters, or professional caretakers
- 23 percent are enrolled in day-care centers or preschools

Some kinds of help are more helpful than others.

Good centers are also more likely to have caregivers with some training in child development and early childhood education. It is not surprising, given the different developmental needs of babies and older pre-schoolers, that parents of the younger group tend to choose care in homes, while parents of the older ones choose centers."

Conversation with a Working Mother

Eight years ago Louise Lague, now forty, nearly sabotaged a successful journalism career in order to have a baby. For years, as a journalist, she was paid to interview celebrities and dance at the White House; then she became associate editor for *People*, a plum job indeed. But all that glitter could not prevent her from heeding her biological clock, and, in the dead of winter, she proudly brought a beautiful boy into the world.

Did you return to work right after you had the baby?

Not immediately. At work I had the option to be on unpaid maternity leave for up to a year. Since I didn't know what motherhood was like, I just took a guess that six months at home would be enough. I had the luxury of being flexible. After four months *People* called and offered me a part-time job, two and a half days with no late hours, doing the weekly "Chatter" page. I jumped at it.

So, the decision to leave the baby and go back to work was not a hard one?

No. After four straight months of mothering, I knew I needed some time away from him. Mothering is completely emotional and physical; there is nothing intellectual about it. I needed help, but I couldn't afford it unless I worked. We lived in a tiny, expensive, overheated Manhattan apartment and *I needed out*, at least some of the time. For me, a part-time job, not a full-time job, was perfect.

A mother's decision to work or stay at home is intensely personal. You have to search your soul. I always look at full-time working mothers and wonder, Gee, how can they do that? But people are different. Some are endlessly patient with their children, others need the isolation and rewards of work. We all have different mental balances. I can't not work and I can't work full-time. I was lucky. Part-time jobs are hard to find.

When you first left the baby for work, were you able to be philosophical about it?

Did I feel guilty? Yes, but not *that* guilty. I still had plenty of time with the baby. Routinely he'd get up at 5:30 A.M. for the day. I'd count the hours between the dawn's early light and 9:30 A.M. which I left as quality time to get the guilt out. When I got to work at 10:00, I'd put my head on my desk and rest awhile. Then, after work we'd be together another two or three hours before his bedtime.

Just like home: mealtime in the kitchen of a friendly caretaker.

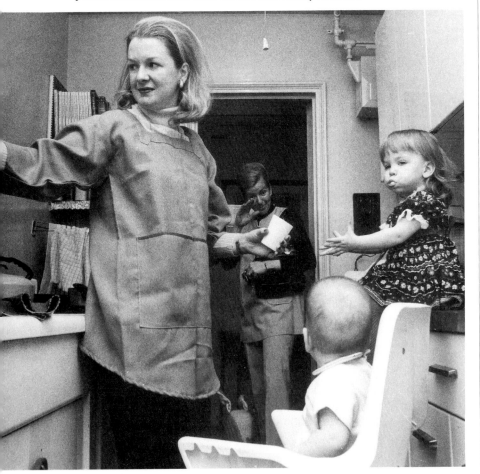

MATERNITY LEAVE ABROAD

SWEDEN

Parental insurance enables either parent to take up to 12 months leave without loss of income. Insurance benefits correspond to 90 percent of gross income for nine months and a fixed daily rate for the remaining three months.

FRANCE

Employers are required to provide at least three months maternity leave for the first and second child with no loss of income or job. For the third child the mother is guaranteed six months leave.

BRITAIN

The national health program requires a standard 29 weeks of maternity leave for the mother, only 18 of which are paid by the government. Employment is guaranteed following the leave although the job may be a comparable one with another company.

JAPAN

A maximum of 4 months maternity leave is common, and it is paid out by individual companies, not the national government. But many Japanese women still believe that their first responsibility is at home with the child. Consequently, many women quit the work force after giving birth.

SOVIET UNION

The Soviet government finances 1½ years of paid leave for the mother only, and job security is guaranteed.

How did your baby react to your disappearing act?

I think he was fine. We had a wonderful girl taking care of him.

What tips have you learned from experience about hiring babysitters?

I think you have to trust your instinct. Never interview a sitter without the baby in hand. Watch how she handles him or her. Personality is important. Ask yourself, Do I like her?

Check the references *very* carefully.

Did you live happily ever after with this first sitter?

At first she came to me only on the days I went to work. But it soon became clear that I was really going crazy, because all the errands and cleaning were waiting for me on the days I was home. So it turned out I was working at home and working at work. After three months we agreed that she would come five days a week. When I was at work, she took care of the baby; when I was home, she would come and clean while I played with the baby.

What happened when the second baby came along?

I kept working until I was seven months pregnant. We then moved to the suburbs. I had no help and no work for two months which, with only a three-year-old in tow, was wonderful. Together we settled into the new town, did the children's library, etc. But this time I was smart. I knew that the day the baby was born I needed Nanny again, and this time I had saved money for it.

In the suburbs the sitters are different. Everyone has an extra bedroom, which you don't have in the city, and you take someone to live in. I advertised in the local paper for one of those twenty-year-olds, and I hired one who moved in the day before my next son was born. And I have been doing that ever since.

Did you continue your part-time job in the city?

No. When we moved to the suburbs, I went completely freelance and left the staff at *People.* I didn't want to commute regularly.

You have worked in an office away from home and in a home office. What are the advantages and disadvantages of both?

The advantage of an office outside my home is that people, including Nanny, hesitate to call on me. I don't hear any babies crying or children fighting. I can concentrate completely on my work without distraction. Working at home, I have everyone trained to leave me alone, but I can still hear what's going on. Also, I am tempted to go downstairs and start dinner. But there are definite advantages of working at home. You have no commute, and you can take a break and give your kids a hug for a few minutes during the day. These intimate moments are, after all, by far the best part of mothering.

Truly Professional, Almost Perfect: The Nanny

Nanny is my nurse
She wears tissue paper in her dress
and you can hear it
She is English and has 8 hairpins
made out of bones
She says that's all she needs
in this life for Lord's sake

Nanny says she would rawther I didn't
talk talk talk all the time
She always says everything 3 times
like Eloise you cawn't cawn't cawn't
Sometimes I hit her on the ankle with a tassel
She is my mostly companion

Kay Thompson, *Eloise*

A thoroughly modern nanny helps baby "wave bye-bye" to mother.

THE CHILDREN'S NURSE AND HER DUTIES

Long before the supermom concept was born, new mothers were cautioned against doing it all alone. Here is Harper's Bazaar's advice, given in September 1909:

"There is little place for a small child in the well-regulated modern household where money is not plentiful. That is, if the master and mistress of the household have aspirations after elegant living, even on a small scale.

"The elegance referred to may not be of an extreme order. But if the house or apartment is in charge of two maids, who do all the work; if the meals are to be served in courses, and afternoon tea is considered an essential part of the program; if there is an occasional modest dinner or luncheon given, for which no outside help is to be hired; if the mistress of the house belongs to a club or two, and has a few social aspirations and consequent social duties, the stork would better stay away!

"If I were at this date the possessor of an infant or a small child I think I would try very hard to get hold of two maids who could be trained to follow the plans that were pursued by the mothers of a generation or more back.

"In those simpler days a woman thought herself fortunate in having two maids for a household of three. It required some scheming to arrange the work, but when this was once done the household machinery ran smoothly. And I see no reason why the same plan should not be followed now.

"If the baby is very young, it should be a matter of course that the mother should bathe and dress it and take most of the intimate care of it. In these circumstances she should not expect that the second maid should do any waiting, unless it be at dinner-

Traditional nannies take starched infants for an airing.

We all know what nannies are: Perfect, British women in blue suits who know everything there is to know about child care, and often everything there is to know about parenting as well.

Today's new twist is that American nannies are starting to enter the work force, as schools pop up all over the country to educate nanny-aspirants in such essentials as nutrition, exercise, first aid, travel, dress, etiquette, regional and ethnic foods, and family dynamics and problem-solving. There is now a burgeoning demand for graduates of such programs: Not long ago, *Time* reported that some two thousand families wrote to the American Nanny Plan of Claremont, California, to ask about hiring one of its thirty-six graduates.

American nannies are not cheap: The average starting salary is $200 a week plus room and board, and the figure can go up to $350 in large cities. Typically, American nanny-school entrants are from small rural towns and receive from eight to fifteen weeks of training. They may be the beginning of a tremendous new resource, particularly for two-career families and single parents. Competent and well-trained, they offer much-needed consistency amid the welter of other child-care options.

Eloise said: "Oooooooo I just love Nanny I absolutely do." Today's Eloises love Nanny, too—and so do her parents.

A grandmotherly nanny delights her charge.

Fashions may change but not the pleasure of a stroll in the park (overleaf).

An exuberant au pair perfects her language skills at the same time as the toddler in her lap.

The All-Too-Rare Au Pair

Au pair, meaning "on a par," is the term for young Europeans who come to live with a family for a year as an all-purpose mother's helper. Sponsored by the American Institute for Foreign Study (AIFS) or the Experiment in International Living, candidates must be between the ages of eighteen and twenty-five and speak fluent English. Currently, some 3,200 such young people are matched with American families on the basis of background, shared interests, and a host of other characteristics.

Most au pairs are bright, energetic young women (although men are eligible, too) who like to take care of children and have some babysitting experience. They enjoy the adventure of living abroad and seeing what sights they can while in the United States; they also expect to be given time off to take some college-level courses.

An au pair can be an ideal solution to the baby-care problem—and a very favorable financial arrangement—for a family with a home large enough to include a private room for live-in help. Whereas a nanny can easily cost $20,000 a year, the cost of an au pair (including a placement fee, a monthly stipend of $100, and a maximum of $300 toward tuition) runs about $8,000–$8,500. However, there are important differences to keep in mind: While a nanny, although highly paid, is an employee, the au pair must be considered as a temporary member of the family. Conversely, while a nanny can be left in complete charge of the household if both parents are traveling on business, an au pair cannot.

The exchange of cultural values touted in the AIFS and Experiment brochures is probably not going to benefit an infant or toddler as much as it will the parent, but the au pair's customary enthusiasm and enjoyment of the job can be a boon to all.

Requests for an au pair must be made at least two and a half months in advance.

Man to man.

BETTER SAFE THAN . . .

Babysitters joined the ranks of insured employees on January 26, 1950 when the American Associated Insurance Companies of St. Louis, Missouri, issued the first babysitters' insurance policy. It covered sitters available through the Missouri State Employment Service and bonded them for up to $2,500.

New Yorker cover by Perry Barlow.

Babysitter to a Nation

It is safe to say, without being the slightest bit salacious, that Perry Mendel, America's graying gentlemanly "first grandfather," is obsessed with women—young women, healthy women, ambitious women, energetic women, *working* women. As founder, chairman, and chief executive of Kinder-Care Inc., the nation's leading commercial child-care organization, Mendel's fixation is understandable. Without women in the workplace, he would not be the head of a company that netted $34.2 million on revenues of $380 million in the first nine months of 1987, up from a profit of $28 million on $235 million the year before. At sixty-five, Mendel finds himself the point man for an industry of considerable economic and sociological importance—despite the fact that it barely existed twenty years ago.

Mendel has taken Kinder-Care from a standing start to its current status as a company that is nearly twice the size of its nearest competitor; consistently profitable, it has engaged in steady expansion to become, as analyst Franklin Morton at Baltimore's Alex Brown & Sons puts it, "a machine that in 1987 opened a new day-care center every three days."

But to get to where he is today, Mendel needed a grand plan. To make really big money, he decided to develop child-care centers on a

HOW TO ESTABLISH A DAY NURSERY

An idea whose time has come? The Woman's Home Companion *thought so in 1910.*

"The advantages of a day nursery in the neighborhood are so many and so apparent that argument is scarcely needed on its behalf.

"I have in mind a day nursery started by a few women in a small town of not more than six thousand people in New England. The idea grew out of a condition—that is, a dearth of household help. There were several women who were anxious to go out and do day work, but they did not care to leave the baby. To take the baby along was not practicable, so a day nursery filled a want and with one accord half a dozen women decided to organize a day-nursery association to start it on a small scale.

really big scale. If McDonald's and Holiday Inn could turn their food and lodging concepts into national institutions, why couldn't he develop a nationwide child-care operation? One measure of his success, whether he likes it or not, is that Kinder-Care has become part of the national vocabulary: Some jokingly refer to his operation as "McChild" or "Kentucky Fried Children."

With a $200,000 stake, Mendel opened Kinder-Care No. 1 in Montgomery, Alabama, in 1969. His 1.5 percent ownership in the company was worth about $9 million at the end of 1987.

The typical Kinder-Care center is a single-story, air-conditioned building on a half-acre plot. Its little red steeple with its black plastic bell is as recognizable as the golden arches of McDonald's.

Mendel still considers that Grandma and Grandpa are Kinder-Care's "major and strongest competitors," but his success has spawned its share of imitators. La Petite Academy of Kansas City, Missouri, and Philadelphia-based ARA Inc. are the two largest. But there is still room for growth.

"As of 1986," Mendel points out, "there were 20 million mothers in the labor force. Currently, 64.7 percent of all mothers with children under eighteen are working outside the home, and by the year 2000 that number will be more than 80 percent."

Kenneth Englade, excerpted from *Continental*

Sing me a song and I'll clap to the music—but not for long.

"'One room for a day nursery is enough to start with,' said one of the prime movers in this particular day-nursery association, 'and it should be located conveniently in the neighborhood of the families who are to reap the benefits of it. A clean room, a caretaker who likes children, preferably one who knows something about nursing, a bed for a baby or two to take a nap in, a table, a stove, a couple of high chairs and a rocker were all we had to start with. The first day we had three children all belonging to one mother who went out to work, earned a dollar and a quarter, and paid to the nursery five cents for each of her children.

"'The local paper published an account of our enterprise, the village painter made us a sign, the grocers and butchers sent us provisions and soup-meat, furniture was donated as we needed it, and we gave various entertainments to raise money to meet the expenses.

"'Our day nursery is now two years old, and has a daily attendance of twenty-five children. Our nursery is a cheery room having curtains at the windows, plants in bloom, and all the homelike comforts. We give the children a breakfast of cereal and milk when they arrive. Dinner consists of soup, baked potatoes, baked apples, rice pudding or its equivalent, and supper consists of bread and milk. In the bedroom are three clean little beds for the babies' naps, and we have bibs and gingham pinafores for them to wear while they are in the nursery.

"'We also have mothers' meetings sometimes in the evenings, and we have some socials for the fathers and mothers, and at holiday-time the whole town is interested in the children of the day nursery having a good time. From our little nursery that started in one small room we have developed a really splendid work that is helpful to all, rich and poor alike.'"

The Baby in the Gray Flannel Romper

Some little ones fly on business trips; others are driven to the office every day, have lunch with a parent, gather for a "nap meeting" in the mid-afternoon, and drive home again at 5:00 P.M. They are the lucky ones: Their mothers or fathers work for one of the 150 or so large American companies whose commitment to their employees extends to providing day care.

Office day-care centers can be on-site or near-site—a mile or so away—and facilities range from basic to extravagant. The *Wall Street Journal* reported on one of the latter serving several major firms at Hacienda Business Park in Pleasanton, California. Features include radiant heat to warm the babies, a "tactile crawl area" and toddler-height windows, not to mention "dramatic wooden castles with recessed lighting."

"It's the wave of the future," Hayden Eaves, the managing partner of the developer, told the *Journal.*

Eaves is undoubtedly right. Although only about three thousand of America's six million employers currently provide any form of child-care assistance—be it money, referral services, or an arrangement with a sick-care program—child care is likely to be on a par with employee health insurance by the end of the century.

Less formal office care is also expanding. Increasingly, babies can be brought to the office for a day when other arrangements have fallen through. They may also be cared for in an office on a full-time basis, if the management is agreeable and flexible enough to deal with an occasional crisis. When it works well, in-office care is mutually beneficial: The baby acts as a communal stress-reliever and the parent is able to concentrate on the work at hand, free from nagging worries.

Infants are the best office regulars because they sleep most of the time; over-threes are next best because they are old enough to understand that when the office staff gathers around one big table it is not family dinnertime. In-between toddlers, however, may need a child gate to set territorial boundaries.

Bringing baby to the workplace is not a new phenomenon, for mother *or* father.

LITTLE FOOTNOTES

NANNY'S TABLE RULES

Always eat a slice of bread and butter first; then you may have jam on the next slice.

Don't eat with your mouth open.
Never speak with your mouth full.
You mustn't play with your food.
It's very rude to make a noise swallowing your milk.
Leave a little piece on your plate—for the fairies.
Say Grace before leaving the table.

"Some parents hire a babysitter when what's really needed is a lion tamer."

Bertrand Russell

"A group of recent mothers were discussing which month of pregnancy had been the most trying. One said the second, another said the ninth. At that moment a husband turned up and made the statement that he thought the tenth month was the most difficult. 'Because,' he said, 'that's the month the father carries the baby.'"

Hal Price
Bartlett's Unfamiliar Quotations

LAYING IT ON THE LINE

A training school for nursery-maids that was opened in connection with the new Babies' Hospital in New York in 1889 made it very clear that admission was not granted to the "broken-down, drunken or hopelessly dull and ignorant, nor to those who are careless, untidy, untruthful and impertinent." The school has since closed.

TICK-TOCK

Child-care advice in rhyme, from a book entitled For the Young Mother, *written by Murtle Eldren and Helen Lo Cron in 1921:*

The clock is Baby's truest friend
  As every Mother ought to know!
From early dawn to evening's end,
  It points the way to go!
'Wake up!' it says at six o'clock,
  'Wake up and have your morning
    meal!'
  And later, 'Time to bathe, (tick,
    tock!)'
And, 'Oh, how happy you will feel!'
  Then, 'Eat again,' then, 'Sleep,'
    then 'Take
  Your daily airing,' thus it goes—
So Mother ought, for Baby's sake,
  To take the clock's advice! It knows!

D. Beekman, *The Mechanical Baby*

THE WAY IT WAS

The daughter of a noble family of relatively modest means in nineteenth-century Russia recalled the following: "Relations between parents and children were defined quite precisely. Children kissed their parents' hands in the morning, thanked them for dinner and supper, and took leave of them before going to bed. Every governess spent most of her time trying to keep the children, as much as possible, from bothering the parents."

David L. Ransel,
The Family in Imperial Russia

GETTING THE PRIORITIES STRAIGHT

The first nursery school in New York City was established in 1827 "to relieve parents of the laboring classes from the care of their children while engaged in the vocations by which they live, and provide for the children a protection from the weather, from idleness and the contamination of evil example besides affording them the means of early and efficient education."

Famous First Facts

HOW DOES YOUR
BABY GROW?

An Amazing Process

---※---

That first shuddering inflation of breath opens up far more than those tiny, hitherto unused lungs—a whole new world of sensational power, in which the newborn spends the first few months catching up with the motor development that other mammal babies have at birth, then steadily outstrips them. For parents, babyhood is a time filled with protective caring, with providing food, exercise, security, companionship— all those tried-and-true virtues that are the building blocks of life. Every baby will grow, no matter what; understanding what happens makes the process all the more wonderful.

Physical Milestones

Can you chart your baby's development? Should you? Any number of books will tell you when a baby should sit up, roll over, or begin forming words. Most will also caution that not all babies develop at the same rate, and so you should not worry if your child is not following a precisely laid down developmental timetable.

Dr. Lawrence Balter, who we interviewed for this and the following chapter, confirms this very sensible advice. Still, he says, babies do progress toward toddlerhood on a fairly consistent course, passing predictable physical and mental milestones at a satisfying rate. Though one baby, for example, may crawl at seven months and another at nine months, no child will walk first and crawl later (though some bypass crawling altogether).

We sought out Dr. Balter because of his reputation for providing sound, comforting, and practical advice to parents feeling trapped in the morass of conflicting views about child rearing. A professor of educational psychology at New York University, he is the author of two books, *Dr. Balter's Child Sense* (1985) and *Who's in Control? Dr. Balter's Guide to Discipline Without Combat* (1988). He is, as well, a regular columnist and contributing editor for *Ladies' Home Journal*, reports on parenting and child-related issues for WABC-TV Eyewitness News in New York, and hosts nationally syndicated radio programs about parenting.

We asked Dr. Balter to outline a baby's physical development in the first two years of life, and were rewarded with reassuring, sensible guidelines.

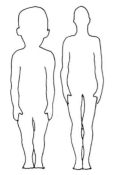

The baby's head is startlingly big in relation to the body when compared to adult proportions.

At each stage of development. a healthy baby is content, even angelic.

What Happens When

What can infants see at birth? At one month? At three months?

Babies can see at birth, although not very well. If it were appropriate, a newborn would certainly need glasses for myopia. But the eyes develop very rapidly and by seven or eight weeks infants can discern different shapes and colors, and by three months they have developed stereoscopic vision.

When do newborns recognize their mother, father, or primary caregiver?

Although Dr. Balter does not dismiss the claims made by many mothers that their babies know them right away, he explains that this varies from baby to baby and mother to mother. It is hard to determine but likely that babies "recognize" their mothers during the first few days of life by feel and smell rather than by sight.

How well does a baby hear?

Tiny babies can hear, of course, but probably not very well. They respond best to soft tones and singing. Loud, sharp noises may upset them.

Do babies have any sense of taste?

Babies can distinguish between sweet and sour tastes, but they have not developed the sophisticated flavor preferences that make up the complicated abstraction we call a palate.

Infants are most comfortable in a small space, where they naturally assume the fetal position.

Once babies begin to look around and glimpse life, they will never stop stretching their boundaries.

When can babies grasp objects?

Reflexes enable very young babies to curl their fingers around adults' fingers. At about two months they begin to initiate grasping, but the operation is not a smooth one. By four or five months they can hold an appropriate object after reaching for it or having it placed in their hands.

When do babies begin sitting up unsupported? When can they pull themselves into a sitting position and a standing position?

Sometime around five or six months a baby will sit unsupported for brief periods when placed in a sitting posture. Not until they are seven or eight months will babies try to pull themselves into this position, using their hands for help. At about ten months their muscles are sufficiently developed so that they can sit up all by themselves. At about this time, too, they begin pulling themselves up to stand, holding onto the side of a table or playpen.

Hands and knees are the speediest means of getting from here to there.

A TREATISE
OF THE
MANAGEMENT OF
FEMALE COMPLAINTS
AND OF CHILDREN
IN EARLY INFANCY

BY ALEXANDER HAMILTON, M.D.
M, DCC, XCV

Differences in the structure of
NEW-BORN CHILDREN
from that of
GROWN PERSONS

The bones are soft, spongy, and imperfect. Those which are afterwards single are generally divided into several portions; and almost all the bones have their extremities or edges in the state of gristle. The bodies of children, therefore, have not an exact regularity of shape, and are not well supported. Their different parts are not so steadily moved; and the organs lodged in the cavities are not so well defended.

The Nose, from the state of its bones, is also much exposed to injuries; and

What do you mean—it's bedtime?

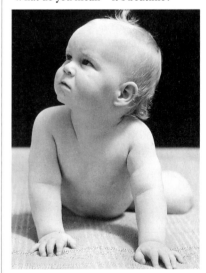

When does a baby crawl?

As a rule, babies begin by creeping. They sidle along the floor more or less on their bellies, often propelling themselves backward before mastering the forward direction. Creeping usually begins at about seven months, closely followed by full-fledged crawling around the eighth or ninth month.

When do babies walk?

Dr. Balter reminds parents that walking is a very different story from crawling. Walking generally occurs sometime between ten and fourteen months, but depends as much on a baby's confidence, temperament, and physique as on physical development. Sturdy, active children may walk earlier than quiet, passive ones, who may be more content to sit in one spot and observe what is happening close at hand.

the insensibility of its nerves renders it highly irritable; but the bad effects which would often be the consequence of this structure are probably counteracted by the mucus which constantly covers the inside of that organ.

The Lungs, hitherto small, collapsed, and supplied with little blood, immediately after birth, begin to perform the operation of breathing, and to receive the whole blood of the body; which functions continue during life. These organs are at first weak and veritable. The Heart acts with considerable force and quickness.

The Liver is of a remarkable large size in proportion to other parts, and is not so well defended as afterwards. The Gall Bladder is nearly in the same proportions.

The Kidneys are lobulated; and the Renal Glands are larger in proportion. The Urinary Bladder, and other organs in the Bason, are differently placed, as that cavity is very imperfect, from the gristly state of the bones of which it is composed.

RANGES IN WEIGHT AND HEIGHT FOR BABIES

Age (MONTH)	GIRLS		BOYS	
	Weight (LB.)	Height (IN.)	Weight (LB.)	Height (IN.)
BIRTH	5–8	18–21	6–9	19–22
6	13–17¼	24¼–27½	14–19¼	25–28¾
12	17¼–22½	27½–31	18¾–24	28¼–32
18	19½–25½	30–33¾	21–27	30½–34¾
24	20¼–28	32–36	23–29½	32½–37

Look at me!

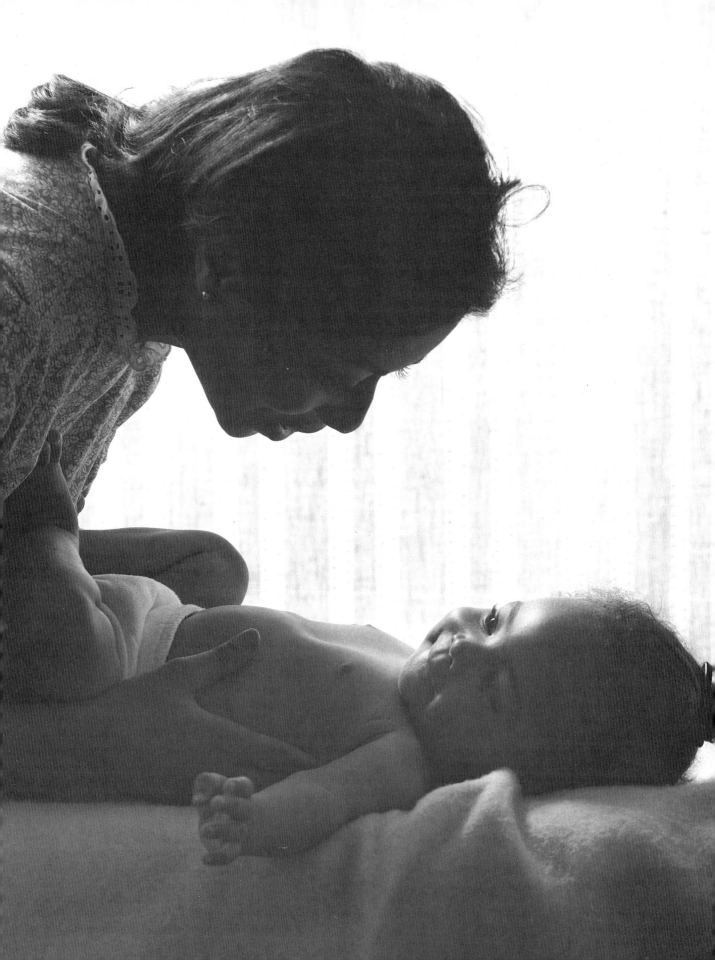

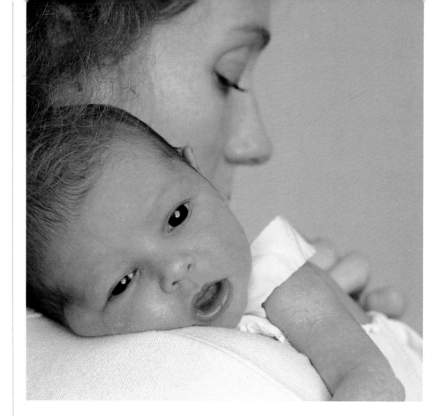

The gentle touch of a mother's hands helps baby to grow emotionally and physically.

The Experience of Touch

As reported by Daniel Goleman in an article in *The New York Times* of February 2, 1988, "premature infants who were massaged for fifteen minutes three times a day gained weight 47 percent faster than others who were left alone in their incubators—the usual practice in the past. The massaged infants also showed signs that the nervous system was maturing more rapidly: they became more active than the other babies and more responsive to such things as a face or a rattle."

Tiffany Field, a psychologist at the University of Miami Medical School, who conducted the study, concluded that, since the massaged infants ate no more than the others, their weight gain must be due to the effect of the contact on their metabolism. After eight months, the babies who had been massaged did better on tests of mental and motor ability and continued to hold their weight gain.

Field embarked on the massage experiment because of research carried out by Dr. Saul Schanberg of Duke University, whose studies of infant laboratory rats showed that a particular pattern of touch by the mother rat, particularly licking, inhibited the baby rat's production of beta-endorphin, a chemical that affects the levels of insulin and growth hormone, and quickened their growth.

According to Goleman, this led Schanberg to believe that the brain effects found in rats would also hold for humans, because the basic neural and touch systems are the same.

From the Wet Nurse to Presterilized Formula

Until this century, most babies were breast-fed for the simple reason that there was no real alternative. As early as the Middle Ages, it was recognized that unmodified cow's or goat's milk was not ideal for human babies and should be used only as a last resort.

Mothers who were able generally nursed their babies for at least a year. In medieval Europe, two to three years was normal, depending on the sex of the child (girls were suckled longer) and the amount of competition from successive babies.

Women who could afford it usually hired a wet nurse, a practice frequently followed, though frowned on by philosophers and moralists throughout the ages. Hebrew prophets thundered that nursing was a mother's duty. Plutarch stressed its emotional benefits, while Tacitus deplored the fashion among Roman matrons of handing their babies over to "any old Greek servant." Much later, in 1839, a book titled *American Lady, Parental Duties* felt it necessary to remind readers that "the first of the parental duties which nature points out to the mother is to be herself the nurse of her own offspring."

Advice abounded on the selection of a wet nurse. It was generally agreed that she should be in good health and of sound constitution, should not drink too much wine, eat highly spiced food, nor sleep with a man. Above all, her milk must be abundant and of good quality.

As early as the second century A.D., the "fingernail" test for breast milk was devised, which continued to be used as a criterion into Victorian days. A drop of milk was put on a fingernail or a laurel leaf. If it spread slowly and retained its drop form when shaken, it was "good," but if it spread quickly, it was considered too watery.

In some cases, when neither mother nor wet nurse was available, desperate measures were called for. The practice of putting a baby to suck directly from a goat or an ass continued in French foundling hospitals well into the nineteenth century.

Diane de Poitiers
François Clouet, c. 1510–1572. Oil on wood, probably c. 1571, 36¼x32 inches. National Gallery of Art, Washington: Samuel H. Kress Collection.

GUESS WHAT THESE WOMEN HAVE IN COMMON

"Miz" Lillian Carter
Margaret Mead
Queen Elizabeth II
Princess Grace of Monaco
Sophia Loren

Glenda Jackson
Natalie Wood
Vanessa Redgrave
Buffy Sainte-Marie
Carly Simon

They breast-fed their babies.

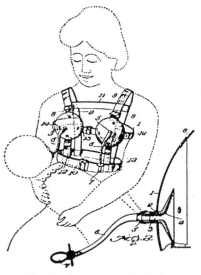

The "anti-embarrassment device" once used to keep feeding time under wraps.

Modern mothers, when they are able, offer the best brand of all.

Infant feeding vessels are known to have existed as far back as 2,000 B.C., though it is only in the past sixty years that cow's milk has become a major source of baby food. In medieval times, a small polished cow horn with a pierced end and two parchment "nipples" was popular. Early glass feeding bottles were boat-shaped, with a rubber teat at each end, one of which was pierced to make a nipple. Once bottles became upright, mothers were severely cautioned to sterilize them in huge stovetop tanks resembling canning pots, in which six or eight at a time were purified with copious amounts of boiling water.

Inevitably, today's throwaway society has developed a completely disposable feeding system in which a presterilized nipple, bag, and bottle collar are used just once—and discarded.

TUNISIA

Mothers concoct a dish called bsissa, *a mixture of chick-peas, wheat, and aromatic fenugreek—similar to, but less spicy than the staple of the same name relied upon by generations of pilgrims to Mecca.*

ZAIRE

Babies born here dine on sorghum flour and banana juice or pap made from cassava or maize with a sauce of cassava leaves and palm oil.

HAITI

Mothers grind up dried corn and combine it with soft, well-cooked green and red beans to make a baby food called ak-a-mil.

NEPAL

The very young are nourished with "magic flour"—a mundane mixture, despite its name, of toasted rice and lentils.

Warfare at the Supermarket

"On the subject of feeding my first child, I was what you might call a real pain. For the first six months of his life he got nothing but breast milk, accompanied by the occasional rhapsody about nourishing him from my own body. When I put him on solids, I carried a little food mill everywhere; it became traditional at family gatherings to see me hunched over a plate of steamed carrots, grinding them and mixing them with yogurt.

"I knew those days were gone forever when I found myself recently splitting a bag of Cheez Doodles with my kids. (You know everything about Cheez Doodles by the way Cheez is spelled. I mean, would you buy a sauce for your asparagus called Holl-N-Daze?) It was not companionable; none of us were talking, just scarfing down those little curlicues like attack dogs at feeding time. Finally my first child, he of the breast milk and pureed carrots, looked up and grinned, a salty orange grin. 'Mommy, I like this stuff,' he said.

"The father of the children remembers a time when I was a careful shopper and a devoted cook. He forgets that at the time, my Tupperware was not being used as bathtub toys, my vegetable steamer basket had not become a pond for the plastic dinosaurs and nobody was using

"He absolutely refuses to eat the less expensive substitute."

There is nothing like a little sweetness to banish the blues.

the garlic press as a gun. (It was also a time when I sublimated my true nature and pretended that I thought Ring Dings were revolting, which is a lie.)

"I once had a theory that if you fed children nothing but nutritious foods, with no additives, preservatives or sugar, they would learn to prefer those foods. I should have recognized the reality at the first birthday party, when tradition triumphed over nutrition and I made chocolate cake for the guest of honor. He put one fistful in his mouth and gave me a look I would not see again until I brought a baby home from the hospital and told him the baby was going to stay. The cake look, roughly translated, said, 'You've been holding out on me.' He set about catching up. The barber gave him lollipops, the dry cleaner a Tootsie Roll. At the circus he had cotton candy, which is the part of the balance of nature designed to offset the wheat germ.

"The other night for dinner he was having vegetable lasagna and garlic bread, picking out the zucchini, the spinach, even the parsley— 'all the green stuff'—and eating only the parts of the bread that had butter. 'Know what my favorite food is, Mom?' he said. 'Sugar.'"

Anna Quindlen, excerpted from *The New York Times*

EARLY ENLIGHTENMENT

What may very well be the first book in English devoted entirely to exercises for infants aged five months to one year—Baby's Daily Exercises—was written in 1927 by Dr. Edward Theodore Wilkes, then assistant pediatrician at the New York Nursery and Child's Hospital.

In stressing the importance of exercise during the first year of life in determining a baby's future physical development, Wilkes pointed out that "exercise in infancy is not a new idea.

"Even in some lower animals there is an instinct to exercise the young while playing with them. Bears, lions, and birds are known to do this. The instinct of parents to play with their babies helps to develop and exercise the babies' muscles. . . . Louis Pasteur once said, 'When I look upon a child I have two emotions, one of love for the child that is before me, and the other of respect for what he may some day become.' It is for the sake of what your infant 'may some day become' that you must develop his body to the utmost."

Up, up and away!

Wee Workouts

"Socialization is more important than anything," says the Tumbling Tots instructor at the 92nd Street "Y" in New York City. "Development of simple motor skills opens children's minds and at the same time they are learning to be with other children in a social setting."

The instructor begins by tossing colored balls around the room. "A child will follow a brightly colored ball where he or she may not go alone," she says, indicating the cloth and wire tunnel she is teaching the babies to crawl through. The tunnel is dark inside and might be scary, if it were not so much fun to follow the bouncing ball. "They discover the fun of the tunnel before they have time to be frightened," she explains.

Classes end with parachute games. All the children sit on a multi-colored parachute while the adults, holding the outer edges, walk in a circle singing "Ring Around the Rosy," turning the babies slowly until they "all fall down" in a great, giggling pile.

To watch these twelve- to seventeen-month-old babies and their parents or caretakers play with the balls, slides, and other equipment is actually to witness the development of a child's personality. Some babies are naturally more curious—or are they just encouraged to be so? Others tend to cling and are more easily frightened. Could this be because a parent hovers like a dragonfly over the child's every move, even in a protected setting like a padded gym?

All together now, reach out as far as you possibly can.

HOW A BABY BECOMES A MUMMY

For centuries, babies were swaddled for health and safety reasons. In 1472, an Italian doctor named Paolo Bagellardo told how to do it:

"The midwife should cover the infant's head with a fine linen cloth in the fashion of a hood. Then, placing the infant in her lap, its head towards her feet, she should raise its arms and, taking a soft linen cloth, wrap its breast and bind its body with three or four windings of the band. Next she should take another piece of linen and draw the hands of the infant straight forward so that the infant acquires no humpiness, and then, with the same bands, bind and wrap the infant's arms and hands so that they will become correctly shaped.

"Next she should turn the infant over on its breast and take hold of the infant's feet and make its soles touch its buttocks so that the knees will be properly set. Then she should straighten the infant's legs and with another band and little cloths bind and wrap up the legs and with yet another wrap up the hips. Next she should take the entire infant and roll it in a woolen cloth or garment like a cape lined, in winter, with sheepskin or, in summer, a simple linen cloth will suffice.

"Put the child in a mild room . . . and then let it sleep."

It's time for happy landings when tiny tots all fall down, swathed safely in a great big parachute.

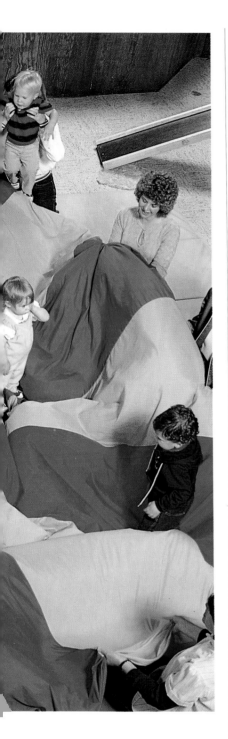

Several teachers of exercise for tots report finding parents harder to handle than the children. Parental overprotectiveness can prevent a child's natural curiosity from developing; it also inhibits the teacher and ends up frustrating both teacher and child.

Another common problem: parents who want their babies to be perfect at everything they attempt—which is a lot to ask of someone less than two years old. Instructors agree that such pushing has the effect of discouraging a child from trying new things.

More often than not, however, the experience of exercising with an infant is joyful. One parent describes benefits for herself as well as her son. "I feel more relaxed here, more able to let him do things that I might be afraid to let him do at home," she says, as her twenty-two-month-old son navigates a ladder laid on a slant, aided only by the rails at his side. She watches him carefully but never touches him, and as he climbs off, she applauds—and he flashes her a smile before wandering over to the trampoline.

Instructors for the Wee Wizards Program (eighteen to twenty-four months) notice huge changes in ability in the course of the thirteen- to fifteen-week semester. "They are growing so fast, and learning so fast, that the amount they accomplish is incredible," says one teacher. "Mastering things that were too difficult only a short while ago gives a tremendous boost to a child's self-esteem."

On to the Polliwog Class, where the adults are helping sixteen-month-olds to jump into the pool to the tune of "Humpty Dumpty" and to paddle after floating toys tossed a few feet away. There is much giggling and splashing in this corner of the pool. "It's a nice activity to share with a child," says the smiling instructor. It alleviates some of the parents' fears about having their baby in the water and helps them learn good safety practices.

Across the country, similar programs are being offered, and independent businesses have entered this new and growing arena.

Gymboree, an international franchise, has some 350 centers in the United States, Canada, France, and Australia. Joan Barnes founded this infant-toddler movement education program in 1973 when she wanted an interactive play program for her children and found none available. Playorena, founded by Susan and Michael Astor in 1985, has seventy-five franchises, chiefly in the eastern United States, where children "playercize" and have fun learning skills.

Instructors in all these classes emphasize that a baby who really dislikes an activity, such as swimming, should not be forced to participate, and that no child can do everything well, especially the first time. They advise parents to let their babies develop at their own pace while they enjoy the learning process, the time together, and the bonus that comes with any toddler exercise program: Tuckered-out babies nap *very* soundly afterward.

LITTLE FOOTNOTES

※

HEAD START

Among some American Indian tribes, it was once standard practice to flatten the heads of infants artificially as a symbol of rank and status. A wooden board, heavily padded with buckskin, was strapped to an infant's frontal bone every night for the first six months of life, and after that, hand pressure was continued to achieve the coveted shape.

Ancient Egyptians, it seems, admired their Pharaoh Akhnaten's curiously cone-shaped head so much that they molded the pliable heads of their infants in similar fashion. Across the Mediterranean, the Greeks preferred a nice, round head, and a good midwife knew how to shape the newborn accordingly.

———

"I find that the most successful approach to the subject of babies is to discuss them as though they were hams; the firmness of the flesh, the pinkness of the flesh, the even distribution of fat, the sweetness and tenderness of the whole and the placing of bone are the things to praise."

Samuel Marchbanks

FORGET THE BOTTLE, GIVE HIM A BURGER AND FRIES

The Guinness Book of World Records *gives the Large Diaper Award to the heaviest baby on record who was born weighing 22 pounds, 8 ounces. The child arrived in Italy in September 1955. The parents were reported to be of normal size, normally— though we suspect the mother was probably abnormally heavy immediately prior to the birth of the child. No information is available on whether the baby bounced.*

ARGUMENTS OFFERED IN FAVOR OF BREAST FEEDING

The milk is the right temperature with no waiting.

It comes in attractive containers.

The cat can't get at it.

———

A baby is an angel whose wings decrease as his legs increase.

French proverb

HOLD THE MANICURE

To cut a baby's nails before it is a year old will make it grow up a thief.

English rural superstition

A TURN-OF-THE-CENTURY "EASTENDERS"?

A mother was bathing her baby one
　　　night,
The youngest of ten, a poor little mite.
The mother was fat but the baby was
　　　thin,
Nought but a skellington wrapped up
　　　in skin.
The mother turned round for the soap
　　　from the rack,
She weren't gone a minute, but when
　　　she got back,
Her baby was gone, and in anguish she
　　　cried,
"Where 'as my baby gorn?"
　　　　　—The angels replied,
"Your baby 'as gorn down the plug'ole,
Your baby 'as gorn down the plug.
The poor little thing
Was so skinny and thin
'E should've been bathed in a jug.
Your baby is perfectly happy,
'E won't need no bath anymore,
'E's workin' 'is way through the sewers,
Not lost, but gorn before."

London music-hall song

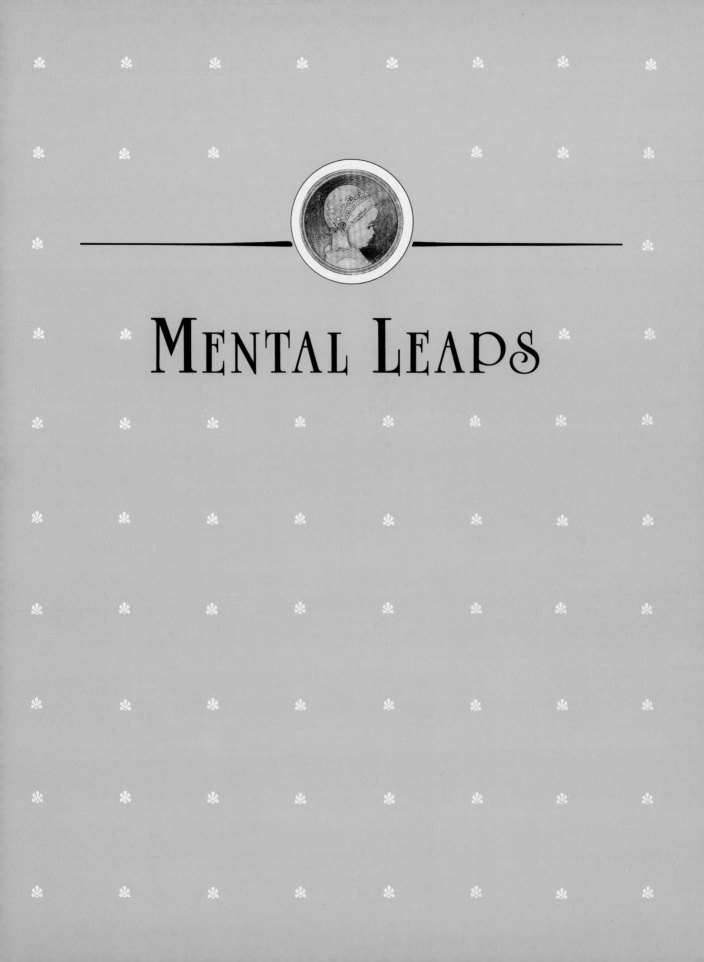

MENTAL LEAPS

WHEN NORMAL IS REMARKABLE

❖

Though at birth a human infant's brain is only 25 percent of its adult size, the phenomenal growth process begins immediately. Properly speaking, each baby is a genius—constantly observing, constantly practicing, constantly learning. There is no limit to infant curiosity, and a baby will often show equally dazzling speed of comprehension. Some of us are tempted to hasten the process along by more overt means than simple nurturing, but it is usually enough to let the infant proceed at personal pace; just the feat of learning to talk makes every baby a Quiz Kid.

Pink elephants have a way of being here one moment—and gone the next. At this young age, an infant will not remember a toy once it is hidden from view.

The Journey Begins

We asked Dr. Lawrence Balter to trace a baby's mental journey through the first two years, as he did for a child's physical growth in the preceding chapter.

Dr. Balter urges parents to be responsive to each child in whatever ways appear most appropriate for that baby because, as with physical development, cerebral development depends greatly on the individual child, and to a considerable extent, also, on how parents or caregivers respond to him. Some babies are naturally more active than others; some are more verbal; others are passive and reflective. Parents should try to be in tune with their child's particular temperament and rhythms and respond accordingly. Remember, too, that a second child may be very different from the first—and a fifth child, for instance, may be totally unlike any of the other four.

Important as it is to be responsive to a baby, Dr. Balter stresses that not everything a child does directly reflects the parents' handling. Being loving, attentive, gentle, and caring are crucial to healthy development but in no way guarantee a "perfect" baby. At the same time, of course, the baby who is neglected or ignored has a much poorer chance of developing into a happy, secure child than does a well-loved infant who has been cherished since birth.

When do babies begin to have memory?

Dr. Balter asserts that babies have what he calls "emotional memory" from their first day of life. Lacking the code of language, they cannot store memories as older children and adults can, but they remember things in different ways. By the time they are two or three months old, infants are able to remember some things for a moderate period of time. They "remember" their mother's voice and face, they "remember" their crib, perhaps, or their favorite hanging toy, or are immediately quieted by certain songs. Context is very important to infants, when it comes to memory. A toy or music box presented to a child in a strange crib or carriage may not give the ready satisfaction it brings in a familiar setting.

When do babies start getting involved in the world around them?

From the minute they find themselves in it, babies begin exploring the surrounding world. During the first few weeks these explorations are extremely limited, but by three months or so, babies are very much integrated into their own worlds, mostly through their own initiative— and the help of loving adults.

When do babies begin to show affection?

The newborn snuggling into mother's arms is, in some ways, showing affection as well as seeking comfort. Some theories support the idea that a baby smiles as much for survival as to show contentment, because adults cannot help but respond with affection to that winning smile.

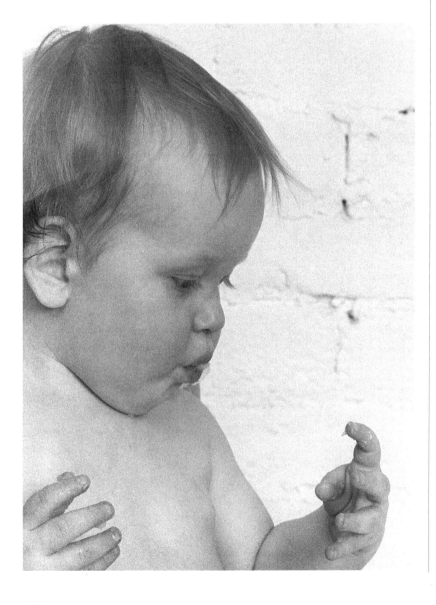

A tiny drop of water fascinates the baby at left, while a slightly older child wonders why some flowers are pink and others lavender (above).

This, in turn, can be construed to mean that the infant is seeking affection. Babies are born knowing how to suck, a mechanism that satisfies more than hunger. Sucking evolves into kissing (and sometimes biting, which is not usually aggressive on the baby's part), just as early clinging and clutching evolve into hugging.

Being actively affectionate with a baby is extremely important, Dr. Balter insists. Parents may feel it is a one-way proposition at first, but, in fact, their affectionate behavior quickly brings interaction between them and their child, and this is vital for healthy development. Babies who have not been cuddled, held, played with, sung to, and generally adored may be depressed, withdrawn children by the second half of their first year—a condition that, unless the situation changes radically, can only worsen as they grow older.

You'd be mad, too!

Can you spoil a baby?

There is no way to spoil a baby under a year old, says Dr. Balter. An infant who cries or whimpers is not trying to be manipulative—merely communicating distress and unhappiness with a particular situation. By responding to an unhappy baby, parents are teaching that they are there to give the child what he or she needs. This response instills a sense of trust and confidence that should remain with the child throughout childhood and beyond.

When do babies develop a fear of strangers?

In the early months of life, babies have no concept of separateness from their parent or primary caregiver. They may *prefer* this person to others, but will not protest if given into someone else's care. By the age of six months, babies recognize their parents as distinct from other people and may protest loudly if handed to a "stranger." By this time, too, babies have developed a sufficient attachment to their mothers for such a separation to suggest that they might lose this attachment.

During the second half of the first year, babies become apprehensive and wary of strangers, which is why many experts believe that the hardest time for a mother to return to work is when her child is about a

Pack a bag and close the door firmly, then everyone will get the message.

Not running away—running free.

year old. At this age, the child is keenly aware of having been left but lacks the mental capacity to understand that the absence is only temporary. Children who are left with third-party caregivers during the first six months develop attachments to the caregivers that lessen their anxiety when separating from their mothers.

How do children learn to separate from their parents?

By the time babies are eighteen months old, they are actively investigating the world. Parents and caregivers become apparatus upon which the toddler keeps emotional and physical tabs. Children of this age will run away, knowing that they will always be "caught" and brought back. Toddlers test their separateness again and again—an activity which, by the time the child is two, has usually evolved into negativism. Two-year-olds are what Dr. Balter calls "compulsively noncompliant," but parents can take comfort that this is merely a normal stage of development—another step away from babyhood and toward independence.

Baby Talk

When babies learn to talk—usually around one year of age—they assume the unique characteristic that separates humans from animals: the ability to communicate through speech. Parents await that first precious word eagerly—although within a year or two, when the child seems to start *every* sentence with "Why . . . ?", they may find themselves yearning for the days of gurgles and coos. At the magical moment of a baby's first meaningful utterance, however, an entirely new relationship springs up between parent and child. Things will never be the same.

Contemplate for a moment the astounding language feats performed by every healthy baby in the world between birth and age two. In this short span of time, babies not only learn how to manipulate their fast-developing speech equipment by coordinating tongue, vocal chords, lungs, and the muscles of the throat and mouth, but they perform the amazing mental accomplishment of sorting out human noise into comprehensible language. Most amazing of all, babies learn to speak.

The first subtle stages of the process go by so fast that parents may miss the signals that their baby is already treading the path toward

MILESTONES

Individual babies vary greatly in language development, but linguistics researcher E. H. Lenneberg identifies specific stages and approximate ages:

- 12 weeks—smiles in response to talk and makes cooing sounds.
- 16 weeks—turns head in response to human sounds.
- 20 weeks—makes sounds like vowels and consonants.
- 6 months—cooing changes to babbling.
- 8 months—increasing repetition of some syllables.
- 10 months—appears to distinguish between adult words by showing differing responses.
- 12 months—speaks first words such as "ma-ma" or "da-da"; understands some adult words.
- 18 months—says and uses between 3 and 50 words.
- 24 months—uses 2-word phrases; knows more than 50 words.

"If you're supposed to be so smart, name me five newly created African nations!"

Watching mother's lips, a baby learns the music of words.

conversation. Scientists, however, have identified a series of developments that almost all babies reproduce. Some move through the sequence more rapidly than others, but almost all infants fit the pattern sooner or later.

Some researchers claim that even newborns can distinguish between meaningful human language and miscellaneous adult vocal noise, but there is no doubt at all that babies during the first year of life show an intense involvement with word-like sounds. Two-month-old babies can distinguish between very similar syllables, such as the difference between "ga" and "ba." Moreover, they recognize these syllables even if pronounced with differing accents (babies in Boston still know a "ba" from a "ga" even if a Mississippi Delta farmer is speaking).

Yawning.

BODY TALK

As any parent soon learns, babies command a wide range of communication techniques long before they speak their first word. The guide to baby body language that follows is adapted from Edward Tronick's *Small Talk*.

- ARMS CLASPING: shows self-comforting when things are too much to deal with.
- SQUIRMING BODY: the first signal of discomfort; crying soon to follow.
- CHIN TUCKED: a sign of sadness.
- KICKING FEET: shows alertness, may be either happy or in distress.
- CLAPPING HANDS: in older babies, shows happiness, excitement, and pleasure.
- CLENCHED HANDS: clenching alone probably shows tenseness; if clenched and pounding fists, probably only excitement.
- HAND TO EARS: a sign of self-comfort.
- GRASPING HANDS: very young babies grasp what they want to learn about.
- HANDS WITH PALMS UP: asking for something.
- POINTING HANDS: a sign of interest.
- SHIELDING HANDS: babies protect themselves by hiding or ducking behind a hand with the palm out.
- SUCKING: babies suck on things to learn about them and for sheer physical pleasure.
- YAWNING: may show stress in addition to fatigue.
- TONGUE MOVING IN AND OUT: the tip of the tongue moved in and out between tight lips shows stress.

The baby's own sounds, apart from the crying response, begin at around two months, most typically with cooing. By the age of four or six months, the stage of babbling begins, and it seems to be the same for children of all cultures around the world: Japanese babies babble in the same way as do the babies of Urdu speakers. Vowel and consonant sounds start to emerge, often in a rhythmic intonation that sounds superficially like speech. Hidden in the babble are virtually all the sounds that go to make up any human language, from the guttural to the most mellifluous, and even including the strange clicks of some African languages. Only as babies begin to tune in more closely to the specific sounds of their immediate language environment does the range narrow. The final stage of babbling involves mixing different syllables in the same utterance.

Pointing.

DID HE HAVE POSTAGE?

Even the most gifted or intelligent babies may move at their own pace. Audrey Grost writes of her son Michael (whose overall ability is considered to be rarer than one in a million) in her book Genius in Residence.

Michael refused to talk until the age of nineteen months, when he began with full sentences rather than single words. Meanwhile, however, he was a furious scribbler on paper.

"As Mike displayed neither the desire nor the intent to talk," Grost comments, "we wondered if he planned on writing us a letter."

At some point—and here is the real miracle—babies begin to make the cultural and intellectual connection between the sounds they are able to produce and the response these sounds evoke from adults. Babies are not slow to realize that saying "ma-ma" makes someone in the room very happy.

By the age of twelve months, most babies have learned that words emerging from the babble are really powerful ideas. When spoken by a baby at the right time and to the right people, words have the power to produce toys, to turn on the lights, to get attention, or to result in food.

After that essential, mysterious process of equating certain sounds with abstractions takes place, the infant is ready to enter the world of spoken human society. Language prompts the development of both memory and anticipation, and the ability to manipulate the environment. As one set of baby experts says, "Language is the sign of thought and thought is the country of the civilized self."

The first words acquired are heavily weighted toward specific names such as *Daddy* or *Rover*, but babies also learn general terms such as *father* and *dog*, as well as such useful tools as modifiers *(big, pretty, all gone)*, action words *(go, up, out)*, social words *(please, no, want)*, and function words *(is, where)*.

As babies move through their second year, they rapidly gain sophistication in speech skills. They learn more and more words, and they begin to combine words into phrases that function as sentences. Remarkably complex ideas and desires can be expressed with no more than forty to fifty words in two-word combinations.

By their second birthday, most children have crossed over into the land of talkers. They have passed through physical changes and assimilated learning at a breathtaking pace. Now they are ready to converse with the rest of the human race.

Grasping.

The Intellectual Baby

Many thousands of parents long to know if their babies are among the brightest and best, and how to foster (some critics might say "force") intellectual development as early as possible. It is clear to even the most impartial observer that some babies are smarter than others. But as no one can agree on exactly what standards to measure by or what effect parents may or may not have on the intelligence of their babies, any answers tend only to raise fresh subjects for debate.

On one side are experts and parents who feel that young babies should grow, mature, and explore their worlds in peace and quiet, relying on a warm, happy family setting to allow each to develop at the pace that best suits *them*. If the child turns out to be mentally gifted, these gifts will emerge in time and at a rate that will be healthy and comfortable for the baby.

Ranged on the other are parents and advocates convinced that all babies are capable of intellectual feats undreamed of in the past, and that, if parents work hard enough at nurturing their mental capacities, almost any baby can become a precocious little genius.

The conflict is not easy to resolve. In the first place, there is not even much agreement on how to determine which babies are intellectually advanced and which are not. Even if young babies *could* take a written intelligence test, the standard IQ measurements have been badly discredited in recent years. Still more basic is the disagreement over the nature of intelligence and whether or not parents or any outside force can have much effect to either enhance or dull a child's mind at such an early stage.

One view holds that intellectual development occurs in a series of definite stages related to the age and maturity level of the brain. Until the age of two, according to this theory, babies are occupied with developing sensory and motor skills, and little else is possible. Between the ages of two and six, children develop perception and language, and between six and twelve they learn conceptualization and abstraction. Children cannot effectively be trained to skip or speed up this unvarying sequence, although some naturally move through the stages more rapidly than others.

An opposing viewpoint, attractive to parents who are ambitious for their babies, sees unlimited potential in every child, awaiting only the proper stimulation to be unleashed. Active nurturing of the baby's potential mental abilities is not only possible, but positively required of a responsible parent. If the proper environment is provided, especially gifted babies will result.

There is, of course, a commonsense middle ground. When parents provide intellectual stimulation as well as comfort and love, smart babies will flower, even though not every baby will become a genius.

A NEW IMAGE OF MOM

"Nobody is excused from the excellence trend. Babies are not excused. Starting right after they get out of the womb, modern babies are exposed to instructional flashcards designed to make them the best babies they can possibly be, so they can get into today's competitive preschools. Your eighties baby sees so many flashcards that he never gets an unobstructed view of his parents' faces. As an adult, he'll carry around a little wallet card that says '7 × 9 = 63,' because it will remind him of mother."

Dave Barry's Greatest Hits

Awesome potential for accomplishment is latent in a baby's steadfast gaze.

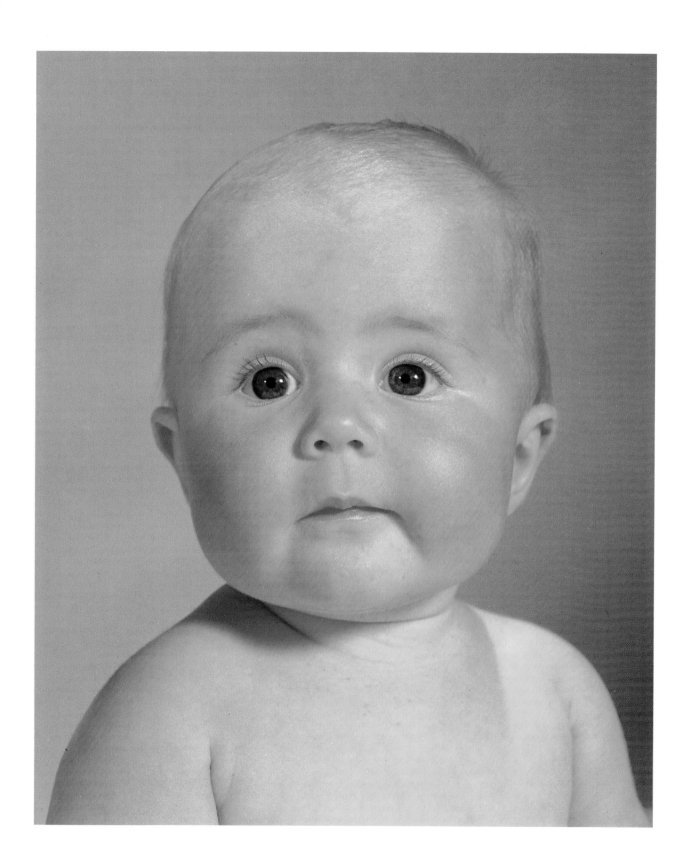

THE 30 PERCENT FACTOR

Some child development researchers have come to believe that any baby who moves more rapidly than usual through the "normal" stages of development may well be advanced, although claims for higher intelligence cannot be based solely on such comparisons. The measurement proposed by Eleanor Hall and Nancy Skinner of Columbia University for identifying gifted babies is a factor of 30 percent: babies who are "about 30 percent more advanced than average on most items" provide reason to believe that they may be gifted or talented. Some items from the researchers' list of advanced cognitive skills:

Cognitive Language	Normal Months	30% More Advanced	Cognitive Language	Normal Months	30% More Advanced
Social smile at people	1.5	1.05	Has vocabulary of 10 words	18	12.6
Vocalizes 4 times or more	1.6	1.12	Has vocabulary of 20 words	21	14.7
Visually recognizes mother	2	1.4	Jargon is discarded, 3-word sentences	24	16.8
Searches with eyes for sound	2.2	1.54	Uses I, me, you	24	16.8
Vocalizes 2 different sounds	2.3	1.61	Names 3 or more objects on a picture	24	16.8
Vocalizes 4 different syllables	7	4.9	Is able to identify 5 or more objects	24	16.8
Says "da-da" or equivalent	7.9	5.53	Gives full name	30	21.0
Responds to name, no-no	9	6.3	Names 5 objects on a picture	30	21.0
Looks at pictures in book	10	7.0	Identifies 7 objects	30	21.0
Jabbers expressively	12	8.4	Is able to tell what various objects are used for	30	21.0
Imitates words	12.5	8.75	Counts (enumerates) objects to three	36	25.2
Has vocabulary of 4–6 words including names	15	10.5	Identifies the sexes	36	25.2
Names one object ("What is this?")	17.8	12.46			
Follows direction to put object in chair	17.8	12.46			

"If you think of her as Isaac Newton, you won't mind her dropping things on the floor."

ON THE BIRTH OF HIS SON

Families, when a child is born
Want it to be intelligent.
I, through intelligence,
Having wrecked my whole life,
Only hope the baby will prove
Ignorant and stupid.
Then he will crown a tranquil life
By becoming a Cabinet Minister.

Su Tung-P'o
11th century

Parents As Teachers

"Whenever the question of educating children is raised, thoughts usually
turn to schools and schoolteachers—an unfortunate association of ideas,
for parents are, and have always been, their children's first and most
important teachers. What parents teach, or fail to teach, intentionally or
unintentionally, profoundly influences their children's entire lives. Home
is, in a practical sense, currently and traditionally, a child's first school.
Here, a child's first learning pattern is established; here the seed is
planted, or not, for advanced education. And here each child acquires
an assortment of strengths and advantages, or handicaps and vul-
nerabilities, that predispose him to success or failure, to happiness or
unhappiness."

Sidney Ledson, *Raising Brighter Children*

The Artistic Baby

Does a baby's melodious babbling mean a new Mozart has been born, or does furious activity with magic marker and paper indicate the talent of another Mary Cassatt? How do parents recognize artistic or musical talent in a very young baby?

The question is almost as hard to answer as giving a definition of what constitutes creativity. Yet, though most young babies lack the physical skills to produce what we would recognize as music or art, many babies are capable during the first two years of life of stretching their motor and mental equipment to the limit in order to sing, dance, and scribble. In recent years, too, close observation has shown that art and music are elements in a baby's environment that really *can* make a difference.

Parents need to distinguish carefully between artistic *achievement*, which can only come in a child's later years, and artistic *aptitude*, which is possible to spot and even stimulate during the very first months of life.

The only guide to assessing artistic achievement is still the critical judgment of a professional, and such a process should wait until the child has gained enough control over motor skills to be able to have a fair trial.

Meanwhile, it is possible to observe and nurture. Babies with superior talent usually begin to perform in more sophisticated ways at an earlier age, and to learn new skills more rapidly, even without exposure to stimulation. When they receive lots of artistic or musical input, talented babies may respond with rapid strides.

Caught in the act, a youthful artist studies the scene.

The melody is not always in harmony; sing it again, Sam.

Artistic or musical aptitude may or may not be related to rapid advancement in other areas. For example, a baby may gain advanced control over scribbling and spend hours at it while refusing to walk or talk until well past the usual ages. Most artistically and musically talented babies, however, exhibit better than usual concentration and are able to reproduce long, even complex, patterns of activity more often than the average infant.

Baby Music

Sound is one of the first stimuli of the outside world that a baby reacts to; even the heartbeat of a fetus will change in response to sounds. Music is sound with pitch, rhythm, tone—sound with a pattern that newborns seem to like and parents to provide quite naturally. What is so spontaneous as a lullaby?

Within their first four months, babies begin to create sounds that can be classified as a primitive form of music. There is a noticeable rhythm to some infants' thumping and banging, and most babies go through a stage called babble-singing, which is babbling that has pitch, tone, and pattern. Some babies are able to generate their own patterns, becoming, in effect, infant composers. Between the ages of six and eighteen months, babble-singing grows more complex and as babies near their second birthday, singing comes ever closer to "real music." Almost all babies are able to sing along with favorite tunes fairly recognizably by the end of their third year.

Baby Dancing

Babies naturally move their bodies to the music as they vocalize. At first, musical movement is not much more than turning toward the source of a song or swaying or rocking along with a familiar tune, but by the age of eighteen months, most babies are clapping hands in time. Soon, as the baby gains more and more control over large motor skills, dancing appears.

Artful Scribbling

Though very young babies *respond* to art, to shape, color, and form, all but the most rudimentary forms of graphic expression must wait until a child's mental and motor skills are relatively well advanced. Most babies begin to scribble by the middle of their second year, but the "pre-representational" stage, in which a child gains command of the discrete elements of eventual drawing, is not typically achieved until age three.

Most babies begin to identify the business end of crayons or magic markers and manipulate them to produce shapes and figures when they are around two. The creation of symbols on paper, crude though they be, is a remarkable artistic accomplishment for a child who has changed from a helpless bundle of nerves and tissues into a being capable of distinguishing between itself and the world—the first prerequisite for art—and capable of using tools to carry out an abstract design.

Colorful splashes by a three-year-old radiate life and energy and well deserve the name of *art*.

LITTLE FOOTNOTES

HOP TO IT!

"It is related that a woman once asked Freud, 'How early can I begin the education of my child?'

"'When will your child be born?' asked Freud.

"'Born?' she exclaimed, 'Why, he is already five years old!'

"'My goodness, woman,' the famous psychoanalyst cried, 'don't stand there talking to me—hurry home! You have already wasted the best five years.'"

Morris Mandel, *A Complete Treasury of Stories for Public Speakers*

MAD DOGS, NOT ENGLISH

Should a baby born in Burma cry out "Ma ma ma ma ma," he or she might not be calling out for Mother. Depending on the inflection, Baby could be saying, "Help the horse—a mad dog is coming!"

The Book of Strange Facts and Useless Information

"If children grew up according to early indications, we should have nothing but geniuses."

Goethe

BABY TALK

Many decades ago, the Phonographic Institute Company of Cincinnati took upon itself the task of publishing A Text-book for Babies on the Art of Learning to Speak.

In page after page of advice the parent is urged to instruct the child carefully and patiently. "The little student," asserts the Institute, "is to be taught to repeat the sound of E, E, E, E, again and again, slowly, and not too often at a sitting until its little organs are thoroughly trained to their work of adjustment for this sound, and strengthened by the repeated effort."

How heartrending it must have been to the devoted parent when the sound most frequently formed by those thoroughly trained little organs was almost certainly not E, E, E, E, but a self-taught and emphatic "NO!"

"The soul of a child is like a clean slate on which nothing is written; on it you may write what you will."

Aristotle

A LOT OF LEARNING . . .

Rare case histories show that baby geniuses can perform incredible mental feats. It is perversely comforting to note, however, that early preparation does not necessarily lead to a long and productive life. Two examples from the "enlightened" eighteenth century:

Little Frenchman Jean Louis Cardiac could recite the alphabet by age three months and read Latin by the age of four, translating it into either French or English. By age six, he read Greek and Hebrew, and was well immersed in the study of arithmetic, history, and geography. He died in Paris at the age of seven.

Another sad, but in his day famous, case was that of Christian Friedrich Heinecken, who was reputed to have mastered numbers and all the principal events of the Bible before his first birthday. At three, he was proficient in history, geography, Latin, and French. By age four, he was dead.

The Book of Lists

"Once I drew like Raphael, but it has taken me a whole lifetime to learn to draw like a child."

Pablo Picasso

PLAY AND LEARN

Noah's Ark and Nursery Rhymes

Remembering back to their own childhoods, adults have always tried to enrich their babies' lives with songs and stories, to beguile them with toys and pictures, to create magical worlds of the imagination within the confines of every day. Featured here are some of the charming enticements offered children over the ages, but despite their appeal, a baby probably gains equal pleasure—and possibly even more profit—from exploring the kitchen cupboards and banging an old frying pan on the floor. Play is one job a baby will never quit, nor cease to learn from.

A Few of Our Favorite Things

Starting with the earliest terra-cotta rattles, parents have always improvised toys for their children. Toys are largely an accessory to the child's imaginary play world, or a means to practice developing skills. In Cyprus, archaeologists found toy wine carts, forerunners of toys designed to let children imitate adult occupations. A hundred years ago, there were shovels and coal trucks for boys, with mops and baby dolls and tiny cast-iron stoves for little girls. As women move into the work world and men immerse themselves in child care, however, parents demand ever more versatile toys. Today we have supermarket-sized toy stores with gleaming aisles filled with talking dolls, climbing equipment, motor vehicles, and computer games.

The toymakers' offerings may vary, but babies have not changed. As infants, they like toys they can chew and toys that make noise. A little later, as they learn to walk, they enjoy toys they can push and pull. When we look at toys of enduring popularity, it seems clear that they evolved in response to babies' needs. Not surprisingly, such toys have been in every nursery throughout history.

A rainbow top from the 1920s can spin red, blue, yellow, pink, and green into a vibrant haze of color.

Early Rattles

The first rattles were dried gourds with the seeds left inside. Tribal priests used rattles to intimidate enemies, heal the sick, and ward off evil spirits.

Quite apart from this ceremonial use, however, the evidence suggests that there have always been rattles intended specifically for babies.

The ancient Egyptians made clay rattles shaped like birds and pigs. No ears or legs protruded and the edges were carefully rounded. Often they were glazed blue—a color that was believed to have magical properties—and covered with a protective layer of silk.

During the Victorian era rattles became quite sophisticated. Often given as christening gifts, they were finely crafted of precious metals, ivory, and mother-of-pearl. Gold and silver rattles, ornamented with bells, were attached to coral or agate "gumsticks" for teething. Collectors speculate that these costly toys were primarily intended to impress the parents.

Compared with these objets d'art, the pink-and-blue rattles we give babies now seem mundane. Sniffed one collector, "I have yet to see a plastic one that can be described as anything else but cute and hygienic."

Just Follow the Crunching Ball . . .

Balls were probably our most primitive playthings. Prehistoric babies in their caves amused themselves with smooth, rounded stones. The Egyptians made balls out of painted wood, colored leather, papyrus fiber, and plaited reeds. Some very beautiful glazed balls, striped turquoise and purple, have been found in children's tombs.

The Celts made lightweight balls from sheep bladders filled with air. American Indians used deerhide, while the Japanese improvised with tightly bound tissue paper and string.

These balls were undoubtedly fun to play with, but something was missing. It was not until the nineteenth century, with improvements in rubber processing, that balls began to bounce.

"There were Noah's arks in which the Birds and Beasts were an uncommonly tight fit, I assure you; they could be crammed in anyhow, at the roof, and rattled and shaken into the smallest compass. By a bold poetic license most of these Noah's arks had knockers on the doors: inconsistent appendages, perhaps, as suggestive of morning callers and a postman, yet a pleasant finish to the outside of the building."

Charles Dickens

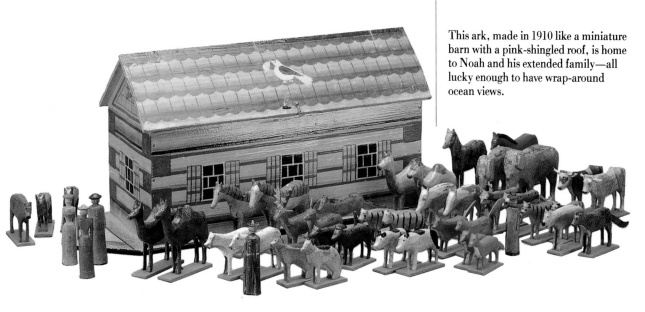

This ark, made in 1910 like a miniature barn with a pink-shingled roof, is home to Noah and his extended family—all lucky enough to have wrap-around ocean views.

In the eighteenth century, the Dutch exported huge quantities of dolls to England, which gave rise to the following rhyme:

What the children of Holland take
       pleasure in making,
The children of England take pleasure
       in breaking.

Wet Whistles

In 2800 B.C., the Mesopotamians made pink clay whistles shaped like pigeons. Horse, sheep, and alligator whistles have been found in other cultures, but it seems that, throughout history, birds have been consistently favored.

During the seventeenth and eighteenth centuries, the Moravians manufactured the *Wasserpfeife*, or water whistle. The hollowed-out body of the bird was partly filled with water, and gave forth an interesting warble when a child blew through the tail.

Swiss bird whistles were wooden, with beaks that opened and closed, and tails that moved up and down. Chinese and Japanese water whistles twittered delicately, while Korean whistles sounded like mourning doves.

Some of us continue to play with bird whistles after we grow up, but they are known as "duck calls."

Ancient Pull Toys

A pair of pull toys was excavated from the foundation of a Persian temple built in 1100 B.C. One was a limestone porcupine on a wheeled sledge, the other a lion, similarly ensconced and wearing a magnanimous smile. In other countries we find rocking pottery birds, toy bulls, stuffed dromedaries, and low-slung mice on wheels, all designed to be pulled along on a string by a child.

As skills increased and babies grew more sophisticated, toymakers went on to imitate adult transportation, with miniature armies of lead warriors on horseback, gladiator carts, and bronze chariots that even Ben-Hur might have envied.

Archaeologists were amused to discover that little Romans carved the names of their favorite racing drivers on their toy chariots—like children everywhere, they must have set up "pretend" races with each other. What were the noise effects, one wonders?

It's a bird, it's a . . . well, in fact, it's a goat on wheels, upholstered in plaid, and it's a turn-of-the-century push toy from the collection of the Museum of American Folk Art.

The Bear Facts

The Teddy Bear was born in 1902. Where he was born is another matter, and the distinction has been claimed by two countries.

According to the American version, President Theodore Roosevelt went to Mississippi to resolve a state boundary dispute. While he was there he went hunting. In an effort to be helpful, the locals trapped a bear and tied it to a tree for him, but the president refused to shoot an animal in such an unsportsmanlike manner.

On November 15, the *Washington Post* ran the story and the next day published a cartoon by Clifford Berryman. This showed the president standing with his back to the bear and was titled, "Drawing the Line in Mississippi."

With entrepreneurial spirit, Rose and Morris Michtom, a pair of Russian immigrants living in Brooklyn, made some stuffed bears and displayed them in the window of their candy store. The bears were an instant success, and the Michtoms sought and received the president's permission to call them "Teddy Bears." By 1910, these cuddly toys were so popular that toymakers feared dolls were going out of style.

Meanwhile, a German woman named Margarete Steiff was producing the first European model. Her plump, mohair bears, with the trademark button in the ear, made their debut at the Leipzig Fair in 1903.

Both the American and German toymakers insisted that they made the first Teddy, but the mixture of evidence suggests the events really did occur simultaneously.

Maybe it was just a bear whose time had come.

QUESTION: *If Theodore Roosevelt is the President with his clothes on, what is he with his clothes off?*
ANSWER: *Teddy Bare.*

According to a survey cited by Peter Bull in The Teddy Bear Book, *45 percent of British bear-owning children call their bears "Teddy." Prior to 1903, American children referred to their toy bears as "Bruin." Austrian bears are called "Brum" bears, and French bears go by the name of Martin.*

Doll Magic

Anybody can make a doll. The requirements are simple: a head and body, two eyes, a nose, and a mouth. Inventive parents have created them out of scraps for centuries, and whenever technology yielded a new material, the dollmakers were not far behind.

In earlier times, people relied on nature. Egyptian dolls had wooden spoon-shaped bodies and ringlets composed of mud beads strung on thread. The Russians made moss men, wood dolls with pine-cone arms, moss mustaches, and bark hats. In America, the Iroquois Indians made their babies' dolls from corn husks, carefully leaving the faces blank to prevent the dolls from coming to life.

Dietary staples found their way into the dollhouse. The settlers used apples for dolls' heads, pinching and kneading them into facial features

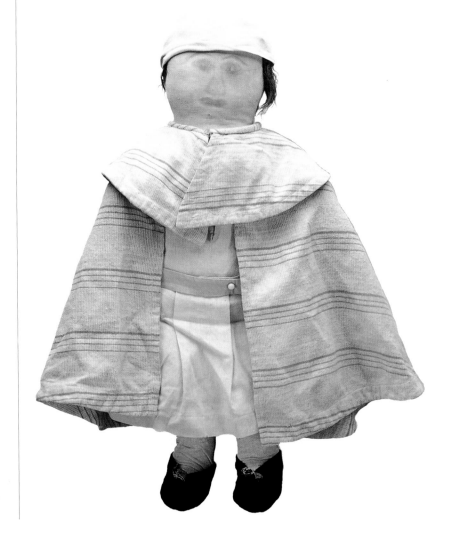

This homemade doll, decked out in a stylish cape and elegant black velvet shoes, was made in Iowa around 1910.

that darkened and wrinkled as they dried. They also fashioned dolls with dark brown faces made from hickory nuts, chestnuts, walnuts, and painted pecans. Even the turkey wishbone was pressed into service, with a small beeswax ball for the head.

In the antebellum South, slaves made cloth topsy-turvy dolls. These dolls had a white baby's head and torso attached to a black baby's head and torso, with a long calico skirt around the middle. Little girls could play with whichever doll struck their fancy, while the other lay concealed beneath the skirt.

In 1710, the Germans perfected the art of making china. Although it was originally intended for teacups, dollmakers quickly recognized its potential. They made beautiful dolls with molded black hair and blue eyes, but china was prohibitively expensive, and the dolls were not widely available until the following century.

The first china dolls to be mass-produced and disseminated throughout Europe were the *Badekinder*, or "bathing dolls." These one-piece china dolls were hollow, and could float. Despite their fragility, they were intended as bath toys. Perhaps because they spent so much time in cold water, the dolls were dubbed "Frozen Charlottes."

Masters of subtlety, the French preferred bisque (unglazed china) for their elegant "lady dolls." These had elaborate wardrobes, and came equipped with silk parasols, a dolly trousseau, and a traveling trunk. Around 1870, a French dollmaker named Jumeau had an inspiration. Instead of giving children dolls which looked like adults, why not make a doll who looked like a baby? With her lovely bisque head, heavy eyebrows, and paperweight eyes, the Jumeau *bébé* swept both continents. Dollmakers moved on to even more realistic "character" dolls, with names like Dolly Dimple, Tantrum Baby, and Baby Grumpy.

In America, printed cloth dolls were rolling off the presses for use as product incentives. Mothers were soon stitching up New York Biscuit "Brownies," the Quaker Crackel doll, and Miss Malto-Rice. Not to be outdone, a Southern woman, Miss Ella Smith, brought out the "Alabama Indestructible Baby." According to legend, one of these dolls had survived being run over by a truck.

The next doll craze was Kewpies. Irresistible imps, they had molded cowlicks, googly eyes, and tiny blue wings. Then in the 1920s, Grace Putnam came up with the "Bye-Lo Baby." Modeled after a three-day-old infant, this doll was so successful that it became known as the "Million-Dollar Baby."

Such prowess among dollmakers makes us wonder: Has there ever been a flop? Has any doll *ever* been unpopular?

Historians can point to one: the metal doll. Manufactured in Switzerland in 1921, this unbreakable doll with ball-jointed limbs just never sold. Unwittingly, the toymaker had violated one of the tenets of dollmaking. It is not enough for dolls to have a face, two eyes, a nose, and a mouth. They also have to be cuddly.

"In the same way as birds make a nest of anything, children make a doll of no matter what."

Victor Hugo

I once had a sweet little doll, dears,
The prettiest doll in the world;
Her cheeks were so red and so white, dears,
And her hair was so charmingly curled.

Charles Kingsley, *Song IV*

Collection of the Museum of American Folk Art

The best playthings do not always come from the toy store.

A New Boom—Toys?

The late twentieth century has been bonanza time for toymakers. The Baby Boomers have finally settled down to start families, and American toy companies could not be happier. According to the National Center for Health Statistics, almost 42 percent of all babies born today are first children. More babies are being born into two-income families, and their grandparents are living longer.

Putting it all together, this means that we have more babies now than ever before and more relatives who are ready and willing to spend money on them. Or, to express it another way, far-sighted individuals who bought the right toy stocks are reaping fortunes.

But those who cannot afford to clean out the toy store should not despair. A survey of the one-year-olds of our acquaintance reveals that babies are quite open-minded. Opposite, we give the results of this startling survey.

BABIES' CHOICES

#1   Mom

#2   Stereo knobs, TV volume control, and the VCR

#3   Philodendrons (Warning: These are poisonous, so be sure to hang them up high, or better still, get rid of them altogether)

#4   Ice cubes, hors d'oeuvres, or whatever "they" are having for dinner

#5   The telephone. Babies cited its "soft, chewy cord," "funny sounds coming through the receiver," and "the interesting noise it makes when you drop it on the floor"

Collection of the Museum of American Folk Art

A cuddly friend must always be there in times of need.

Mother Goose Frieze.
Mabel Lucie Attwell, England, c.1910. Wallcovering. The Cooper-Hewitt Museum, New York.

Little Jack Horner
Sat in a corner
    Eating a Christmas pie;
He put in his thumb
And pulled out a plum
    And said, "Oh, what a good boy
        am I!"

*According to legend, Little Jack
Horner was actually Thomas Horner,
steward to the Abbot of Glastonbury
during the reign of King Henry VIII.
Rumor had it that the acquisitive king
would soon be reaching for some of
the Glastonbury holdings. The nervous abbot, hoping to appease the
royal appetite, sent the king a special
gift: a pie containing twelve deeds to
manor houses. On his way to
London, the not-so-loyal courier
Horner stuck his thumb into the pie
and extracted the deed for Mells
Manor, a plum piece of real estate,
where his descendants live to this day.*

Everybody's Mother: Mother Goose

They have been called cradle sonnets, jingles, *lullynges,* and Tommy Thumb's little stories. The British call them nursery rhymes, and Americans refer to them as Mother Goose songs. The poet Walter de la Mare called them "tiny masterpieces of word craftsmanship [that] free the fancy, charm the tongue and ear, delight the inward eye." We all know them, the cheerful ditties we learned from our parents that we sing to our children—and sometimes find ourselves humming unexpectedly on the way to work.

Every civilization has them, and their similarity from one culture to the next is striking. Where do they come from? How long have they been in existence?

Nursery songs have always been a part of domestic life, like kneading bread or hemming petticoats or braiding the children's hair. Passed down orally from mother to child to grandchild, they were considered too trivial and unimportant for public notice. It was not until the eighteenth century that the first books appeared. The Tommy Thumb stories were published in London in 1744, in tiny books no bigger than a child's hand. Soon after came the chapbooks, ten-page pamphlets illustrated with woodcuts, sold by "chapmen" who peddled them door to door for a few pennies.

Authorship of the first Mother Goose collection has been hotly debated. The physical evidence points to a Frenchman, Charles Perrault. A man of varied interests and a checkered career path, he grew disenchanted with practicing law and turned to writing fairy tales. His

book *Contes de ma mère l'oie* (Tales of My Mother Goose) was published in 1697 under the name of his ten-year-old son, Perrault d'Armancourt.

The Goose family of Boston, Massachusetts, tells a different story. According to them, an English ancestor by the name of Elizabeth Foster married Isaac Goose, a man old enough to be her father, and instantly acquired ten stepchildren. She then bore six of her own, a continuous flow of babies in need of distracting and soothing.

One of these children, Elizabeth Goose, married a printer named Thomas Fleet in 1715, and they went to live behind his print shop on Pudding Lane. When the first grandchild arrived, Elizabeth's mother appeared with an armload of swaddling clothes and some seasoned nursery songs. Unfortunately for the neighbors, she sang out of key.

People have never been noted for being enthusiastic about their mothers-in-law, and Thomas Fleet was no exception. When his repeated requests that she stop singing met with no success, he sulked off to his print shop. There, he transcribed the very ditties with which she tormented him and published them under the title *Songs for the Nursery or Mother Goose's Melodies for Children* in 1719.

On the title page was a drawing of a long-necked gooselike creature, honking at full volume. How Grandmother Goose reacted to this unflattering depiction, we will never know, and no copies of the book are available to satisfy our curiousity or substantiate her descendants' claim to fame.

The Mother Goose debate to one side, there is little doubt that the rhymes themselves have been with us for centuries. Ironically, it seems that only the alphabets, game rhymes, and lullabies were actually *intended* for children. Most of our nursery rhymes were derived from folk

Rock-a-bye baby,
  on the treetop,
When the wind blows,
  the cradle will rock.
When the bough breaks,
  the cradle will fall.
And down will come baby,
  cradle and all.

The author of this well-loved lullaby was reportedly a Pilgrim who sailed on the Mayflower. *The Wampanoag Indians, who befriended the colonists, carried their infants in cradleboards on their backs. In temperate weather, they suspended the cradles from tree limbs so that passing breezes could rock the babies while their mothers tended the maize and beans. With typical motherly indulgence, the cradles were decorated with shells, beads, and porcupine quills. For sober-minded Puritans, the sight of a birch tree festooned with such cradles must have been memorable indeed.*

ballads, drinking songs, and romantic verse. Still others were sly satires on political figures.

Exposing young children to such adult themes may seem strange, but in the seventeenth and eighteenth centuries, children were treated (and dressed) like miniature adults and were carried about with their parents on daily business, to market and tavern alike.

Lovers of nursery lore have traced the rhymes back further, finding references in Shakespeare, tenth-century Latin books, and Norse mythology. The lyrics in "counting off," or elimination, rhymes, such as "eeny, meeny, miny, mo," have been linked to the Druids, a group of Celtic priests who practiced magic in ancient oak forests.

Just how far back do the rhymes go? As long, one suspects, as there have been mothers and babies.

The rhymes survive because they are essential. There will always be restless children to entertain and babies who will not go to sleep. How better to amuse them than by singing pretty songs with interesting words? The rhymes also express the natural playfulness of mother and child, serving as an excuse for tickling, kissing tiny fingers, and tugging on baby's toes.

Being able to recite a short poem in its entirety gives the young child a sense of mastery. The rhymes can also be a source of comfort. For a toddler, each day holds tremendous novelty and new tasks to master. Sitting in mother's or father's lap, reciting the safe, familiar words provides a respite—a quiet interlude with no surprises.

Perhaps this is why, as adults, we recall them with such clarity. We associate them with the warmth and acceptance we knew holding hands with our mother, who once held hands with her mother. No doubt children throughout the world experience a similar bond.

And perhaps, somewhere back in antiquity, the hands meet.

Ride a cock-horse to Banbury Cross,
To see a fine lady upon a white horse;
With rings on her fingers and bells on
 her toes,
She shall have music wherever she
 goes.

Before the suffragists came along, women were sometimes compelled to obtain their ends by unusual means. Consider the case of Lady Godiva. Her husband, Leofric, earl of Mercia, imposed a heavy tax on his subjects. Distressed by their hardship, Godiva pleaded their case. Her husband listened politely for a few days, then with mounting annoyance, and finally he offered a dare.

"Ride naked through Coventry, and I'll do as you ask."

Confident his wife would never commit such an act, Leofric returned to his ledgers. Undaunted, Godiva galloped through town on a handsome white horse, clad only in her coppery tresses, while all the folk in Coventry stayed indoors with the shutters locked, to spare her blushes. The earl conceded, and lifted the tax.

And if she hears music wherever she goes, it is probably the townspeople singing her praises.

Jack, be nimble,
Jack, be quick,
Jack, jump over
The candlestick.

The lace makers of Wendover in Buckinghamshire were a lively bunch. Every year on November 25, they celebrated the Feast of Saint Catherine,

Nursery Rhymes
Designed by Walter Crane, England, c.1875–1885. Wallcovering. The Cooper-Hewitt Museum, New York.

their patron saint. *Costumed as men, singing special love songs for the occasion, they visited neighbors, who served them wiggs—buns flavored with caraway seeds—and hot pot—a drink of warm beer thickened with rum and whipped eggs. Afterward, they held a banquet and set off fireworks, especially Catherine wheels. In conclusion of the evening, they played leap-candle. A candlestick with a lighted candle was set on the floor. A player's jumping over the candle without extinguishing the flame augured good luck for the following year.*

There was a little girl
Who had a little curl
Right in the middle of her forehead;
And when she was good,
She was very, very good,
But when she was bad she was horrid.

This poem is the work of the American poet Henry Wadsworth Longfellow. He composed it one day when his daughter Edith refused to submit her hair to a curling iron. For many years afterward, Longfellow, the author of such works as Evangeline *and* "Paul Revere's Ride," *denied having written the verse.*

When pressed by his friends, he owned up, albeit somewhat crossly.

"When I recall my juvenile poems and prose sketches," he said, "I wish that they were forgotten entirely. They, however, cling to one's skirt with a terrible grasp."

The House That Jack Built
Designed by Walter Crane, England, c.1875. Wallcovering. The Cooper-Hewitt Museum, New York.

Sing a song of sixpence
A pocket full of rye;
Four-and-twenty blackbirds
Baked in a pie.

When the pie was opened
The birds began to sing;
Was that not a dainty dish
To set before the King?

This rhyme has been linked to a culinary curiosity of the sixteenth century. Apparently it was not uncommon practice to conceal treats and prizes in baked goods. One recipe from an Italian cookbook of the period provides instructions for serving a pie with live birds inside. When the pie was cut, the birds would burst forth and fly into the air, serving the twofold purpose of entertaining the guests and extinguishing the candles. Unusual though this may sound, it is not so different from the contemporary practice of having a full-grown woman clad only in feather boas jump out of a cake.

LULLABIES FROM OTHER LANDS

Like nursery songs and counting games, lullabies have been handed down for generations. References to them are found in Roman literature, and in 1398 an Englishman named John de Trevisa described how: "Nouryces vse lullynges and other cradyl songes to pleyse the wyttes of the chylde."

Lullabies are tender songs, full of reassurance and love. Elements of family life and the changing seasons may be woven in, along with the mother's hopes for her baby. The soft words and soothing melody, combined with a rocking motion, are used to calm the infant and lull him or her to sleep.

WEST AFRICA

(The Akan tribe)

Why do you cry?
You are the child of a yam farmer.
Why do you cry?
You are the child of a coco-yam farmer.
Why do you cry?

Someone would like to have you for her
    child,
But you are my own.

JAPAN

(Province of Izumo)

Sleep, sleep, O sleep, my child!
If you sleep I will go home to fetch your
    mother!
If you stay awake the *Gagama* [a
    goblin] will catch and bite you!

(Province of Musashi)

Sleep, sleep, sleep, my child!
When was my baby made?
In the third month,
in the time of the blooming of cherry-
    flowers.
Therefore the color of the honorable
    face
of my child is the color of the cherry-
    blossom.

TUNISIA

Sleep, sleep.
Sleep is winning over you.
O little cheeks like poppies.
Sleep, sleep, slumber,
O little flowers of my eyes.

Ring around the rosy . . .

RUSSIA

Sleep, my little sun,
Sleep, little grain of wheat.

Sleep, my own one,
Little goldfish.

You cozy warmer,
Grow, little helper,
You'll surely be my little envoy,
And go whither I send you.

Sweet and Low

When I was a toddler, my grandfather took me for slow promenades around our neighborhood in Houston, carrying a pearl-handled cane and cutting a fine figure in his white linen suit and white Panama hat. The aroma of his cigar would perfume the air as we ambled along on hot afternoons in the shade of broad trees, past rows and rows of white picket fences with bursts of cool green ferns springing through the slats.

When we came home again, we would go out on the back gallery and drink buttermilk cool from the ice box, and he would sit me on his knee and sing to me, verse after verse of "Froggy Went a-Courtin'" and "She'll Be Comin' Round the Mountain" and many more songs of his childhood that I am sorry to say I have forgotten. But I have never forgotten his bony knee and the pony rides he gave me while we sang together.

Naturally, when my own babies came, I emulated my grandfather. From the time they were tiny, I sang to them—"I Can't Get Started" is one of my favorite songs in this world—and I also gave them "Mood Indigo" and "Blues in the Night," and "Summertime" from *Porgy and Bess*. In due course, they learned the verses to "Froggy" and "She'll Be Comin' Round the Mountain," and it pleased me greatly to think that my children were learning songs my grandfather taught to me in the 1930s and had learned himself on his own grandfather's knee in the 1880s. I felt that I had nothing richer to give them.

When my grandfather and I sang "She'll Be Comin' Round the Mountain" while I sat on his knee, I used to wait eagerly for the verse in which "she'll be drivin' six white horses." As a child, I had the image of a fierce and strong woman standing in a buckboard, driving those horses like crazy, with her white hair flying out behind her in the wind. I can see it to this day, and it is almost as exciting to me now as it was then. I hope my own children have wild, exciting pictures like that from this music. These are the totems of our people, I believe, and it is in our songs that they are passed on from one generation to the next.

So I think we should all sing to our children the songs that we love, the songs that mean something to us. Whatever it is, your baby will love the old stuff.

How well I remember! It's the middle of the night, my baby is in my arms, restless, sleepless, blue, and we drift together into the middle of the darkened living room. I ask my baby if she would care to dance, and she doesn't say no, so I attach the tiny fingers of one of her tiny hands to my extended thumb and put her little noddy head next to mine. "Yoooou," I slowly croon, and turn and swing, "ain't been . . . bloooo-oou . . . nooooo-nooooo-nooooo." And what do you suppose? Suddenly, there we are, out together, dancing cheek to cheek, sharing an old song, passing it on.

Richard Atcheson

SING ALONG

Close observation of the musical activity of babies raised in three distinctly different home environments led researchers D. Linda Kelley and Brian Sutton-Smith to develop the comparisons that follow. It seems that babies of professional musicians (P), babies in musically oriented families (M), and babies in nonmusical families (N) go through some (not all) of the same behaviors at differing ages.

- Making *glissando* (downward sliding-note) sounds
  P—6 mos.; M—10 mos.; N—none
- "Singing" 3-note melodies
  P—8 mos.; M—15 mos.; N—none
- Clapping in time
  P—8 mos.; M—8–9 mos.; N—none
- Dancing
  P—9 mos.; M—none; N—18 mos.
- Singing alternating thirds
  P—9 mos.; M—18 mos.; N—none
- Attempting to reproduce parents' songs
  P—11 mos.
- Beginning songs
  M—18 mos.; N—20–21 mos.
- Singing with accurate pitch and rhythm
  P—11–12 mos.; M—none; N—none

Reading together counts more than words can tell.

Reading to Your Baby

First off, a word in your ear: There really is no such thing as a book for a baby under six months of age. For those who want a literary gift for a newborn baby, the best solution is a starter for the child's library bookshelf, such as the Beatrix Potter books, or A. A. Milne's *Winnie-the-Pooh* in good hardcover editions.

Around six months, when the baby can sit unsupported, is a good time to start trying books that can be "read" aloud while parent and child turn the pages jointly. Babies learn only gradually that books deserve gentler treatment than their other toys, so it is worth choosing ones that do not damage easily. The best are board books, with rounded corners and sturdy bindings that can be wiped clean. There are many with clear, bright colors and minimal, undistracting backgrounds. *Max's First Word* and other titles in Rosemary Wells's Max series, for example, can be enjoyed both by a very young child and by older ones, who return with pleasure to "read" them to a younger sibling.

From twelve to eighteen months, babies love to be busy. This is a perfect time for activity or touch-and-feel books, such as *Pat the Bunny* and *The Telephone Book*. Peek-a-boo books offer a real thrill, and an undoubted star for this age is *Where's Spot?*

Children nearing two love to look at pictures of animals, and of other children doing the same things they do. Helen Oxenbury, John Burningham, and Anne Rockwell each has a series of board books featuring a toddler's slice-of-life. Jan Ormerod's *Messy Baby* is funny and contemporary; Eloise Wilkins's cherubic, old-fashioned children are still ideal. Finally, remember that the soothing repetition characteristic of classics like Margaret Wise Brown's *Goodnight Moon* helps to calm parent as well as baby after a long day at the playground or the office.

Carol Curtis

Collection of the Museum of American Folk Art

LITTLE FOOTNOTES

A TINY VICTORIAN'S ABC

The text of Arthur's Alphabet, *a "toy book" published in London in 1877.*

A for ARTHUR, *careful and good,*
Learning his lessons, as little boys should.

B is BABY, *cheerful and gay,*
Too young to learn, but ready for play.

C *is the Cart in which Baby sits down,*
Playing with Arthur at driving to town.

D *is the Dinner brought up on a tray,*
For which Master Baby's quite ready today.

E *is Nurse Emma, who sits in her place,*
Teaching dear Arthur how he should say grace.

F *the Footman; this shows how he stood,*
To say Mamma wants them if both have been good.

G *for Gratitude; Arthur stands there,*
Emma to thank for her kindness and care.

H *for the Horses the carriage that drew,*
In which Arthur is riding, and Baby went too.

I *for the Indian, who comes from afar,*
From a country in which there has often been war.

J *is for Jug, by Baby o'erthrown;*
Dear children, don't meddle with things not your own.

K *for the Kiss Baby took with great joy,*
When Mamma had forgiven her dear little boy.

L *is the Lady Mamma went to see,*
Who said: "Arthur and Baby must come and see me."

M *for the Monkey, smartly arrayed,*
That danced on the organ the Savoyard played.

N *is the Nosegay of flowers so gay,*
That Arthur brought home for Nurse Emma one day.

O *for the Orange which Baby holds tight,*
While Arthur cries for it;—dear boy, that's not right.

P *is Papa, who came in and said,*
If Arthur is greedy we'll send him to bed.

Q *for the Quarrel that happened one day,*
When Arthur took Baby's big bounce-ball away

R *is the Rod, that to Arthur was shown,*
To teach him to leave poor Baby alone.

S *is the Stool, on which Arthur must sit,*
Till he has got over his covetous fit.

T *for the Toys, with which he must not play,*
For in well-earned disgrace is poor Arthur today.

U *for Uncle, who came home from sea,*
And Arthur, forgiven, here sits on his knee.

V *is the Vessel, with sails all unfurled,*
That has carried dear Uncle half over the world.

W *is the Watch, Master Baby's great joy,*
Which Mamma now holds up to amuse her dear boy.

X *is for Xerxes, and Uncle has said:*
"I'll tell you about him, but now go to bed."

Y *is the Yawn, given by Arthur at last;*
So they put him to bed, for his bed-time was past.

Z *the Zoological Gardens must be,*
which Arthur and Baby were taken to see;

And when our young friends have learned this book through,
I think they deserve to be taken there too.

THE
BABY GURUS

WHAT'S UP, DOC?

Doctors Spock and Brazelton stand out among a long line of medical men who have counseled parents on the care, feeding, and raising of the young. The practice dates back as far as the fourteenth century, though those earlier doctors' pronouncements reached a much smaller audience, and were chiefly concerned with remedies—often disastrous—for diseases, rather than methods of improving children's health or their relationships with their parents. Certainly no practitioner before Spock so profoundly reassured parents as he did when he urged them to trust their common sense.

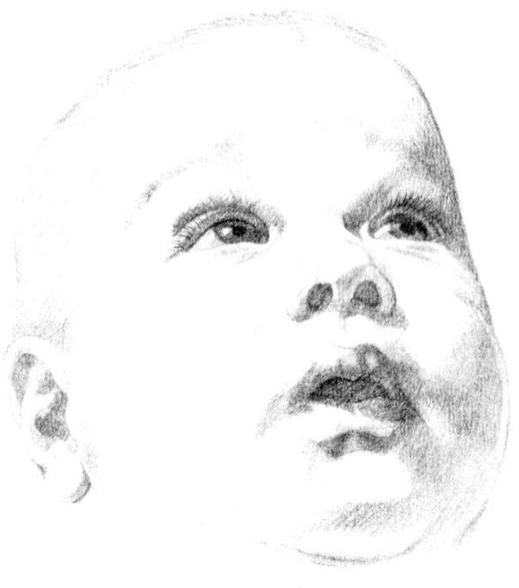

Benjamin Spock, M. D.

"All babies are born with a capacity to love, which then must be developed.

"In the period between about one and three years children acquire a very definite sense of themselves as separate people, with emphatic wishes of their own. . . . Babies don't just assert their rights; they overassert them. They say no to their parents' requests not only when they really don't want to do something, but also when they're actually willing, just to make the point that their wishes must be considered.

"When a parent is timid or reluctant to give leadership, the children—especially those of the same sex—feel let down. . . . When parents are afraid to be definite and firm, their children keep testing the limits—making life difficult for the parents and also for themselves—until the parents are finally provoked into cracking down. Then the parents are apt to feel ashamed, and back off again."

William Sears, M. D.

"The period from birth to three years of age sees the most rapid development of your child's brain. . . . An infant's desire and capacity for learning is first manifested in the newborn period by his state of quiet alertness, a state in which he is most receptive to outside stimuli. An extension of this state of quiet alertness is the tremendous power of concentration infants and young children have. The ability of the young

These sensitive drawings by New York artist and mother Judy Clifford capture the essence of babyhood in a way that everyone who has ever loved a baby can share.

child to learn several languages simultaneously and without confusion, a feat which is much more difficult for an adult, demonstrates a child's great capacity for learning.

"The message I wish to convey . . . is that home education does not mean saturating your child with information. It means creating an environment which allows his individual desires and talents to flourish at his own individual pace, the result being increased self-esteem."

Selma Fraiberg

"Long before the child develops his inner resources for overcoming dangers he is dependent upon his parents to satisfy his needs, to relieve him of tension, to anticipate danger and to remove the source of a disturbance. . . . To the infant and very young child the parents are very powerful beings, magical creatures who divine secret wishes, satisfy the deepest longings, and perform miraculous feats.

"The discovery by the normal baby of his separateness from his mother is the result of a gradual process. . . . The first phase in this process takes place around the middle of the first year. It will be two more years before this process reaches the stage of personal identity, expressed in the first shaky and uncertain 'I.' "

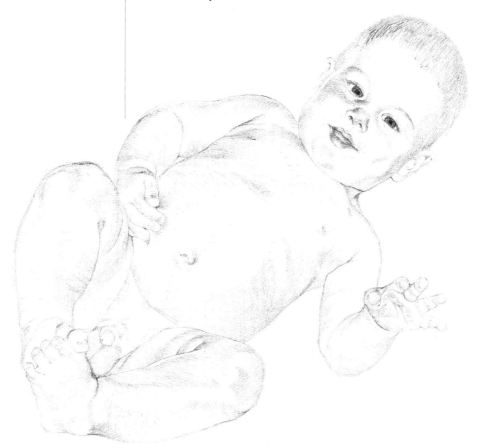

Burton L. White

"After you have decided you want a well-developed child, then what? How do you achieve that goal? . . . In our present society, neither the child who will achieve superbly nor the one who will be seriously behind by the first grade seems to show any special qualities during the first year of life. But in our studies we have concluded that rearing children well becomes much more difficult once they begin to crawl.

"The goals we recommend parents work toward during the first eight months of life can be grouped under three headings:

1. Giving the infant a feeling of being loved and cared for.
2. Helping her to develop specific skills.
3. Encouraging her interest in the outside world."

Penelope Leach

"He is, after all, a brand-new human being. You are, after all, his makers and his founders. As you watch and listen to him, think about and adjust yourselves to him, you are laying the foundations of a new member of your own race and of a friendship that can last forever. You are going to know this person better than you will ever know anybody else. Nobody else in the world including your partner, however devoted, is ever going to love you as much as he will in these first years if you will

His mother's eyes,
His father's chin,
His auntie's nose,
His uncle's grin,

His great-aunt's hair,
His grandma's ears,
His grandpa's mouth,
So it appears . . .

Poor little tot,
Well may he moan,
He hasn't much
To call his own.

Richard Armour

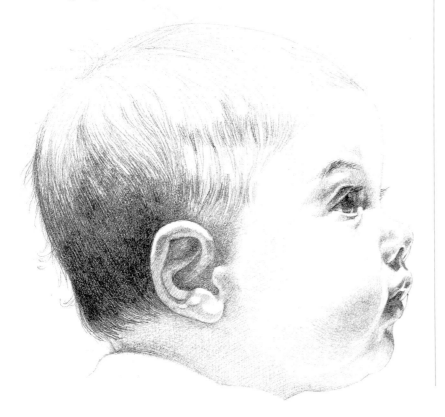

let him. You are into a relationship which is unique and which can be uniquely rewarding.

"If you provide the space, equipment and time for your child's play, he will see to the development of his thinking for himself. He is the scientist and inventor; your job is merely to provide the laboratories, the facilities, and a research assistant—you—when he needs one. What he actually does with the play materials you provide or allow is his business. He needs the true scientist's independence to work as he pleases, involving you or showing you results only as and when he thinks fit."

Stanley Greenspan, M.D., and Nancy Thorndike Greenspan

"It is a thrilling experience to nurture your child's uniquely human capacity for emotional growth and understanding. You can see your infant's initial interest in the world, which is, after all, a 'sensory interest,' involving sights, sounds, and feelings, broaden to become an interest in people, particularly yourselves. This interest grows into love. The love grows into a desire to have an emotional dialogue, to communicate emotions and receive the communication of emotions. This emotional dialogue grows into the desire to interact in ever more complicated ways, such as understanding more about people—how they function, what they mean—and eventually leads to the ability to construct an internal mental life—that is, to imagine experiences for oneself.

"When you read and respond to your baby's specific emotional communications, he is learning that his actions and emotional expressions result in reactions from the world. . . . This link gives him a beginning sense that he can have a pleasurable impact on the world—a most important foundation for optimism and trust—and also that there is a relationship between what he does and how "the world" responds. This cause-and-effect understanding is the essence of reality testing. Your baby is not born knowing he can cause something to happen; he must be taught by your reciprocation of his emotional responses."

T. Berry Brazelton, M. D.

"The most common questions with which young parents confront me in my pediatric practice are: 'Am I doing the right things for my baby?' and 'How will she know that she is loved?' The first question is generated by a desire to take all the right steps in childbearing at a time when our culture is no longer very sure of its goals. . . . Perhaps the fact that there are so many different points of view is good in some ways. At least young parents needn't be burdened by the feeling that there is just one answer and that they can't find it. . . . All I can recommend is: 'Do what makes you and your baby feel the best and gives you the nicest time together.'"

How to Find a Pediatrician

A new baby is usually seen by a pediatrician while still in the hospital and will need a checkup two weeks later, so it is a good idea to have chosen a doctor well before the birth.

There are several ways to find a reputable pediatrician.

- Ask other parents of small children for their doctor's name.
- Ask your obstetrician or internist for a recommendation.
- Call your local hospital and speak to the chief pediatric resident.
- Get a list of names from the county medical society (although, as a service to the physicians, they often supply the names of the *newest* doctors in the area).

Today, it is considered perfectly acceptable to interview several doctors before selecting one. According to Dr. Fern Perlman, a pediatrician who practices in Westport, Connecticut, this is very common and very sensible—for both doctor and parents. "I would say that in the last five years, 100 percent of our new parents have come in for interviews," she says, adding that she and the other doctors in her group encourage it. This is the time for parents to begin establishing an all-important rapport with the doctor, to ask questions about how the practice is set up, and then to go home and calmly evaluate each doctor before making a decision.

Dr. Perlman suggests that parents consider the *three A*s when selecting a pediatrician: ability, availability, and amicability.

Ability, measured in terms of credentials, is the easiest to establish. Was the doctor educated at an American medical school? Is he or she a board-certified or board-eligible pediatrician? Is the doctor also affiliated with a good hospital (teaching hospitals are generally preferable), and is it a hospital you want to use?

Availability is fairly easy to determine as well. If the pediatrician practices in a group, all the participants will almost certainly be covered twenty-four hours a day, 365 days a year. This means that the members of the group take turns being on call evenings and weekends. If the doctor practices alone, it is impossible to be always available, though many solo practitioners have arrangements with other doctors to ensure that they are covered.

If both parents work, it is a good idea to ascertain if the doctor has weekend or evening hours for regular, routine checkups. Availability also includes telephone consultations. A doctor or nurse should always be available for phone calls, at least at some point during the day. Some doctors have "telephone hours," time set aside every day just for phone calls; others have a certain time each day for calling back parents who have left messages; still others call parents back when they can fit the call into the daily schedule. An interview is the time to find out how phone calls are likely to be handled. Pediatric nurses, who frequently answer

the phones, are well qualified to give medical advice about many childhood ailments, but parents should be able to speak to a doctor within a reasonable period of time *on the day they call.*

Amicability, the final category, is probably the most important. Parents *must* feel that the doctor is sympathetic to them and to their individual situation. New parents have hundreds of questions and should never feel inhibited about asking them. They should feel that the doctor wants to work *with* them to see their child through all stages of his development—not just medical crises.

Dr. T. Berry Brazelton sums up the relationship between parents and pediatrician as a subjective one, in which the essence of the routine visits is "the exchange of feelings and insights." If parents and doctor establish a good, comfortable relationship, well seasoned with mutual respect, they will find that they have become the sort of working team that functions efficiently in emergencies, and happily year in and year out as the child grows up.

LITTLE FOOTNOTES

---※---

MEDICINE MEN STUDY ASTROLOGY

In the seventeenth century, it was believed that inherited diseases stemmed from the occult influences of the stars, which ruled all life on earth. So firmly fixed were these astrological beliefs that the minute and hour of each baby's birth as well as the day, month, and year were entered in detail in family Bibles. Physicians could then prepare potions for their patients, keeping the all-important planetary conjunctions in mind.

BOTTOMS UP!

Malaysians protect their babies from disease by washing them in beer.

COUGH REMEDY

According to Barbara Kaye Greenleaf in Children through the Ages, *treatments for whooping cough included "carrying the afflicted child through a cloud of smoke, placing a live frog in his mouth, or holding an old spider over his head while saying the charmed words: 'Spider, as you waste away, Whooping cough no longer stay.'"*

TINCTURE OF SLEEP

The ancient Sumerians were familiar with the soothing properties of opium, but it did not appear in Europe for more than five thousand years. In 1472, Italian physician Paolo Bagellardo denounced the practice of dosing children to induce a restful night. "Our common people give infants a little of the stuff called 'Quietness,'" he wrote in his popular Book on Infant Diseases, *but it seems this was a boiled-down extract of black poppy seeds, not opium itself, which was introduced by Paracelsus in 1521. It at once took pride of place in the pharmacy of the period, replacing such alternatives as hare's brains and ground hedgehog, which lacked opium's charisma—and effectiveness.*

TIME HEALS ALL

With the invention of the printing press in the fifteenth century, several eminent physicians published "regimens" for children. One, Bartolomaeus Metlinger, even suggested that certain problems might be left to heal themselves without medical intervention—brave advice for a time when physicians felt almost obliged to administer drastic remedies.

DISPENSING A LITTLE DOPE

The practice of drugging little babies lasted into the early 1900s. Dr. Harvey W. Wiley, a baby doctor of some repute, writing in a 1912 issue of Good Housekeeping, *urged parents to steer clear of the dozens of "soothing syrups" readily available which contained opium, morphine, chloroform, and even cannabis. He noted that "the promiscuous use of deadly, habit-forming drugs is a constant threat, not only to the health but to the life of the infant, paving the way for later addiction. Far better," he added, "to listen to the infant's cry for a while than to have it forever hushed."*

TOUGHENING-UP TECHNIQUES

Colonial babies were plunged into cold water every day and dosed with such medicines as Daffy's Elixir and snail-water. Another medicine with the trade name of Venice Treacle was said to have been invented by Nero's physician, though its ingredients, which include a dozen vipers, white wine, opium, and "spices from both the Indies," sound more appropriate for a witches' brew.

Alice Morse Earle,
Child Life in Colonial Days

GETTING AROUND

WITH BABY

Up to the minute in the early 1900s, a Montana family shows off a horseless carriage—and a new baby.

...AND BABY MAKES THREE

❖

Nobody stays at home anymore, and baby goes everywhere—carried close in front and back body slings by walking parents, propelled in carriages and strollers, strapped into car seats, bicycle seats, on planes, in trains, on boats. Babies are brought into restaurants, installed in hotel nurseries, and taught to behave nicely while riding in supermarket carts. Before their feet touch the ground, many babies have covered more territory than their great-grandparents ever did, who may have spent a lifetime walking around the block and around again.

Three—for the Road

The basic human needs are simple: food, clothing, shelter. But many parents would add the right to be mobile, even with babies in tow.

Traveling with children, in fact, has become commonplace. Researchers at the U.S. Travel Data Center, who keep track of such things, found that children accompanied adults on 34 percent of all travel in the United States during 1987. Americans undertook nearly 405 million trips with kids during this one year alone. Of course, travel with babies *is* different than the unfettered freedom of two on the road.

It will behoove parents to make up their minds early on that the baby is the new tour director, and no matter how damaging it may be to the adult ego, the group will move at a rhythm dictated by its youngest member. Moreover, while a parent may view a trip as a chance to do something new and exciting, for the baby one place is much like another so long as it is cozy, clean, comfortable, and has food available on demand. The Grand Canyon, Niagara Falls, or Chartres Cathedral have nothing to compare to a snuggly blanket and a warm bottle.

There are some stages when travel is easier or harder. Although it can seem as if newborn babies require their own tractor-trailer load of equipment to walk around the block, it is in some ways easy to travel with the very young. They tend to be relatively passive and motion seems to help them sleep (and, if good luck reigns, they sleep a lot), which means they can be toted along to museums, ball games, and other fun places without too much trouble.

Babies between about six months and a year are another story. At this stage, children are active and demanding and have ceased to slumber peacefully. Travel becomes more of a problem. It is still possible, but a child of this age really takes over the pace.

Slightly older babies, of between one and two, for example, are somewhat simpler to travel with, because they are beginning to respond ever so slightly to logic and persuasion. They may be diverted by some of the sights and sounds, provided the duration of any single part of a trip is not prolonged. As children near the "terrible twos," however, smart parents plan to stay close to home.

Modern society has done much to accommodate travel with children, providing such necessities as the disposable diaper and a whole range of handy gadgets as well as facilities specially designed for the very young. These days, parenthood *is* compatible with mobility.

A BABY'S PERFECT DAY

This 1924 excerpt from Woman's Home Companion *shows just how far "experts" have come in their thinking about the mobility of babies.*

"You must be ever watchful of the interested efforts of the older children to be helpful in 'amusing the baby.' If they wish to take him to the park or the street or even on a quiet country road, be mindful of the dust (usually refuse) which is so much nearer the level of his perambulator than of your nose. You who have guarded his little nose so jealously from kisses, from handkerchiefs, from dogs, from ashcans, cannot take needless chances with the dust of the streets . . .

"Do not take him for a motor ride in the evening 'to cool him off.' You will also refuse the temptation to take the baby on picnics. He may sleep from habit, but he will show fatigue afterwards. Never fear monotony for babies. It is a priceless thing."

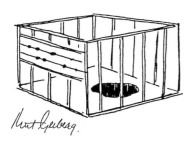

Sling and Go

Sometime during the 1960s, American parents rediscovered the sling, but the idea is age-old.

All over the world, mothers long ago learned to wrap up a baby in a fold of cloth close to the body and then go about the daily business of seeing to tasks related to food, clothing, and shelter.

A baby wrapped in a sling, which began as an extension of a mother's clothing, leaves the hands free for other jobs, and is the simplest method ever devised for moving a young baby from one place to another. In Africa and Asia, children are taken along routinely in many adaptations of the sling. The baby is wrapped securely close to the mother and left to snooze, suck on fingers, or otherwise amuse itself while the parent goes about the business of life.

The modern adaptation of the sling is slightly more high-tech, but the results are the same: Babies feel comfortable and parents have maximum freedom. A baby in a sling can go virtually anywhere the

WHAT TO LOOK FOR

Personal baby carriers come in three versions: the soft front sling, a backpack style with rigid frame, and convertibles that can be used either front or back.

When shopping for equipment, look for:

- Neck and head support for use with very young infants
- Double-stitched or reinforced seams
- Roomy arm and leg holes that don't impede circulation
- No breakable hardware or sharp, abrasive edges; make certain there is nothing that can pinch or cut
- Padded frame and straps
- A simple strap system (no one wants to be a contortionist)
- Enough adjustments to keep the baby's weight close to the adult's center of gravity

Slung from daddy's shoulder, a two-week-old attends Harvard graduation.

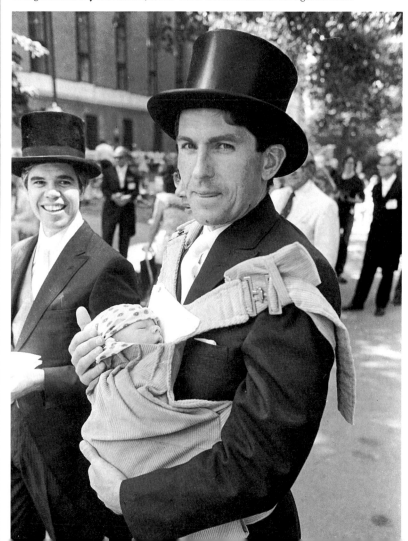

Sweet dreams!

ROYAL PILLOWS

American interest in royal babies is nothing new, it seems. In July 1901, Harper's Bazaar informed its readers:

"Italian mothers and nurses always carry a small child on a pillow: this pillow is curiously fashioned so that the baby is cozily slipped into a case and then safely kept there by being tied in. The royal Italian child has enough pillows to change every day in the month if necessary, but one was made especially to use at the formal presentation of the infant, soon after birth."

parent can walk. Hiking a nature trail, strolling barefoot on the beach, or ambling through shops are equally possible.

Small babies can be carried in a front sling shortly after birth, although some sort of head support is recommended for newborns. When babies are old enough to hold up their heads without support (about three months of age), the backpack adaptation becomes a possibility, and can accommodate babies up to thirty pounds, if necessary. Some styles of carrier are convertible for either front or back use.

THE ELEGANT PRAM

The sling may be practical and the umbrella stroller handy, but for sheer style and elegance, nothing surpasses the classic English-style perambulator—better known as the pram. The picture that comes to mind invariably includes visions of nannies in starched caps and aprons pushing babies in the park on a balmy spring day.

These Rolls-Royces of baby conveyances are large, usually elaborate, and definitely a sign of affluence. They were actually invented in New York in the mid-nineteenth century by a man named Charles Burton, but Americans failed to take to the idea, perhaps because they did not like being crowded off the sidewalk by the wide-bodied carriages.

Burton took his pram to Great Britain, where he opened a factory. His fortune was made and the future of the carriage assured when Queen Victoria ordered a Burton pram. Soon afterward, Queen Isabella of Spain acquired a pram, and thousands of less-exalted mothers decided they had to have a similar contraption for their precious offspring.

The first successful baby carriage in the United States was marketed in 1858 by the F. A. Whitney Carriage Company in Leominster, Massachusetts.

When a baby really takes your fancy, the pram can be fancy, too.

STROLLIN'

The lightweight stroller may be one of the more useful inventions of modern industrial society. Either of the two styles—standard or the smaller "umbrella"—provides mobility with convenience, keeping wear and tear on both parent and baby to the minimum.

Standard strollers provide nearly as much durability and comfort as a full-sized carriage, but take up far less room, can be collapsed for carrying, and are less expensive.

Umbrella strollers fold up to practically nothing (they can be easily carried in one hand when not in use), but are instantly expandable for service.

Features to look for:

- The certification seal of the Juvenile Products Manufacturers Association, showing that the equipment meets or exceeds safety standards
- A wheel base wide enough and wheels large enough to provide stability; some strollers tip too easily
- Good seat restraints and secure, childproof brakes
- Hinges, scissor joints, and springs protected from baby fingers
- Sturdy fabric that can be removed for cleaning
- A high-quality, removable canopy or weather shield
- A collapsing system that works smoothly with one hand
- Handles that adjust for height
- A reclining seat with several positions, all of which are stable with a baby on board
- An adjustable foot rest
- A place for packages that is over the rear axle and doesn't affect the stroller's stability

Snugly ensconced in 1903's latest fashion in carriages, a baby in Harrisville, New York, is all ready for an outing.

WHEN BABIES CROSS THE OCEAN

*A baby on "Love Boat"? Well, proba-
bly not, but once upon a time many
people traveled by ocean liner, and
taking baby along was a common oc-
currence. In 1904, Emma Duff Gray
gave readers of* Harper's Bazaar *some
hints on how babies might comforta-
bly sail the seas:*

"Those who ought to know say that
the families are legion who would
make a rush for the first ocean
steamer on which they could secure
berths, if it were not for the baby.

"But what is to be done with the
baby? To take the child with them and
ignore all possible happenings is a
foolish solution of the problem, because crossing the ocean, even at the
most favorable season, they cannot be
sure of avoiding lurches, rollings,
heavings, and draughty exposures.

"The following easy way in which
an infant may safely travel over even
the longest ocean voyage must, therefore, make a forceful appeal: Buy a
strong, light-weight basket, about two
and a half feet in length, one and a
quarter feet in width, and a foot or
more in depth. Pad such a basket securely with the softest cotton batting,
over which a soft sheet of wadding is
tacked in place, or a thick fleecy piece
of Canton flannel. This done, cover
the padding neatly with a soft, firm,
pink or blue silk; or cover with French
chintz having a rosebud pattern running over it. As the basket would be
continuously exposed to a damp at-
mosphere, the chintz would prove
most enduring. The basket could be
edged with silk or other cords, such as
the upholsterer would advise as the
proper vogue in color and weight.*

"In this basket the infant may be
laid in much the same manner as he
is put to bed, only with a warm hood
on his head. . . . A basket of this kind
may be put directly on the deck, or in
a steamer chair, and by means of
blankets and other baby belongings
the infant will be as warm and cozy
as can be.

"Infants are apt to sleep a great
deal, especially in the sea air, and because of the basket they do not need to
be disturbed to be put to bed. As the
basket is deep, they will not fall out of
it, not even when the ship pitches. And
because the basket is sufficiently padded their tender skin will not be
bruised, nor will the rolling or other
motion of the vessel act otherwise than
as the rocking of a cradle."*

A mother sits in the sun on the *Rotter-
dam*, bringing her baby born abroad
home to America.

Aboard the liner *Majestic*, in the 1920s, even a babies' party was set out in style.

Words of Experience

Cathy McCarthy, a long-time flight attendant ground-based since she became a mother, shares some insights into air travel with babies:

When parents pack for a trip with baby, they frequently bring along more than they are leaving behind. Is there any way to avoid bulging bags?

I never pack more clothes than we will use in three to five days. On a weekend trip I pack one duffle for the four of us. Remember that you can often travel in the same clothes both ways. And there is no need to bring a huge box of diapers. There is practically nowhere in the world these days that doesn't sell disposable diapers. Pack seven or eight and plan on buying more when you get there.

You often hear that parents should ask for bulkhead seats facing the front wall when traveling with small children. Do you agree?

Unless you are flying an overseas airline that has special bassinets that fit onto the wall, it's hard to think of any reason why you would ever want a bulkhead seat. Perhaps if you had a dedicated climber who loves to pull the hair of the passenger in front, a bulkhead seat might be useful. Otherwise, why would you want to stare at the wall in front of you, hassle with stick-in trays rather than having the convenient pull-down variety, and most likely be the last to be served?

How do you keep a wriggling toddler from driving everyone crazy?

Toys, new toys and lots of them. I would suggest going to the store before the trip and buying inexpensive toys that your child has never seen before. Leave them in the wrappers: opening them takes up time and also is part of the fun.

Trick number two: food and lots of it. Snacks, junk food, anything to keep them munching. It is a treat because they don't usually get that at home.

Do babies and toddlers sleep when they travel on planes at night?

Yes, particularly on early-morning flights, the so-called red-eyes.

When a plane is taking off and landing, what should you do for safety? What about pressure in the ears?

The seat belt should only be fastened around the parent. If you belted the baby along with you, the baby would be crushed in an impact. If oxygen masks appear, put yours on first, then attend to the baby.

Hurting ears can be helped. Lots of times ear-wax buildup is the major source of pain when the altitude is changing. As a stewardess I have moistened paper towels with very hot water from a special tap, stuffed them into Dixie cups, and placed these over a baby's ears. It

In 1935, taking a baby on a trip by commercial air flight was a big adventure, as recounted by Jean DuPont Miller in August 1935 for readers of The Parents' Magazine:

"It was necessary for me to cross the continent eighteen months ago with my twenty-months-old baby. My husband, who had been flying for seven years, suggested our going by air. We crossed in thirty-one hours, leaving Newark, New Jersey, at nine o'clock in the morning and arriving at the airport in Oakland, California, at one o'clock the following day. Small Joan had three meals and one night's sleep in a traveling environment. She arrived at her grandparents' home with none of the usual marks of a long and tiresome journey.

"The first thing to remember is the fact that large transport planes are well equipped as to ventilation and heating. . . . From Chicago on I found that we were adequately provided with heavy wool steamer rugs. . . . In the Eastern States, where we did not once ascend to 2,000 feet (though today's planes average 7,000 and 8,000 feet), the heating units themselves were then, and now are, ample.

"Except in the stretch across the Rockies, and from Newark to Cleveland, stops were made on an average of every hour and a half. Varying in length from ten minutes to half an hour, these periods are a great relief to a little child and one of the major advantages of air travel for a youngster. There is time to stretch small legs, to get a drink of milk or fruit juice and attend to other necessities.

"On a long air trip it is possible through the courtesy of the company to radio ahead to the airport restaurant where the dinner stop is made

Sometimes, for a stewardess, it can be O.K. to kiss the client.

and have the proper type of meal waiting for a child. In the case of one who eats slowly, this is highly advisable. Light lunches are served on the planes, and while they might not contain all the essential vitamins of a child's regular diet, they are purposely kept light and digestible. I remember bouillon, lettuce sandwiches on whole-wheat bread, fruit cup, and hot chocolate. (Coffee for grown-ups, of course.)

"While large transport planes have the same toilet facilities as a train, the very strangeness of the surroundings will probably nullify their use. For a well-trained child the stops at the various airports will be sufficient."

seems to loosen the wax and ease that intense, painful pressure. Normally, if you keep the bottle or breast reserved for takeoff and landing, and keep a toddler chewing, the problem will be manageable.

How can someone traveling alone eat a meal and hold the baby?

You can't. Eat before or after and pray that the plane is on time. If you are traveling with a toddler, you can take comfort when you remember you have packed all those wonderful junk food snacks!

Are there any tips to offer that make a plane trip easier?

Nowadays, when there are so many delayed flights, it is wise to join an airline's "club" so that you can weather the delay with a TV, drinks, and the comfort of soft furniture. An alternate plan is to look into the day rate a nearby hotel will charge for four hours of rest in one of their rooms. If your flight is delayed beyond four hours, then you have a hotel room for the night already in hand.

LITTLE FOOTNOTES

TRAVEL DATA

In 1987, Americans took nearly 1.2 billion trips (defined as travel at least ten miles away from home) and more than a third included children. The United States Travel Data Center has broken down the statistics on how adults traveled with children:

One male, one female	13%
Two females	12%
One female	5%
One male	2%

PRECIOUS CARGO

"A woman arrived in the United States after a long stay in Europe. She had with her a young nine-month-old son. When she came to customs, her heart sank as the official looked at the large pile of luggage.

"'What articles of value have you acquired abroad in the past twelve months?' he demanded.

"'Well, there's the baby . . . ,' began the woman.

"He looked at the sleeping infant, and then with a wave of his hand said, 'Lady, original works of art are exempt from duty.'"

Morris Mandel, *A Complete Treasury of Stories for Public Speakers*

NO SQUIRMING EN ROUTE

The traditional cradleboard used by the Navajo and many other native North Americans was basically a baby-tending device, but it also served a valuable function as a form of infant transportation.

A cradleboard consists of a board about 10 by 40 inches, a footboard about 10 by 5 inches hinged to it by a leather thong or string, a two-part cover attached to each side of the main board, and a hoop arching over the head of the infant lying on the board.

Once wrapped in a blanket and tightly laced inside the board's cover, the baby could safely be hung from a saddle or, more typically in recent times, carried by hand.

James S. Chisholm, *Navajo Infancy*

AIRBORNE DELIVERY

A baby girl has the distinction of being the first child born while traveling in an airplane. Her mother, Mrs. T. W. Evans, gave birth to her over Miami, Florida, on October 28, 1929.

Famous First Facts

GO! GO! GO!

Sears' Fall Catalogue for 1910 offers this $5.45 bargain: "In our Solid Comfort Davis Collapsible One-Motion Go-Cart are combined the latest and best ideas, durable construction and perfect comfort. It is one of the strongest, most rigid and lightest running vehicles of this kind that has ever been constructed.

"The framework is made of Bessemer spring steel, the joints and corners reinforced and firmly riveted, and finished in black enamel.

"The hood, seat, back, sides and dash are upholstered in fabricord (imitation leather), dark green or tan color, as desired. The pusher handles are made of solid steel, fastened to the body by a strong brace. The hand grips are fancy-turned, enamel polish finish, with nickel plated ferrules. The automatic security foot brake is fastened to the frame within easy reach and locks and unlocks with a slight pressure of the foot. The wheels are made of steel, anti-rust finish, 10 inches in diameter, fitted with crescent shape rims, with 1/2-inch rubber cushion tires."

"In America there are two classes of travel—first class, and with children."

Robert Benchley

THE WORKING BABY

Is There a Star in the Family?

So you think she ought to be in pictures? Well, once a baby has been born it's not too soon to try to get her a job, though it may be a considerable amount of bother. Producers of commercials use lots of babies and there may be an infant part in some movie, if they are casting, somewhere. The photographs that follow are by Barbara Campbell, a professional photographer who specializes in shooting babies (of both sexes) for commercials. You may recognize some of them; maybe your little miracle ought to be one of them.

Ready on the Set

Alexis Nicole Colapinto, age six months, and Alexander Evan Cohen-Smith, age one year, arrive with their mothers at Barbara Campbell's photography studio. Both children have worked with Campbell before, Alexis on a national ad for Baby Fresh baby wipes and Alexander on the cover of a catalog for Hasbro Toys.

The studio is spacious, lined with windows that let in the slightly sooty sunlight of downtown Manhattan. The shot is already set up. "When you work with children you have to be ready before they are," says Campbell. "Their attention spans are so short that if you are diddling around with equipment, you'll lose them."

She has hung a huge expanse of white paper from the high ceiling and spread it over several yards of the pale wood floor. A masking tape X marks the spot where the baby will sit. The lights are arranged and the camera is on a low tripod, loaded and all set.

Campbell pokes her head into the toy- and prop-filled waiting room to signal "baby wrangler" Erica Bogin that she is almost ready. (A wrangler is responsible for helping mothers prepare the child and keeping the little stars quiet on the set and attentive to the camera.) This time the photographer tells Bogin that neither child needs blush—both have rosy cheeks today—but that their hair should be fixed with styling mousse. She leaves to attend to the final details of the day's shot, and Bogin goes to work on Alexis. While Mother holds her up, Alexis faces Bogin, who smiles and coos at her. Alexis responds in kind and forgets to notice that Bogin is tousling her hair. Once the strands have been arranged so that they stand up where they should and lie down every-

---

Looking steadily at the camera, model Alexis is every inch the pro.

According to a sampling of baby-model managers and agencies, babies of twelve to eighteen months are currently most in demand. Other desirable characteristics are listed in order of importance:

· Blond with blue eyes
· Brunet with fair skin
· A light-skinned Black
· Oriental
· Outgoing and willing to go to anyone
· Not an only child

As for the ideal baby-model parent, he or she:

· Owns a car
· Is intelligent and follows directions
· Has an answering machine
· Does not work at a job outside the home
· Can be inconspicuous on the set

where else, it's show time. Alexis is placed on her mark, and the flashbulbs start popping.

Mother sits on one side of the starlet and Bogin on the other. Unlike some photographers, Campbell believes that mothers are essential to good baby photography, and she encourages them to stay with their children throughout the process. "If the mom is not next to the baby, the baby is looking for the mom all the time, and not at the camera," she says. "Babies are like animals in that they are extremely sensitive to the mood of those around them. If the mother is relaxed and having a good time, the baby will sense that, and will relax and have a good time, too. It is supposed to be a pleasant experience."

Campbell begins to talk to Alexis immediately. She pulls toy after toy from a stockpile to her left and keeps up a steady stream of nonsense chatter, focusing and shooting all the while.

She then asks Mother to place a tiny pink and white headband on Alexis's head. That done, she requests several small adjustments and shoots frame after frame—until Alexis pulls the headband down around her neck and begins to chew on it. Another photographer might have been nonplussed, or even angry, at such insubordination. Not Campbell. Mother takes the slightly soggy prop away gently, and the flashbulbs continue.

Alexander watches the procedure for a while, then gets bored and returns to his toys. He will be prepped just before he goes on camera. Trial and error have taught Bogin that prepping a year-old boy too far ahead is an exercise in futility.

About fifteen minutes have elapsed, during which Campbell has taken seventy photos of Alexis and contrived to keep her tiny model continuously amused and attentive. When she is done, Barbara Campbell thanks Mother, applauds the baby, and begins her preparations for the next session.

Bogin has sat with her star throughout the shot. Only when it is over does the wrangler leave Alexis with her mother and return to the waiting room. It is time to ready Alexander for his performance.

Does a Six-Month-Old Need a Manager?

"A manager is like the hub of a wheel," says Barbara Jarrett, a baby-model manager based in New York. "The spokes are the agents, and the rim of the wheel, where the tire goes, represents the opportunity for the baby. The wheel spins and the manager receives calls from many areas." The better known and more respected a manager is, the more calls she—almost all of them are women—will get, and the more likely it is that she will receive a call for a baby just like yours.

The main advantage of having a manager over being a free-lancer

Please don't eat the geraniums—until the shoot is over!

Future directors get experience on the set (overleaf).

who contacts agents directly is that it reduces the amount of work the parents of a prospective star have to do for themselves.

When you have a manager, you have one person to depend on, and one person to blame when things go awry. A manager keeps track of people with whom you have dealt, will deal, or might deal in the future. And whereas an individual cannot register with more than one agency, a manager gets calls for modeling jobs from many agencies, thus broadening a baby's opportunities. In addition, a manager makes the calls and mails out the letters and photos that keep your baby's name in front of the right people. And when you consider that new shots must be taken and sent out every four weeks as the baby grows and changes, that represents a lot of stamps the manager is licking for you.

Customarily, a manager receives a commission of 15 percent in addition to the agent's 10 percent.

"No one needs a manager," says Jarrett. "No one needs anything. But a manager makes it a lot easier."

And a good one can make you a lot wealthier.

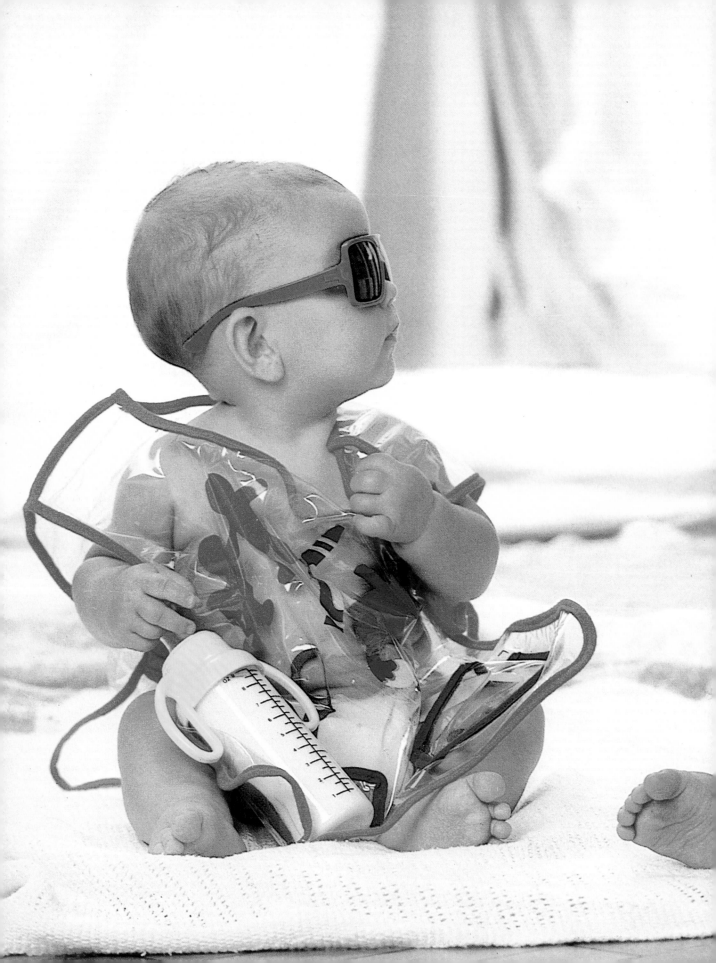

Leading Man, Leading Lady, Leading Baby?

Over 3.8 million American babies were born in 1987, the highest rate in two decades. Nearly half of them were first children, born to the original postwar baby boomers. These "echo boom" babies wreaked blissful havoc on their parents' once self-oriented, career-dominated lives; they also began to take center stage on screen. In *Baby Boom* for example, Diane Keaton played a fast-track career woman who was derailed but eventually found happiness after inheriting a baby from relatives—the neat plot was picked up for a television series. Carrying the trend one step further in *Three Men and a Baby*, the bachelor lives of Tom Selleck, Steve Guttenberg, and Ted Danson were dislocated, then hugely enriched by the focal character—who else but a baby left on their doorstep. These movies marked the beginning of a trend rich with possibilities. . . .

Our Gang gathers around the seven-month-old center of attention at Hal Roach's ranch in June 1929.

Cover models already, these twins are posing for the number-one spot in *American Baby* magazine.

BUY ME!

"Sticking a picture of an adorable child into an ad practically ensures that a wide range of humans will at least *look* at it," says psychologist Carol Moog. Some major companies obviously feel that they will do considerably more than that. Among those currently using children as attention-getters or emotional bridges between the product and the viewer's wallet:

Pan Am World Airways   Eaton
Purina   Lotus
First Boston   Weyerhaeuser
Prudential   Merrill Lynch
Sharp Electronics   Dean Witter
Michelin Tire

LITTLE FOOTNOTES

A BARNUM AND BABY CIRCUS

Tom Thumb, the world's most famous tiny person, made his debut with P. T. Barnum when he was twenty-five inches tall and weighed fifteen pounds—comparable to the dimensions of a five-month-old baby. In fact, he was four years old at the time.

Barnum made his first fortune out of presenting Charles Stratton (Tom's real name) as "Tom Thumb from England aged 11" at New York's American Museum in 1842. The show was a wild success—at a rate of $500 a day, split between Barnum and the child's parents—and when Barnum took tiny Tom on a European tour, 80,000 people crowded the docks to see them off.

John and Alice Durant, *Pictorial History of the American Circus*

BOOTING THE BABY

The best known movie baby was probably Baby LeRoy, real name Ronald LeRoy Overacker, who played the role of W. C. Fields's nemesis in several 1930s films. In a famous scene in The Old-Fashioned Way, *Baby LeRoy drops Fields' watch into the molasses at breakfast and Fields later retaliates by kicking him in the rear when he thinks no one is looking. Paramount tried to cut the kick, fearing audiences would disapprove. Fields insisted it be kept in, on the grounds that "There's not a man in the world who hasn't had a secret desire to boot a kid."*

Fields, a notable drinker, once spiked his co-star's milk. During filming of It's A Gift, *LeRoy (who was, after all, only two and half) was holding up production by being "difficult," and his nurse had to feed him his bottle to keep him quiet. Fields asked if he could help, then dispatched the nurse on an errand, and while she was gone, he "dropped a couple of noggins of gin in the bottle and gave it to the baby. LeRoy sucked it up, then passed out. No one could revive the youngster and the day's shooting had to be cancelled. As Fields walked off the set he yelled to the director, 'I told you the kid was no trouper.'"*

Ronald J. Fields,
W. C. Fields: A Life on Film

THE FIRST PRIZE BABY

The first recorded baby show was held at Springfield, Ohio, on October 5, 1854, "more in a spirit of jest than with a serious object." The idea met with instant success and no fewer than 127 babies were entered. The prize baby was the ten-month-old daughter of William Ronemus of Vienna, Ohio, who was awarded a large salver worth $300 (no small sum in those days). Three other prizes were awarded, but history does not relate what they were.

Famous First Facts

IS THAT BABY BOGIE?

Who is that infant whose likeness became the Gerber Company logo in 1928, and has since adorned well over a thousand consumer products, labeled in eleven languages and marketed in fifty-five countries?

Gerber still gets some ten inquiries weekly from folk asking if the baby is Humphrey Bogart. No, it is not: Bogie was born in 1899.

The real Gerber baby is the four-month-old likeness of Ann Turner Cook, now a teacher living in Florida, who has four children and seven grandchildren.

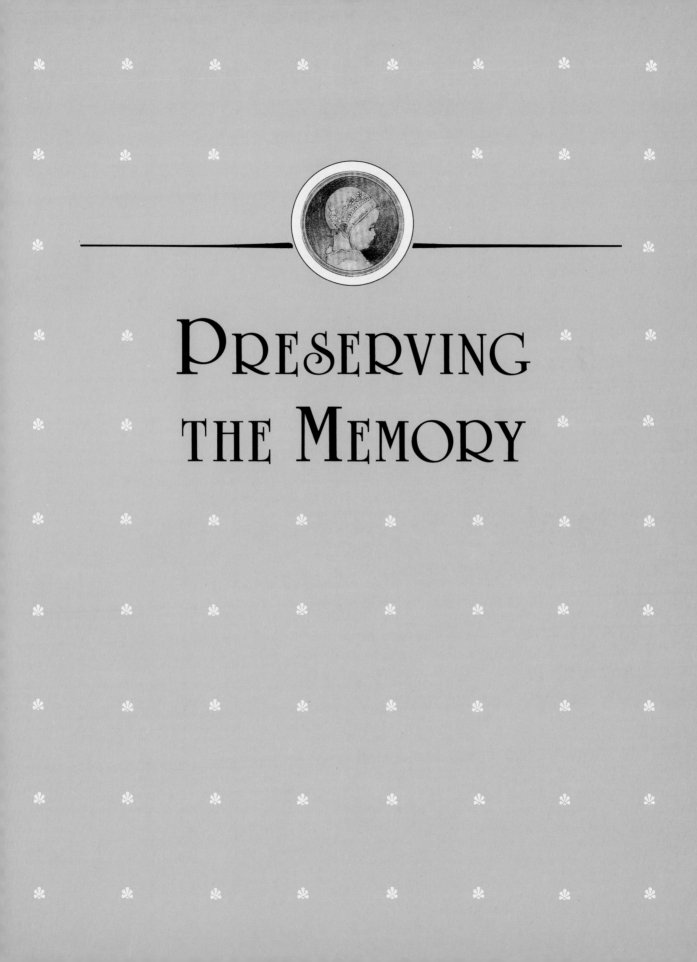

PRESERVING
THE MEMORY

A PHOTOGRAPHER'S OWN ALBUM

There's Dad carrying the newborn and looking as though he might drop him at any minute. Remember when the kids splashed naked in the little wading pool? Oh, what a mess that first birthday party was. Oh, what fun to remember.

Those moments will never come again, but thanks to photographs, we can all go back. And thanks to the superb work of photographer Erika Stone, whose personal baby-picture album follows, we can not only share in her experiences but know exactly how she obtained the effects that are so moving.

Cherished Moments Are Savored Forever

Photos, albums, snapshots! How wonderful it is to be able to remember. It is beautiful to recall memories of the times when my home was filled with laughter and the voices of children—some happy sounds, some not-so-happy sounds, but all of them part of those busy, full-house, fun-filled days.

Now that my home is quiet, the kids and noises gone, I dearly love to pull out those albums or boxes of photos. I am at once temporarily transported away from my workaday cares, able to return briefly to those days when my children were young. And I remember the pride and joy those pictures brought to their grandparents. They eagerly anticipated our arrival, each time with a new batch of photos, to be proudly shared with friends, neighbors, and family.

One day, I, too, will have grandchildren to photograph. What a rich reward it will be to record their years of growth and change on film in much the same way that I did with my children and other parents. It will be wonderful for my children and me to share the ever-changing moments that vanish so quickly. Babyhood, toddling, childhood . . . each period has its own special highlights. They do pass with the blink of an eye. But how fortunate we are to have easy-to-master cameras to preserve those expressions, actions, antics, and experiences.

You, too, can create these memories, can hold onto and treasure the days of your children's youth. Keep your camera loaded and ready . . . for those priceless moments that won't happen again.

Baby on Crocheted Spread
Patterns can be distracting but, in this case, the colorful blanket works. I took a chance and found that the spread really makes this picture. Of course, I got the baby at a happy, flying moment, which is equally important for a successful picture. Her pink outfit was perfect. Had she had a patterned outfit on, the picture would have been too busy.

Two flash units, bounced into soft, white umbrellas, were used, one as a main light and the other as a weaker fill- in.

50mm—f 1:4 lens—Kodachrome 64
125th at f 8

Baby with Puppies

Working with both baby and pets takes patience, alertness, and spontaneity but if you do catch the right moment, the results are worthwhile. Soft, even light is a must because of the ever-moving subjects. I looked for an open shade location and decided to get down to the level of the baby to get my picture. (This might mean lying on your stomach.) The grey stones beneath the subjects reflected some light back into baby's face, preventing deep shadow.

    50mm—f 1:4 Nikkor lens—Kodachrome 64
        125th at f 5:6

Baby on Couch

Catching a baby at the right moment takes practice and patience. Dad helped by catching her attention. Very often, a parent can be helpful in animating a child and I often let them assist in this manner. The striped material on the couch does not distract while a pattern might have. A single flash unit on a stand was placed to the right of the camera at a 45-degree angle.

    85mm—f 2 lens—Tri-X film developed in D 76, 1 to 1
        125th at f 8

Baby Asleep

I chanced upon this picture and couldn't resist documenting it. There was nothing to do but ask the mother for permission to take the picture, take a meter reading, and snap the shutter. Pulling or straightening out the blanket would have woken the baby and the little sticking-up behind would have been down in no time. So have your camera ready and grab that shot. It's a good one for your memory album.

    85mm—f 2 lens—Kodachrome 64
        60th at f 5:6

First Steps
This toddler has just started to walk and is mighty proud of it. As you can see, I photographed him from behind and above, emphasizing his small size and also eliminating disturbing background clutter. The boy's two-toned blue outfit is very effective against the green meadow. I caught the shot at the moment he took a step, showing off his new-found ability. Light is late afternoon, low sun.

    50mm—1:4 lens—Kodachrome 64
      250th at f 5:6

Child Smelling a Flower
Catching a moment such as this one is priceless. The intensity with which the little girl is sniffing the flower is recorded for posterity. Set your speed and aperture before you ask the model to do a task, and be ready to snap when the action takes place. The light was an open-shade area so there were no shadows or light flecks to worry about. The dark, wooded area in the background was thrown out of focus by a fast shutter speed and a fairly large aperture. A distracting background would have spoiled the picture.

    85mm—f 2 lens—Tri-X film developed in D 76, 1 to 1
      250th at f 5:6

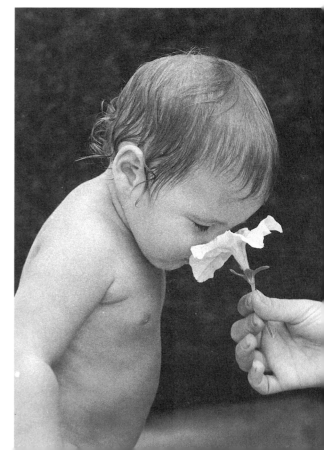

Walking in the Rain

This is the kind of picture for which I use zone focusing. It means setting the distance scale and the lens aperture in advance in such a way that a specific distance zone is in sharp focus.

Because the toddler was walking toward me, I pre-focused on a break in the sidewalk. When the child arrived at that line, I clicked the shutter. This way, I did not have to try to focus while the boy was in action. The wider-angle 35mm lens also had the advantage of giving me more depth-of-field, which helps with an action picture.

35mm—f 3:5 lens—Kodachrome 200
    250th at f 8

Child with Bubbles
Another late-afternoon, backlit shot done with a reflector fill. In this case, I propped a large white cardboard on a chair and reflected some of the sunlight back into the late-afternoon shadows on the baby's body. To catch the bubbles, I photographed at a speed of 250th. It takes repeated tries to catch a good photo when doing action shots. I usually continue to photograph until the baby loses interest.

   50mm—f 1:4 lens—Kodachrome 64
      250th at f 4

Boy with Truck

Very contrasty light sometimes calls for a fill-in flash, which was used here. My Sunpak 422D flash unit can be set for various power ratios, such as full, 1/2, 1/4, 1/8 and 1/16. In this case, I used the weakest output of light (1/16th). With this low light output, I was certain that the flash would not overpower the ambient light for which I exposed the film. To get my correct exposure, I measured the backlit rim of the boy's head and made my exposure accordingly. The soft flash output filled in the shadows nicely.

  35mm—f 3:5 lens—Kodachrome 64
    60th at f 5:6

Splashing in the Pool

Summer is always a great time for pictures but watch out for sunny, contrasty light. On those days, it is best to have your photo sessions in the late afternoon when the sun is low and shadows soften. For this picture, I picked an open shade area under a tree with enough sun hitting the child to indicate a feeling of summer. Note that the background is obstructed and does not conflict with the subject. I used a fast shutter speed for this photo in order to stop the action. The background, because of a larger aperture, is out of focus, which adds to the picture.

  35mm—f 3:5 Nikkor lens—Kodachrome 64
    250th at f 4

Baby in Toilet Paper
One day I found my son Michael in the bathroom in this condition. My immediate reaction, of course, was "No-no. We don't do that." On second thoughts, I recognized it as a potentially good shot, so I quickly set up a flood lamp to bounce light off the ceiling, wrapped him back up in the toilet paper, and shot the picture. Then I told him not to do it again.

Rolleiflex—50mm lens—Tri-X film developed in D76, 1 to 1
125th at f 5:6

Boy Playing with Pots
Finding good props for baby does not need to be expensive. As you can see, this boy is having the time of his life with Mommy's pots and a spoon. The simple closed shutters behind him create a feeling of kitchen and home. A happy moment was caught. One flash unit on the camera was used, bounced off the white ceiling.

50mm—f 1:4 lens—Tri-X film developed in Microdol
125th at f 5:6

Birthday Girl
First birthday is an important event, which you might like to record. My pretty little model had licked the birthday cake and I caught her at a moment of satisfaction with the taste. A single flash on camera bounced off the white ceiling was the light source.

50mm—f 1:4 lens—Tri-X film developed in D 76, 1 to 1
   125th at f 8

PRODUCT/ RESOURCE GUIDE

Having a baby today seems as much a symbol of good taste as of proper timing for the couple turning family. (Everybody's doing it—in style.) This guide has been prepared to help expectant parents in making ready for the new arrival without becoming embedded in a morass of detail. Though it offers a selective sampling that is national in scope, it makes no attempt to be a definitive exploration of the host of resources and references that are currently available. It is simply intended to offer some ideas on where to turn for information and support in specific areas, and hence is arranged in four sections: What to Buy; What to Know; Local Community Resources; and Media Resources for New Parents.

WHAT TO BUY

This section of the guide spans a very diverse range of materials—from books, magazines, and mail-order catalogs worthy of attention all the way to the most appropriate baby furniture to buy, plus a note about door-to-door services and some innovative ideas for gifts that will give pleasure to parents as well as to the new arrival.

BOOKS TO BUY

A sampling of baby-care resource books for not-quite-ready-for-prime-time parents.

BEFORE BIRTH

Beyond Jennifer and Jason: An Enlightened Guide to Naming Your Baby, by Linda Rosenkrantz and Pamela Redmond Satran (New York: St. Martin's Press, 1988).

The Complete Mothercare Manual, with consultants Rosalind Y. Ting, M.D., Herbert Brant, M.D., and Kenneth S. Holt, M.D. (New York: Prentice Hall Press, 1987).

Having a Baby After Thirty, by Elisabeth Bing and Libby Colman (New York: Bantam Books, 1975).

The Maternity Sourcebook: 230 Basic Decisions for Pregnancy, Birth and Baby

Care, by Matthew and Wendy Lesko (New York: Warner Books, 1984).

What to Expect When You're Expecting, by Arlene Eisenberg, Heidi E. Murkoff, and Sandee E. Hathaway (New York: Workman Publishing, 1984).

ABOUT BABIES

Babyhood, by Penelope Leach (New York: Alfred A. Knopf, 1983).

The First Twelve Months of Life: Your Baby's Growth Month by Month, edited by Frank Caplan (New York: Bantam Books, 1973).

Infancy: A Guide to Research and Resources, by Hannah Nuba, Deborah Sheiman, and Kathleen Watkins (Wolfeboro, NH: Teachers College Press, 1986).

Infants and Mothers: Difference in Development, by T. Berry Brazelton, M.D. (New York: Dell, 1983).

The Second Twelve Months of Life: Your

Baby's Growth Month by Month, edited by Frank and Theresa Caplan (New York: Bantam Books, 1977).

Your Baby and Child: From Birth to Age Five, by Penelope Leach (New York: Alfred A. Knopf, 1983).

Your One-Year-Old: The Fun-Loving, Fussy 12-to-24-Month-Old, by Louise Bates Ames, Frances L. Ilg, and Carol Chase Haber of Gesell Institute of Child Development (New York: Delacorte, 1982).

Your Two-Year-Old: Terrible or Tender, by Louise Bates Ames and Frances L. Ilg of Gesell Institute of Child Development (New York: Dell, 1976).

ABOUT PARENTING

A Good Enough Parent: A Book on Child-Rearing, by Bruno Bettelheim (New York: Alfred A. Knopf, 1987).

How to Raise a Street-Smart Child: The Complete Parent's Guide to Safety on the

Street and at Home, by Grace Hechinger (New York: Facts on File, 1984).

How to Win as a Stepfamily, by Emily B. and John S. Visher (Chicago: Contemporary Books, 1982).

Know Your Child: An Authoritative Guide for Today's Parents, by Stella Chase (New York: Basic Books, 1987).

The Magic Years: Understanding and Handling the Problems of Early Childhood, by Selma H. Fraiberg (New York: Basic Books, 1984).

New Parenthood: The First Six Weeks, by Cecilia Worth with Anna Marie Brooks (New York: McGraw-Hill, 1985).

The Nurturing Father, by Kyle D. Pruett (New York: Warner Books, 1987).

Parents after Thirty, by Murray Kappelman and Paul Ackerman (New York: Wideview Books, 1981).

A Parent's Guide to the First Three Years, by Burton L. White (Englewood Cliffs, NJ: Prentice-Hall, 1980).

Parents' Guide to Nutrition: Healthy Eating from Birth through Adolescence, by the Boston Children's Hospital with Susan Baker, M.D., Ph.D., and Roberta R. Henry, R.D. (Reading, MA: Addison-Wesley, 1986).

The Parents' Resource Book, by Gail Granet Velez (New York: New American Library, 1986).

Planning Your Young Child's Education, by J. Robert Parkinson (Lincolnwood, IL: VGM Career Horizons, 1986).

The Private Life of Parents: How to Take Care of Yourself and Your Partner While Raising Happy, Healthy Children—A Complete Survival Guide by Roberta Plutzik and Maria Laghi (New York: Everest House, 1983).

The Complete Dr. Salk—An A-to-Z Guide to Raising Your Child, by Dr. Lee Salk (New York: New American Library, 1983).

Dr. Spock's Baby and Child Care, by Benjamin Spock, M.D., and Michael B.

Rothenberg, M.D. (New York: Pocket Books, 1985).

Toddlers and Parents: A Declaration of Independence, by T. Berry Brazelton, M.D. (New York: Delacorte, 1974).

Who's in Control?, by Lawrence Balter, M.D. (New York: Poseidon Press/Simon & Schuster, 1988).

CONSUMER GUIDES

Consumer Reports Books: Guide to Baby Products, by Sandy Jones with Werner Freitag and the Editors of Consumer Reports Books (Mount Vernon, NY: Consumers Union, 1988).
A useful, comprehensive guide that ranks available products by *Consumer Reports* standards.

The Childwise Catalog—A Consumer Guide to Buying the Safest and Best Products for Your Children, by Jack Gillis and Mary Ellen R. Fise (New York: Pocket Books, 1986).
Recently endorsed by the Consumer Federation of America (CFA), this is by far the most comprehensive guide to consumer purchases and services.

The Ultimate Baby Catalogue, by Michele Ingrassia Haber and Barbara Kantrowitz (New York: Workman Publishing, 1982).

REGIONAL GUIDES

There are also locally published guides/directories on the lines of *Having a Baby in . . .*, which offer reminders, checklists, and useful references for new and expectant parents living in the regional communities.

MAGAZINES AND NEWSLETTERS

A selection of publications of interest to parents. Some are initially distributed free of charge through doctors' offices

and if parents like them, they can sign up for paid subscriptions. Others are available on newsstands or by subscription.

American Baby—A free monthly magazine for expectant and new parents, covering topics associated with pregnancy, newborns, and toddlers in a "brides-type" style. Subscriptions from:

American Baby
352 Evelyn Street
Paramus, NJ 07652

Baby Talk—The first "baby magazine" (it was founded in 1935), this monthly publication is distributed free through hospitals, doctors' offices, and diaper service gift packs; it provides useful if unexciting advice on baby health, nutrition, and welfare concerns in Q&A format for first-time parents. Subscriptions from:

Blessings Corporation
185 Madison Avenue
New York, NY 10016

Child—A bimonthly that celebrates better childhoods and easier parenthoods, wittily written with the sophisticated adult in mind. Subscriptions from:

Child
P.O. Box 11224
Des Moines, IA 50347-1224
Cost: $2.95 an issue; $9.97 per year

Children—Brand-new, wide-ranging monthly for parents with infants and young children, with special emphasis on fitness and health, education and child development. Subscriptions from:

Rodale Press Inc.
33 E. Minor Street
Emmaus, PA 18049
800-441-7761; in PA, 800-841-7768
Cost: $2.00 an issue; $11.97 per year

Growing Child—Available free initially from pediatricians, this ad-free monthly newsletter tailors its issues on child development to the age of the child from infancy to age 6. A catalog of toys and books and an additional newsletter, *Growing Parents*, are also available. For brochure and free sample:

Growing Child
P.O. Box 620C
Lafayette, IN 47902
Annual subscription: $15.95

Mothering—A "progressive" quarterly periodical covering topics of interest to fathers and grandparents as well as mother and child. Solid, well researched articles often include helpful bibliographies. Subscriptions from:

Mothering Publications, Inc.
P.O. Box 8410
Santa Fe, NM 87504
505-984-8116
Annual subscription: $18.00

Pampers Baby Care—A series of digests of selected *Parents* magazine articles, distributed free by the makers of Pampers disposable diapers. (Issues are organized in stages of a baby's growth, so be sure to include the child's age when subscribing.) Subscriptions from:

Pampers Baby Care
P.O. Box 50340
Des Moines, IA 50347-0166
800-247-5470;
    in IA, 800-532-1272

Parenting—Started in 1987, this monthly magazine covers child psychology, assorted product reviews, and regular sections by noted psychologists for parents of infants. Subscriptions from:

Parenting Magazine
Box 52424
Boulder, CO 80321-2424
800-525-0643;
    in CO, 303-447-9330
Cost: $1.95 an issue; $12 per year

Parents—A popular monthly magazine offering parenting advice and information on products, ideas, food, fashions, and issues of concern to parents of children from birth to age 18. Subscriptions from:

Parents Magazine
P.O. Box 3042
Harlan, IA 51593-4207
800-727-3682
Cost: $1.95 an issue; $12 per year

Working Mother—A companion to *Working Woman*, this monthly magazine examines concerns of working supermoms on the job, in the home, and with the kids, in a "how to/can do" style. It also offers baby product reviews and food, health, and safety advice. Subscriptions from:

Working Mother
P.O. Box 51444
Boulder, CO 80321-1444
800-525-0643
Cost: $1.95 an issue; $12.95 per year

MAIL-ORDER CATALOGS

A listing of catalogs in the following general categories (with some overlaps): General Merchandise; Maternity and Infant Clothing; Nursery Furnishings; and Toys and Gifts.

GENERAL MERCHANDISE

The Catalogue's Catalogue
(Children and Mothers-to-be Edition)
    Information Publications, Inc.
    308 Hunters Run Lane,
        Suite 1000
    Mt. Juliet, TN 37122

This $4.95 catalog, obtainable at a reduced rate through an introductory offer, lists many catalogs of interest to expectant parents.

Lillian Vernon Catalog
    510 S. Fulton Avenue
    Mt. Vernon, NY 10550-5067
    914-633-6300

Originally a home products catalog, Lillian Vernon has expanded to include useful baby products, room furnishings, and toys, with such items as high-chair floor mats and baby carryall bags that double as changing sheets.

The Right Start Catalog
    6403 Alondra Blvd.
    Paramount, CA 90723

Offers a $2.00 color catalog filled with infant products from bedding and equipment (carriages and high chairs) to toys and clothes.

J.C Penney Company Inc.
    Catalog Dept./Circulation Dept.
    Box 2056
    Milwaukee, WI 53201-2056

For $4.00 (covered by a $5.00 merchandise certificate), Penney's general merchandise catalog includes maternity and infants' clothing, nursery furnishings, and baby products, along with toys, books, and accessories.

Sears Roebuck & Co.
Order Sears catalogs through your nearest regional selling center:

EAST
4640 Roosevelt Blvd.
Philadelphia, PA 19132

SOUTH
675 Ponce de Leon Avenue, N.E.
95 Annex
Atlanta, GA 30395
or
1409 S. Lamar Street
Dallas, TX 75295

MIDWEST
925 S. Homan Avenue
Chicago, IL 60607
or
Dept. 146
4545 Fisher Road
Columbus, OH 43228

WEST
2650 E. Olympic Blvd.
Los Angeles, CA 90051

Sears offers special "Infants N' Toddlers" and "Toys (Christmas Wish Book)" catalogs in addition to its general merchandising catalog ($5.00 cost is deducted from first order). Some parents find their children treat these big catalogs like picture books.

MATERNITY AND INFANT CLOTHING

Laura Ashley, Inc.
    1300 MacArthur Blvd.
    Mahwah, NJ 07430
    800-367-2000

Known for its English-style home furnishing and loose-fitting patterned clothing, Laura Ashley has added another specialty catalog to its collection: "Mother & Child," featuring clothing for young ones and their "mums." Annual subscription (for entire catalog collection): $5.00; individual catalogs: about $2.00.

Mothers Work
    1309 Noble Street
    5th floor, Dept. WK8B
    Philadelphia, Pa 19123
    215-625-0151

Produced by a nationwide chain of maternity shops, this catalog ($3.00, refundable) offers fashionable clothing for career women at reasonable prices.

Motherhood Catalog
1330 Colorado Avenue
Santa Monica, CA 90404-3381
800-227-1903

This national chain of maternity shops, highly recommended in several publications, now offers a free catalog.

Hanna Andersson
1010 N.W. Flanders Street
Portland, OR 97209
800-222-0544

This free, beautifully produced, color catalog shows imported, mostly Swedish, 100% cotton classic but stylish casual wear for infants through adults.

Biobottoms
P.O. Box 1060
Petaluma, CA 94953
707-778-7945

Known for its designer diaper covers and natural fiber clothing, Biobottoms' free catalog goes all the way to high-tech potties and bike helmets.

NURSERY FURNISHINGS

Peaceable Kingdom Press
2954 Hillegass Avenue
Berkeley, CA 94705
800-444-KIDS

Free catalog of prints reproducing famous children's book illustrations, such as *Goodnight Moon* and *Where the Wild Things Are*.

Boston & Winthrop
148 E. 74th Street
New York, NY 10021
212-410-6388

Color catalog of their complete line of custom hand-painted furniture costs $3.00.

Wicker Gardens' Baby Mail Order
1320 Madison Avenue
New York, NY 10128
212-348-1166

Traditional cribs, changing tables, high chairs, clothing (newborn to 6X), foreign and domestic brands. Free catalog.

Scandinavian Design Inc.
127 E. 59th Street
New York, NY 10022
212-755-6078

Free catalog of white-painted or natural birch furniture and furniture systems for newborns and older children.

Shaker Workshops
P.O. Box 1028
Concord, MA 01742-1028
617-646-8985

A $1.00 catalog lists reproduction Shaker rockers, chairs, tables, beds, including children's furniture, dolls, and toys (available in kits or completely finished).

H.U.D.D.L.E.
11159 Santa Monica Blvd.
West Los Angeles, CA 90025
213-478-5986

Free catalog of furniture designs, such as twin, bunk, trundle, and loft beds, dressers, desks, etc.

Conran's
160 E. 54th Street
New York, NY 10022
(and other stores)
201-905-8800 to order catalog

Free catalog and extensive mail-order service available for Conran's contemporary and country furniture, lighting and accessories for every room.

TOYS AND GIFTS

Heir Affair
625 Russell Drive
Meridian, MS 39301
800-322-4347;
in MS, 800-484-4323

The motto of this $2.00 catalog is "Today's Treasures—Tomorrow's Heirlooms"; also contains such trend-setting items as Beverly Hills Baby Club dinner sets and bibs with tuxedo fronts or gold lamé wings.

F.A.O. Schwartz Ultimate Toy Catalog
1 Yellow Brick Road
Ridgely, MD 21685
800-426-TOYS

At $5.00, this is the most expensive toy catalog around—then again, this is the largest toy store in the world.

Walden Kids
P.O. Box 9455
New Haven, CT 06534-0455
800-821-1541

A $1.00 catalog, offering a selection of toys, games, books, and cassettes—even an arts and crafts segment—all listed with appropriate children's ages.

Childcraft
Catalog Dept.
20 Kilmer Road
Edison, NJ 08818
800-631-5652

Offers a free catalog of "Toys That Teach," an array of amusing educational materials for newborns on upward.

European Toy Collection
Leapin' Wizard Productions
97 Hillcrest Road, Box 203
Ogden Dunes, IN 46368
219-763-3234

Free catalog filled with beautiful wooden blocks, puzzles, and mobiles from Europe.

Abilities International Ltd.
Living Tools for Early Years
1-C Old Forge Road
Elizabethtown, NY 12932-0398
800-225-3868 (or 800-ABLE-TOT);
in NY, 518-876-6456

With toy trains, puzzles that form their own stories, hand puppets, and innovative child-care products, this catalog ($1.00 for a year's subscription) encourages imagination, self-expression, and learning.

Sensational Beginnings
P.O. Box 2009
430 N. Monroe
Monroe, MI 48161
313-242-2147

"The seeing, hearing, touching baby catalog"—and it's free. Well researched and put together by a former nurse who has observed and worked with newborns and premature infants.

CATALOGS OF BABY BOOKS

Books of Wonder
132 Seventh Avenue (at 18th St.)
New York, NY 10011
212-989-3270

Imaginative books for newborns on up. Features a distinguished selection of childhood classics and modern masterpieces. $3.00 for 3 catalogs.

Eeyore's Books for Children
2252 Broadway
New York, NY 10024
212-362-0634

Extensive collection of books, cassettes, records for children of all ages. Catalog: $2.00 (includes periodic supplements).

A Child's Collection
611 Broadway, Suite 708
Dept. A-18
New York, NY 10012
800-652-2665; in NY, 212-228-1260

Free, 48-page catalog, geared for children ages 2–10.

MAJOR PURCHASES
❧

Costs of equipping baby with essentials range on average about $1,500 to $2,500, and many parents spend much, much more. As prices vary widely, most guides recommend comparison shopping, in person or by phone, with a list of specific product brands and models. It is worth investing in furniture that can grow with the child, and be converted or adjusted to meet changing needs.

FURNITURE

Factors for first-time buyers to consider:
- What items are essential?—This will vary depending on where you live and your lifestyle.
- What will be your primary mode of transportation?
- How much space is available for baby?

CRIB

1. Port-a-crib/bassinet—from birth up to 6 months; somewhat of a luxury, but ideal when space is tight: $30–$500.
2. Regular crib—up to 2–3 years (some convertible cribs can become youth beds): $100–$1,000. (Most mattresses are sold separately at extra cost.)

SWING

Can have calming effect on babies up to 6 months; some are motorized, some can play music: $30–$90.

PLAYPEN

Can be portable (Fisher-Price's "Travel Tender" folds into a bag); all models fold flat: $50–$100.

INFANT SEAT

1. Portable chairs for carrying baby around; some play music, some have toys attached: varying prices.
2. Baby bouncer—rocks the baby; depending on accessories: $20–$60.
3. "Jolly Jumper"—a seat whose springs attach to top of door frame, in which baby bounces: $30.

CHANGING TABLE

A most convenient luxury if there is enough space; can have drawers, be quite elaborate: $30–$300.

BABY BATH

Heavy-duty plastic: about $15.

CAR SEAT

Must conform to federal safety regulations (harnesses, etc.)
1. Birth up to 6 months (can be used as infant seat): $40.
2. Regular (up to 4 years): 40–$50.

HIGH CHAIR

Use from 6 months on (when baby can hold head up); wood or metal; more or less padding; freestanding or portable (folds flat): $35–$100.

WALKER

Nonessential but convenient from about 6 months on; adjustable: $30–$60.

BABY CARRIER

1. Frame carrier—baby backpack for 4–6 months on; some up to 4–6 years: $30–$60.
2. Soft, front carrier—Snugli-type, adjustable, fabric pouches, slung against chest: $18–$60.

SAFETY GATE

1. Pressure—expandable (no hardware), wedged to door width.

2. Hinged—screwed into wall, used like a door.
3. Combination—fits with pressure, but also opens, like door: $12–$35.

POTTY SEAT

1. Fits securely over toilet seat; removable: about $5.
2. Freestanding (often with front shield): up to $30.

OUTDOOR TRANSPORTATION

CARRIAGES/PRAMS

Less popular than formerly because strollers are easier to transport and store, carriages can hold a lot of paraphernalia, even a seat for a second child, and are easy to wheel. Those where the carriage can be detached from its wheeled base can do double duty as cots. They are expensive, so it is worth checking individual model prices.

STROLLER

1. Regular—from newborn to 3–4 years. Standard features: swivel wheels, harness (regulation), canopy, folds for storage, converts to carriage so parents can face child; varying weights, 13–30 pounds, multiple-position seat (from flat to upright): $49–$300.
2. "Umbrella" (lightweight, folding, can be carried around by the handles)—from 1–4 years, most useful for short, quick outings. Has canopy, reclining seat, harness (regulation); varying weights, 6–12 pounds: $20–$120.

Note: Consumer guides such as *Consumer Reports' Guide to Baby Products* and *The Childwise Catalog* contain helpful lists of baby furniture manufacturers.

DOOR-TO-DOOR SERVICES
❧

The concept of home delivery is nothing new, but these days a wide range of products and services have added this convenience. Some small companies will deliver homemade baby food and gift-laden bassinets; others provide home exercise classes. Store merchants compete for custom with pickup and delivery on such items as videos and pharmacy goods. Interested consumers can locate such services through local and community newspapers, and the phone book.

Unquestionably, the oldest door-to-door baby service is the neighborhood diaper service, many of which are experiencing a resurgence.

DIAPER SERVICE—OR NOT?

Most parents choose a combination of disposables and cloth diapers, for reasons of cost, hygiene, and convenience.

DISPOSABLE:

Most expensive (prices vary widely, with store brands cheaper than name brands, and cost increases with size). Average: 22 cents a diaper. For 2 1/2 yrs: $1,650.00.

Start with 2 dozen in same size (sizes are newborn, medium/infant and large/toddler, packaged by the dozen or by the case).

SERVICE:

Averages $10–$12 for delivery of 90 diapers per week, or 9–13 cents a diaper. For 2 1/2 yrs: $1,200.00.

Service can deliver additional diapers if needed. Types available: Contoured, prefolded, and flat; gauze, bird's-eye, or terrycloth.

CLOTH:

Fixed one-time cost of diapers, pins, pants, pails, plus laundry expenses. On average, 4 dozen diapers used per week, when washing twice a week. Estimated cost for 4 dozen: $60–$70. For 2 1/2 yrs: about $700.

SOME TREND-SETTING GIFT IDEAS

꧁ ꧂

These suggestions, compiled in consultation with Brook Mason, senior editor at *Child* magazine, are eminently practical, yet all are well made and have style. Best of all, they are "in" for now, and guaranteed to give both giver and receiver a chuckle.

Designer Baby Sheets and Bedding—For Anglophiles, there are Laura Ashley's charming designs of rocking horses on a blue background, or the Queen's sentries on duty, with matching mobiles and wall hangings. Prices from $60.00 on up. Baby Polo features baby-size comforters, sheets, pillows, and wall hangings, with pillowcases starting at $20.00. For a grand Italian splurge, give a set of Pratesi linens, priced appropriately.

"Twinkle, Twinkle, Little Star"—A full-scale book production of the famous lullaby with pull tabs, popup scenes, chimes, and a light in the starry sky. Priced at $9.95, it is available at most bookstores, or from The Macmillan Co., 866 Third Avenue, New York, NY 10022.

Dinnerware—any of Paolo Tiramani's Donvier dinner sets, plastic, durable, and inventively shaped like a boat, a plane, or a turtle. Moderately priced at $14.95 per set.

The Sassy Seat—A must for restaurant-keen parents. Eminently packable, it fits into a diaper bag and can be attached to any table to form a baby seat. Priced at $27.99, it can be paired with one ($9.95), or a complete set, of the Zagat restaurant guides to major American cities. (Little known fact: Zagat guides list restaurants that actually welcome children. Contact Zagat at 212-362-1313 for more information.)

Gloucester Classics' Gloucester Rocker—This is proof positive that rocking horses are out and rocking boats are in. Each boat is made of mahogany and teak, individually numbered, and each new skipper receives membership to the Gloucester Rocker Club. The boat, priced at $325.00, is available at F.A.O. Schwartz, or write Gloucester Classics Ltd., 811 Boylston Street, Boston, MA 02116, for information.

Rock-A-Bye Baby—Hammacher Schlemmer's voice-activated cradle has a sensor which responds to baby's cries by swinging the cradle and playing a song. (Parents can adjust rocking time, speed of swing, and volume of song.) Price: $154.95 postpaid.

Beatrix Potter's Tales—These vintage charmers, published by Frederick Warne & Co., retail for $4.95 each, boxed collection (23 in all) $110.00. Present the book in the arms of Peter Rabbit Cottontail, a stuffed, musical rabbit made by Eolen Gifts, priced at $19.95.

Monogrammed and Personalized Clothing—A company called Grow Up offers clothing to suit your taste. Hand-painted shoes ($10 a pair) and socks ($4 a pair) are among many customized items available. For a list of designs, or to order, call 213-721-6314.

Growing Gourmet's Frozen Dinners for Toddlers—The ideal answer when baby (or mother) is too tired to go out. Ready for the microwave and available in frozen food cases at $2.50 apiece.

Sevi's Great Flying Bird—Imported from Italy by European Toy Collection, this whimsical bird (in sneakers) flaps into motion with the pull of a cord. The mobile is $39.00, and available at upscale toy stores. For information, or to order, call 219-763-3234.

Snugli Portable Bottle Warmer—Hot, but not heated, this product (complete with bottle, vinyl heating pad, and traveling pouch) removes the hassle from feeding baby while traveling. Squeeze the bottle's designated corner, and in 10 to 15 minutes, the nontoxic heat pack will warm up the enclosed bottle. Cost: $14.00.

Wooden Baby Rattle—Made by Mossy Creek Woodworks of Wesley, Arkansas, of sturdy, light-colored wood with tiny beads inside. Baby can grip and bite on it without breaking the sound barrier. Priced at $13.00, available at most toy stores.

The Little Driver—This toy, from Ambi Toys, features a steering wheel that turns, a side-view mirror, a beeping horn, and removable cloth ignition keys. A suction-cup bottom enables it to be played with on a table or attached to the front panel of an infant car seat. Priced at $22.00.

Hear-My-Voice Telephone—Made by The First Years, a division of Kiddie Products

Inc. The telephone features an exclusive chamber that magnifies a child's voice when speaking on the receiver. It is made of plastic in bright, cheerful colors. Retail price: $6–$8. For information: 800-225-0382.

Teddy Care Lamp—Cosco's invention responds to a baby's cries through a room monitor/light in the form of a stuffed teddy bear. Parents can be alerted through portable receivers. Costs less than $75 at most children's furniture stores.

Note: The book, *Generations*, produced by the Smithsonian Institution, is a universal family album celebrating the customs and costumes of child-rearing worldwide. Published by Pantheon Books, priced at $18.95, paperback.

WHAT TO KNOW

The sheer volume of expert information and common-sense advice on preparing for a baby seems to expand as rapidly as the audience it addresses. The listings of corporations, associations, and hotlines that follow are a mere sampling of the organizations offering some valuable solutions to common parenting concerns. Many are presented as a community service at no, or minimal cost.

CORPORATE PUBLICATIONS

As a community service for new and expectant parents, the following baby product and service companies provide concise guides offering advice on the topics listed. Usually written or endorsed by pediatricians, nurses, and nutritionists, they contain useful consumer tips and insights, and are free.

Aetna Life & Casualty
Corporate Affairs Dept. DA23
151 Farmington Avenue
Hartford, CT 06156

Choosing Child Care
Keeping Danger Out of Reach
Save Your Child from Poisoning

Beech-Nut Nutrition Corp.
Att: Marian Ferreri
P.O. Box 127
Fort Washington, PA 19043

Starting Your Baby on Solid Foods

The William Carter Co.
93 Highland Avenue
Needham Heights, MA 02194

Expert Tips on Your Baby's Layette
Layette and Gift Shopping Guide

The First Years
Consumer Relations Manager
One Kiddie Drive
Avon, MA 02322-1171

Bathing Your Baby
The First Years Guide for New Parents
Working and Caring

Gerber Products Co.
Att: Medical Marketing Services
445 State Street
Fremont, MI 49412

Baby's Book
Feeding Baby
Guidelines—Child Safety
A Handbook of Child Safety
Ingredients—Gerber Baby Foods
Nutrient Values—Gerber Baby Foods
So You've Decided to Breast-Feed You
Baby

H. J. Heinz Co.
Communications Dept.
P.O. Box 57
Pittsburgh, PA 15230-0057

Answering Feeding Questions

The Arrival: It's Not All Peaches and Cream
Bright Start: A Guide to Infant Feeding and Nutrition
Fresh Start: A Guide to Infant Nutrition
Planning Baby's Meals
Planning Meals for the Allergic Infant

Johnson & Johnson Baby Products Co.
Consumer and Professional Services
Grandview Road
Skillman, NJ 08558

Baby Care Basics
Common Sense Care for Baby's Tender Skin
Getting to Know Your Newborn
Guide for the First-Time Baby-Sitter
How Your Baby Grows
Parenting Insights
Touch—The Language of Love

Metropolitan Life Insurance Co.
Health and Safety Educational Division
One Madison Avenue
New York, NY 10010

Child Safety
Dental Care: Questions and Answers
Emergency Medical Card
Fire Safety
First Aid for the Family

Health and Safety Educational Materials Catalog
Immunization: When and Why
Personal Health Record
Planning for Safety
Your Child's Health Care

ASSOCIATIONS

A selected list of associations of interest to parents; several are also listed in the specific areas.

ACTION ON CHILD-CARE CONCERNS

Catalyst
250 Park Avenue South
New York, NY 10003
212-777-8900

The Children's Foundation
1420 New York Avenue, N.W.
Suite 800
Washington, DC 20005
202-347-3300

Congressional Caucus for Women's Issues
2471 Rayburn Bldg.
Washington, DC 20515
202-225-6740

BREAST-FEEDING

La Leche League International (LLLI)
9616 Minneapolis Avenue
Franklin Park, IL 60131
312-455-7730

CHILDBIRTH AND PARENTING EDUCATION

The American Red Cross
National Headquarters
430 17th Street, N.W.
Washington, DC 20006
202-737-8300
(Contact regional/local chapters.)

ASPO/Lamaze (American Society for Psychoprophylaxis in Obstetrics)
1840 Wilson Blvd., Suite 204
Arlington, VA 22201
703-524-7802

Association for Childhood Education International (ACEI)
1141 Georgia Avenue, Suite 200
Wheaton, MD 20902
301-942-2443

International Childbirth Education Association (ICEA)
P.O. Box 20048
Minneapolis, MN 55420
612-854-8660

American College of Obstetricians and Gynecologists (ACOG)
Resource Center
600 Maryland Avenue, S.W., Suite 200
Washington, DC 20024
202-638-0026

COMMUNITY CENTERS

Jewish Welfare Board (JWB)
Program Development
15 E. 26th Street
New York, NY 10010
212-532-4949
(Runs YMHA and YWHA organizations.)

YMCA of the USA
101 N. Wacker
Chicago, IL 60606
800-USA-YMCA
(Contact local chapters first.)

FATHERING

The Fatherhood Project
c/o Bank Street College of Education
610 W. 112th Street
New York, NY 10025
212-663-7200

SAFETY

CHILDREN'S HEALTH & SAFETY

American Academy of Pediatrics (AAP)
141 Northwest Point Blvd.
P.O. Box 927
Elk Grove Village, IL 60007
312-228-5005

National Child Passenger Safety Association (NCPSA)
P.O. Box 65616
Washington, DC 20035
202-293-2270

National Highway Traffic Safety Administration
U.S. Dept. of Transportation
400 Seventh Street, S.W.
Washington, DC 20590
800-424-9393;202-366-5972

National Safety Council
444 N. Michigan Avenue
Chicago, IL 60611-3991
312-527-4800

OBSTETRICAL SAFETY

American Foundation for Maternal and Child Health
439 E. 51st Street
New York, NY 10022
212-759-5510

National Association of Parents and Professionals for Safe Alternatives in Childbirth (NAPSAC)
P.O. Box 646
Marble Hill, MO 63764
314-238-2010

PRODUCT SAFETY

Consumer Federation of America (CFA)
1424 16th Street, N.W., Suite 604
Washington, DC 20036
202-387-6121

U.S. Consumer Product Safety Commission (CPSC)
Bureau of Information & Education
Washington, DC 20207
800-638-2772
(Contact also through regional offices.)

U.S. Food & Drug Administration (FDA)
HFE-88
5600 Fishers Lane
Rockville, MD 20857
301-443-3170

HELPFUL HOTLINES

Hotlines can provide consumer information, advice in times of crisis, and referrals for new and expectant parents—though their assistance, of course, in no way substitutes for professional help, particularly in medical matters. The list that follows is just a selection of available hotlines; others can be reached by consulting AT&T's toll-free directory service at 800-555-1212.

Auto Safety Hotline
National Highway Traffic Safety Administration
U.S. Dept. of Transportation
800-424-9393
8–5, M–F, EST
Information on buying infant car restraints.

Beech-Nut Nutrition Hotline
800-523-6633
9–6, M–F, EST
Answers questions as varied as eating during pregnancy and starting baby on solid foods.

Bright Beginnings Warmline
412-647-4546
9–5, M–F, EST; answering service 5–9 weekdays, 1–5 weekends
Offers nonmedical parent support consultation in times of stress.

Child Care Information Service
National Association for the Education of Young Children
800-424-2460
8:30–4:30, M–F, EST
Provides publications and referrals on child care.

Consumer Product Safety Commission
800-638-CPSC (2772)
10:30–4, M–F, EST
(Teletypewriter for the deaf:
800-638-8270;
in MD, 800-392-8104)
Call to report a product hazard or product-related injury, and/or for information on safeguarding family; safety publications are available.

Gerber Consumer Information Services
800-4-GERBER (443-7237)
9–5, M–F, EST
Information on feeding and caring for babies.

Johnson & Johnson Baby Products Co.
Consumer and Professional Services
800-526-3967
10–4:30, M–F, EST
Information on baby skin care.

La Leche League Hotline
312-455-7730
3 P.M.–8:30 A.M., M–F, CST
Information and area referrals for support in breast-feeding.

Lung Line
National Jewish Center for Immunology and Respiratory Medicine
800-222-LUNG;
in CO 303-398-1477
8:30–5, M–F, MST
Nurses answer questions about respiratory allergies and immunological disorders.

Mothers of Twins Club
505-275-0955
8–5, M–F, MST
Advice and referrals for prospective/actual parents of twins.

National Adoption Hotline
202-328-8072
8:30–6, M–F, EST
For information on adoption and referrals to member agencies.

National Safety Council
312-527-4800
8:30–4:45, M–F, CST
Information on safeguarding your home; many publications available.

Parental Stress Hotlines
There are many regional support and referral services for parents under stress, usually listed in local telephone directories' "crisis intervention" categories.

Parents Without Partners
301-588-9354
9–5, M–F, EST
Support and information on single parenting; referral service.

Poison Control Center Hotline
Almost all states have such facilities, which can be called round the clock every day; check local listings and post them by the telephone, just in case.

Twinline's Warmline
415-644-0863
10–4, M–F, PST
Crisis support and general counseling for multiple-birth families; publications available.

CHILD CARE

Not since the baby boom years have so many couples prepared for a newborn, and found themselves needing the help of caregivers, whether in day-care facilities or in their own homes. The quality and professionalism of child-care facilities are still very variable, but the following are useful sources of information.

The Children's Foundation
815 Fifteenth Street, N.W., Suite 928
Washington, DC 20005
202-347-3300

A national advocacy organization that provides information, training, and organizing help to those concerned with family day care. Offers a broad selection of bulletins, directories, and fact sheets on child care and related legislation.

National Safety Council
PR Dept.—Child Care
444 N. Michigan Avenue
Chicago, IL 60611
312-527-5800

Send a self-addressed, stamped envelope for a free copy of *How to Find the Right Child Care Center*.

National Coalition for Campus Childcare, Inc. (NCCCC)
University of Wisconsin—Milwaukee
P.O. Box 413
Milwaukee, WI 53201
414-229-1122

A national membership organization of campus child-care providers, teachers, administrators, and other supporters.

BOOKS

The Boston Daycare Directory, available from Bob Adams, Inc., 840 Summer Street, Boston, MA 02127 (800-USA-JOBS), for $12.95 plus handling, will soon be followed by similar directories for Chicago, Los Angeles, and New York, from the same house.

Employer-Supported Child Care, available from Auburn House Publishing Company, 14 Dedham Street, Dover, MA 02030 (617-785-2220), $16.95 paperback, $27.95 hardcover.

HELP AT HOME

Chief sources of in-home child care are nannies, who have probably had some professional training (and are expensive), and young, usually inexperienced au-pairs, who live as family members, at modest cost.

Organizations that will put parents in contact with agencies, or suggest actual referrals, include:

American Council of Nanny Schools (ACNS)
Delta College
University Center, MI 48710
517-686-9417

A nonprofit coalition of accredited schools which train, test, and find placement for professionally certified American nannies.

Nanny Academy of America (NAA)
171 Lakeshore Road
Grosse Pointe Farms, MI 48236
313-884-7550

Nannys Unlimited Agency
2300 Peachford Road
Atlanta, GA 30338
404-451-0936

Nanny Concepts & Services, Inc.
110 Morgans Landing Drive
Atlanta, GA 30350
404-399-6186

FOREIGN AU-PAIRS

Cultural exchange programs sponsored by respected organizations match young foreigners as au-pairs for a year with host American families. For brochures and information, contact:

Au Pair in America
American Institute for Foreign Study
    Scholarship Foundation
102 Greenwich Avenue
Greenwich, CT 06830
203-869-9090

AuPair/Homestay USA
Experiment in International Living
1411 K Street NW, Suite 1100
Washington, DC 20005
202-628-7134

SPECIAL PARENTS/ SPECIAL NEEDS

Some available resources for special needs include:

ADOPTION

National Committee for Adoption
1930 Seventeenth Street, N.W.,
Washington, DC 20009-6207
202-638-1200

A lobbying organization that also operates an international clearinghouse on adoption issues, with available information and publications, including an *Adoption Factbook*. Its membership is primarily adoptive parents and state agencies.

DIVORCED/SINGLE PARENTS

Parents Without Partners (PWP)
8807 Colesville Road
Silver Spring, MD 20910
800-638-8078; 301-588-9354

An international, nonprofit membership organization with 800 chapters, devoted to the welfare and interests of single parents and their children. Offers a clearing house of information, advice, and publications, and runs a program called TOTS for single parents with children up to age 6.

Single Mother By Choice
P.O. Box 1642
Gracie Station
New York, NY 10128
212-988-0993

Stepfamily Association of America (SAA)
602 E. Joppa Road
Baltimore, MD 212204
301-823-7570

TWINS OR MORE

Gerber Multiple Birth Program
Gerber Products Company
445 State Street
Fremont, MI 49412
616-928-2744

Eases family adjustment to multiple births with gifts of food, clothing, and other needs (submission of birth certificates required to qualify).

National Organization of Mothers of Twins Club, Inc.
12404 Princess Jeanne, N.E.
Albuquerque, NM 87112
505-275-0955

Free brochure with helpful hints for prospective or actual parents of twins; general information and referrals.

Center for Study of Multiple Birth
333 E. Superior, Suite 476
Chicago, IL 60611
312-266-9093

Twinline
Services for Multiple Birth Families
P.O. Box 10066
Berkeley, CA 94709
415-644-0861

A nonprofit agency offering regular news-letters, survival kits, publications, and classes for parents with twins, triplets, or more.

TRAVELING WITH BABY

Advance planning is crucial to successful travel with a baby. Wise (and, ultimately, happier) parents will invest some time and money in information before launching a trip.

Some helpful resources:

Travel with Your Children
80 Eighth Avenue
New York, NY 10011
212-206-0688

An information center specializing in family travel. Specialized publications on sea cruises, skiing vacations, etc., and a newsletter, *Family Travel Times*, published 10 times a year ($35.00). A sample issue is available for $1.00 (to cover postage and handling).

Getaways: Family Vacations
P.O. Box 11511
Washington, DC 20008
703-534-8747

A new family travel newsletter published quarterly ($20.00).

Families Welcome
 1416 Second Avenue
 New York, NY 10021
 212-861-2500

A travel service designed by and for parents, to make family vacations much more fun; offers a free brochure.

Families on the Go
 1259 El Camino Real
 Menlo Park, CA 94025
 415-322-4203

Offers a catalog featuring travel and activity books.

Club Med
 3 E. 54th Street
 New York, NY 10022
 800-CLUB-MED

Known for attracting singles to its fixed-price all-inclusive vacation resorts, Club Med has actually become a leader in family vacations by adding "baby clubs" for infants (4–23 months) and "mini-clubs" for ages 2 to 11.

Adventure Express: Rascals in Paradise
 185 Berry Street, Suite 5503
 San Francisco, CA 94107
 800-443-0799

A free brochure describes vacation tours to such exotic spots as Fiji, Nepal, and Belize. Tours also feature qualified babysitters for infants and accompanying "teachers" for preschoolers.

Premiere Cruise Lines
 101 George King Blvd.
 Cape Canaveral, FL 32920
 407-783-5061

Arranges packaged cruises to the Bahamas combined with visits to Walt Disney World. Babysitting is available for infants and organized activities for children from 2 upward.

OTHER OPTIONS

Home exchanges are another possible way to travel. Contact:

International House Exchange Service
 P.O. Box 3975
 San Francisco, CA 94119
 415-436-3497

Note: Many community-based parents' newspapers provide ideas for weekend excursions to nearby spots and day-long activities and events taking place closer to home.

LOCAL COMMUNITY RESOURCES

As the trimesters turn into months and days, preparation for parenthood involves classes and other active ways of making ready for the new baby. It is time to turn to pediatricians as well as obstetricians for advice, and to explore some of the many other resources each community has to offer.

THE HOSPITAL

A hospital these days is far more than a mere baby delivery station. Most have extended their role to provide a wide variety of programs for expectant and new parents. Many offer birth preparation courses, backed by free publications of all kinds on breast-feeding, baby health, and nutrition, along with informal support groups. Others sponsor seminars on child development and even pre-and post-pregnancy exercise classes.

Common to all hospitals, however, is the custom of dispatching new families home with gift packs filled with product samples and manufacturers' coupons. Such kits are big business, it seems; from 18 to 35 percent of consumers switch brands after trying a gift-pack sample. Hospitals, too, hope to establish some future brand-name loyalty.

THE DOCTOR'S OFFICE

Doctors' visits can yield more than the reassurance of regular checkups or advice on specific concerns. There are often pamphlets, guides, and product samples in the waiting room that cannot be found elsewhere, and doctors, in a sense, endorse them by displaying them. A selection of booklets that could be helpful:

PROCTER & GAMBLE

*Expectant Parents' Information Kit Baby
 Care Guidelines for New Parents
Tender Loving Skin Care—A Guide to Infant Skin Care and Skin Conditions
What Every Parent Should Know
Catalog*, which lists other publications to
 send for.

PARENTING ADVISOR

*Milestones of Infant Development
Why Do I Feel So Guilty?*

Self-Protection Lessons for Your Child
A Guide to Child Health Hotlines
How to Handle Home Emergencies
How to Plan a Great Party
Toilet Training Basics

THE LIBRARY

❧

The local library is an excellent general resource to become familiar with before a new baby makes getting around more complicated. Working parents should also be aware that many libraries have extended evening hours and are open on weekends.

Besides offering books, magazines, newsletters, videos on parenting and baby care, and a variety of consumer guides, most libraries have bulletin boards listing a wealth of community events of interest to parents. Story-telling hours for toddlers are common, and some libraries have introduced weekly playgroups and activities parents and children can do together.

A program of particular note is New York's Early Childhood Resource and Information Center. Started in 1972 as an outgrowth of the New York Public Library System, it offers parents, caregivers, and teachers workshops and seminars as well as the opportunity to learn and interact with their young counterparts through a unique resource, the Family Room. Ms. Hannah Nuba, its founder/director, is also prepared to advise about setting up similar programs in other communities. For information, contact:

Early Childhood Resource and
Information Center
New York Public Library
66 Leroy Street
New York, NY 10014
212-929-0815

Another innovative activity is the "Lapsit" reading program offered by the San Francisco Public Library at several of its branches specifically for parents with children from 6 months to 3 years old. The program involves some 20 to 30 minutes of storytime, finger games, and songs. For information, contact:

The San Francisco Public Library
Main Children's Room
Civic Center
San Francisco, CA 94102
415-558-3510

THE COMMUNITY

❧

Neighborhood organizations come in all shapes, sizes, and religious affiliations. All are reaching out to meet the changing needs of the communities they serve. Some children's museums and theater groups, like the Boston Children's Museum, for example, are luring new and expectant parents to their doors with child development resource centers.

Relying on word-of-mouth is one way of locating appropriate organizations; another is by checking the telephone book, local newspaper, or community newsletter.

COMMUNITY CENTERS

Aside from parks and playgroups, community centers are the chief places where families can meet and interact. Here, they can take exercise, childbirth preparation, or safety prevention classes, participate in workshops, exchange ideas, even laugh with others over child-rearing concerns. Many centers also offer supervised programs where toddlers can play with others their own age. Frequently, neighborhood events are posted on their bulletin boards, along with babysitting services and consumer safety tips.

PROGRAMS WITH RELIGIOUS AFFILIATIONS

Religious community-based programs vary widely, reflecting the needs and composition of the community they serve. Some chapters actively administer child-care and playgroup programs together with religious instruction and parents' support groups. Others simply rent out space to families setting up parenting centers.

The agenda prepared by the Union of American Hebrew Congregations offers helpful and instructive advice to parents, regardless of denomination, who are organizing their own centers. To obtain a free copy of *Jewish Parenting Centers: Setting the Agenda*, write to:

Union of American Hebrew Congregations
838 Fifth Avenue
New York, NY 10021.

THE "Y" ORGANIZATIONS

Jewish Welfare Board (JWB)
Program Development
15 E. 26th Street
New York, NY 10010
212-532-4949

This is the central organization that runs the local YMHA and YWHA programs.

YMCA of the USA
101 N. Wacker
Chicago, IL 60606
800-USA-YMCA

The local chapters provide instruction in safety, child development, fitness, family communications, and parenting. Some may offer curricula with a religious orientation, but all attempt to serve the needs of their immediate community. Families having difficulty in locating their local chapter should contact the Metro "Y" in the nearest major city.

CLASSES TO TAKE

❧

ON CHILDBIRTH

There are at least 21 different ways of having a baby these days. Most methods focus on educating and preparing the couple to go through the great event together. Some emphasize physical exercise, others the spiritual aspects. Parents will decide for themselves, after talking to their doctors and to family and friends with experience.

A very helpful resource for descriptions of the various methods is *The Maternity Sourcebook: 230 Basic Decisions for Pregnancy, Birth and Baby Care*, by Matthew and Wendy Lesko (New York: Warner Books, 1984).

Despite the competition, Lamaze remains the most popular method of giving birth. For complete information, contact:

ASPO/Lamaze (American Society for Psychoprophylaxis in Obstetrics)
1840 Wilson Blvd., Suite 204
Arlington, VA 22201
800-368-4404;
in VA, 703-524-7802
Membership cost: $15.00

ASPO/Lamaze issues a wide range of publications, including newsletters and a bimonthly magazine, and sponsors seminars on parenting issues as well as postpartum get-togethers for mothers and babies. In Lamaze classes, expectant parents learn labor and delivery procedures.

ON PARENTING

Classes in parenthood preparation and childhood safety are offered by local and regional chapters of the American Red Cross. For information, contact:

The American Red Cross
National Headquarters
430 17th Street, N.W.
Washington, DC 20006
202-737-8300

Local chapters differ in the variety and number of classes offered; all, however, provide pamphlets and publications on health and safety concerns.

MEDIA RESOURCES FOR NEW PARENTS

Pickings are irregular, at best, when it comes to finding programs on television or radio, but home videos will more than compensate, covering just about all aspects of parenting, from childbirth to breast-feeding to safety instructions to dramatizations and case studies of what lies ahead in child rearing.

TELEVISION AND RADIO

TELEVISION PROGRAMS

Though the Public Broadcasting System named 1988 The Year of the Child, parents seeking televised advice on parenting skills will be sorely disappointed unless they have cable or wake up *very* early. Early-morning news shows regularly report on lifestyle trends and baby business products, leaving advice to periodic short question-and-answer segments with well-known pediatricians or child development specialists. Afternoon shows tend to discuss more sensational family issues.

Lifetime, a national cable system geared generally toward a female audience and specifically to new mothers, offers some regular half-hour programs:

- "What Every Baby Knows," moderated by Dr. T. Berry Brazelton.
- "Mother's Day," hosted by Joan Lunden.
- "Working Mother," with Cyndy Garvey.

The **Nickelodeon** cable channel is devoted entirely to programming for older children.

Action for Children's Television (ACT)—*The* authority on children's viewing, which publishes books, newsletters, and educational materials to make TV a positive educational tool for young ones. Contact this helpful resource at:
20 University Road
Cambridge, MA 02138
617-876-6620

NATIONAL RADIO SHOWS

Radio talk and call-in shows often air for 30 minutes to an hour on the weekend. Resident child psychologists and other experts are interviewed or answer questions called in by listeners.

- On National Public Radio: "The Children's Journal with Bobbi Connor," sponsored by Gerber Products Co., is an hour-long call-in program for parents on topics ranging from discipline and coping with divorce to helping children live creatively.
- On WABC's "Dr. Lawrence Balter," Dr. Balter answers parents' questions about raising children and practicing discipline through intervention and example setting.
- On CBS radio stations news service: "In the Learning Center," with host Dr. Lonnie Carton, gives 90-second responses or comments on listener questions about child rearing.

A VIDEO GUIDE

Today, videos inform and instruct parents on every aspect of parenting preparation and child rearing in the privacy of their homes. Advice usually comes from such authorities as Drs. Spock and Brazelton, while creative parenting tips and pregnancy exercise programs are hosted by big-screen celebrities such as Beau Bridges, Marie Osmond, and Jane Fonda.

VIDEOS WORTH VIEWING

PARENTING GUIDELINES

"What Every Baby Knows"—A series of four videos moderated by T. Berry Brazelton on pregnancy ($14.95), newborns ($14.95), fathering ($9.95), and toddlers ($12.95), covers the basics in an interesting, homespun fashion.

"Caring for Your Newborn with Dr. Benjamin Spock"—Dr. Spock demonstrates everything from bathing the baby to treating early discomforts while giving advice and guidance. $29.95.

"Creative Parenting: The First Twelve Months"—Host Beau Bridges offers explanations of the stages of baby development and advice on developing parenting styles. $29.95.

"Baby Basics"—Meant for first-time parents, this includes such topics as feeding, baby's sleeping and crying, general health, growth, and the sort of sound advice an older mother might provide. $39.95 plus shipping charges; call Karol Video at 800-526-4773.

SAFETY AND PREVENTION

"The Baby-Safe Home"—Host and noted consumer activist David Horowitz guides parents on accident prevention tips in the home. $29.95.

"Baby Alive"—A 65-minute video (with accompanying book) that teaches emergency CPR, the Heimlich Maneuver, aid for cuts and burns, as well as step-by-step guidance on child-proofing the home. $39.95 plus shipping charges; call 800-328-6700 or write to:

Box 1160
Salt Lake
UT 84110

EXERCISE

"Jane Fonda's Workout for Pregnancy, Birth and Recovery"—A complete fitness program for pregnant women from conception to recovery. $39.95.

"The ACOG (American College of Obstetricians and Gynecologists) Pregnancy Exercise Program"—With an introduction by Dr. Art Ulene, this exercise video is geared toward moderate exercise during all stages of pregnancy. $39.95.

BREAST-FEEDING

"Breast-Feeding Your Baby—A Mother's Guide"—A live demonstration video covering all the major aspects of breast-feeding. $30.00.

RESOURCES FOR CHOOSING CHILDREN'S VIDEOS

Sources of information (and actual videocassettes) include the following:

The Knowledge Collection
2611 Garden Road
Monterey, CA 93940
800-345-1441

Offers a catalog ($8.95) of over 6,000 educational, informational and instructional videocassettes which may be purchased or simply rented by mail with a $45 membership.

Children's Circle Home Video
CC Studios
Weston, CT 06883
800-243-5020;
 in CT, 213-222-0002

Produces faithful video adaptations of favorite children's books for children from ages 2 to 8.

Parents' Choice Foundation
Box 185
Newton, MA 02168
617-965-5913

Publishes a review (*Parents' Choice*) of children's media: books, television, movies, music, and home video cassettes.

BOOKS

A Parent's Guide to Video and Audio Cassettes for Children, by Andrea E. Cascardi (New York: Warner Books, 1987).

Video Movie Guide for Kids—A Book for Parents, by Mick Martin, Marsha Porter, and Ed Remitz (New York: Ballantine Books, 1987).

The Video Sourcebook, 10th edition, just published, costs $199, but is worth consulting at or acquiring for a local library. It is a veritable encyclopedia with descriptions of videos on every conceivable subject, along with complete information on where to obtain them. Contact:

The National Video Clearinghouse
c/o Gale Research
Book Tower
Dept. 77748
Detroit, MI 48277-0748

BOOKS FOR BABY

The concept of the baby book club is a relatively recent outgrowth of existing adult clubs. They provide mail-order convenience at prices that are significantly cheaper than in most retail bookstores. Those listed below offer reading selections that correspond to the baby's age.

Books of My Very Own
Division of Book-of-the-Month Club
Camp Hill, PA 17011-9901
800-233-1066

Book club for infants and children, featuring age-appropriate selections. Introductory offers of 4 books with a poncho: $22.95.

Children's Choice
Scholastic Book Service
P.O. Box 984
Education Plaza
Hicksville, NY 11802
516-433-3800

Children's classics tailored to children age 2 onward. After the introductory offer, parents receive 2 book choices every 6 weeks.

Parents Magazine Read Aloud Book Club
1 Parents Circle
Des Moines, IA 50380-0845
515-284-3520

Award-winning books produced by Parents Magazine Press, designed for reading aloud to children age 2 upward. Introductory offers of 2 books at $3.95 (plus handling charges) are followed by additional 2-book shipments, along with a parents' newsletter and child's activity sheet relating each month's selections.

ON A DIFFERENT NOTE

Some sing, some hum, some simply put the audience to sleep—faster than before. Devices that can distract an infant from crying or lull a tired child to sleep are far from essential, but they *might* help:

Sleeptight, Inc.—A patented medical vibration-and-sound unit that simulates a car driving at 55 mph, costs $69.95. Information from:
SleepTime, Inc.
3613 Mueller Road
St. Charles, MO 63301
800-325-3550;
in MO, 314-946-5115

Playskool's Sleeping Sounds™—This device emits recorded sounds of mother's heartbeat from within the womb, can be attached to the crib side or any flat surface, and shuts off after 20 minutes. Retails for about $20.99 and is widely available.

Sound Starter—A recent addition to Century Products' long list of voice-activated products. This battery-operated swing rocks into action with the first pout or coo of its tiny passenger, and retails for about $64.95. Information from:

Century Products Consumer Service Dept.
1600 Valley View Road
Macedonia, OH 44056
216-468-2000

RECORDS AND CASSETTES

A short list of sources for these more traditional ways of entertaining baby.

Children's Book & Music Center
2500 Santa Monica Blvd.
Santa Monica, CA 90404
800-443-1856;
in CA, 213-829-0215
9–5:30, M–S, PST

With more than 20,000 titles in its catalog, this is the largest such store in the country. Parents can also call a *Dial Songline* (213-385-5312), press a button corresponding to area code and baby's age, then hear 5 different song selections.

Baby Go To Sleep Products
P.O. Box 1332
Florence, AL 35631
800-537-7748

Offers a free 12-page catalog of bedtime stories and sleeping tapes ($12.95 each), which include a mother's-heartbeat tape with a money-back guarantee.

Marlboro Records
845 Marlboro Spring Road
Kennett Square, PA 191348
215-444-1995

Offers award-winning children's records and cassettes by acclaimed singer/songwriter Kevin Roth.

A SELECTION OF POPULAR SONGS AND STORIES

Laurie Sale, owner of Children's Book & Music Center, highly recommends the following:
- *Lullabies for Little Dreamers*, by Kevin Roth
- *Lullabies Go Jazz*, by Jon Crosse
- *Lullaby Magic (I and II)*
- *Babysong*, by Hap Palmer
- *Why, Oh Why?* and *Songs to Grow On, Vol. I*, by Woody Guthrie
- *Music for 1's and 2's*, by Tom Glazer

- *Everything Grows*, by Raffi
- *American Folksongs for Children* and *Birds, Beasts, Bugs and Bigger Fish*, by Pete Seeger
- *Sound Songs*, by Dan Crow
- *Elephant Show Record* and *Stay Tuned*, by Sharon, Lois and Bram

TAKE A PICTURE

With nearly 30 years of experience and more than 800 studios in the U.S. and Canada, Sears Portrait Studios have developed a reputation as *the* specialists in baby and child photography and offer parents a free Children's Portrait Planner, with suggestions on clothing colors and styles that look good and tips on what to bring with the baby to the studio.

Sears studios provide a variety of portrait packages at prices starting from $9.95, in addition to special holiday offers. No appointments are necessary; parents register upon arrival and are told when to return. Sessions vary in length, but generally last only long enough for the photographer to take 6 different poses. If customers are not satisfied with the finished portraits, the studio photographer will take another round of photographs at no additional charge.

Contact the local Sears' studio for additional information.

DATES TO REMEMBER

As they rejoice over their baby's entry into the family fold, new parents have some important dates to mark on the calendar:
- Mother's Day—the second Sunday in May
- Father's Day—the third Sunday in June
- Grandparents' Day—the second Sunday in September

And, of course, Baby's First Birthday. . . .

ACKNOWLEDGMENTS AND CREDITS

ACKNOWLEDGMENTS

The editors wish to express their appreciation to the following: The New York Public Library—General Research Division, Microforms Division and Rare Books and Manuscript Division; Mid-Manhattan Branch and the New York Public Library Picture Collection; Library of the Performing Arts at Lincoln Center; Hannah Nuba, Early Childhood Resource and Information Center. Library of Congress Picture Collection. Henry Clay Frick Art Reference Library. Elizabeth Argo, The Pierpont Morgan Library. The Lexington (KY) Public Libraries.

Janey Fire and Karla Friedlich, Museum of American Folk Art; The American Museum of Natural History; Ann Dorfsman, The Cooper-Hewitt Museum; Bea Snyder, The Hancock Shaker Village; The Jewish Museum, New York; Mary Doherty, The Metropolitan Museum of Art; Kimberly Fink, The Metropolitan Museum of Art Costume Institute; Ira Bartfield, Coordinator of Photography, National Gallery of Art, Washington.

Shmuel Bernham and Jeffrey Rubinstein, Jewish Theological Seminary, New York; Union Theological Seminary; The Catholic Archdiocese of New York.

Bonpoint, New York City; Steven Feinberg, Crane & Compay, Inc.; Janet Cabot, Hill and Knowlton, Inc. for Gerber Products Company; Evelyn Boykan, Gymboree Corporation; Lawrence A. Bilotti, Publicity Manager, Laura Ashley, Inc.; Jonathan K. James, Burson Marsteller for Pampers; Jane Borthwick, President, D. Porthault & Company; Elaine Velaochaga, Publicity, Tiffany & Company; Mary Sue Hartman, Media Resource Librarian, United Airlines.

Professor Leonard Ashley, American Name Society; Allyn Rice Bloeme, Public Relations, Traphagen School of Fashion; Frank O. Brayard; Barbara Campbell and Holly Ann, Barbara Campbell Studio; Mary Dauman; Margaret Gale; Katharine Goodbody; Martha S. Leopardo; Nina Fletcher Little; Brook Mason, Senior Editor, *Child*; Katherine L. McEnderfer, ASPO/ LAMAZE; Bill Miller, Jr.; The 92nd Street Y (YM and YWHA), New York; Bobbie Pascaw, Editor, *Maternity Matters*; Sheila Sheridan, Monkmeyer Press; Kathy Simon, M.I.T. Child Care Office; Erika Stone; Nancy Thomas, Nancy Thomas Studio Gallery; Verdi; Christopher Woodworth-Lynas.

p 13—Isadora Duncan, *My Life*, taken from *The Baby Reader*, edited by Marie Winn, Simon and Schuster, New York, NY. Copyright © 1973 by Marie Winn.

p 15—"The Model Father," by Frederick L. Allen, excerpted from *Harper's Magazine*, January 1923. Copyright © 1922 by Harper's Magazine. Reprinted by special permission.

p 19—"The Model Son," by Frederick L. Allen, excerpted from *Harper's Magazine*, November 1923. Copyright © 1923 by Harper's Magazine. Reprinted by special permission.

p 75—"Naming Names," by Bernard Kalb, from *Esquire*, September 1984. Copyright © 1984. Reprinted by permission of Bernard Kalb and *Esquire*.

p 88—"Circumcision: The Symbolic Wound," and "A Widespread Ritual," adapted from "Symbolic Wound," by Melvin Konner, M.D. Copyright © 1988 by The New York Times Company. Reprinted by permission.

p 101—"The Wee One's Laundry," from *Good Housekeeping*, April 1918. Courtesy *Good Housekeeping*, a publication of Hearst Magazines, a division of The Hearst Corporation.

p 114—"Tale of a Grandfather," excerpted from an essay by Robert L. Raymond, *The Atlantic Monthly*, January 1932. Copyright © 1932.

p 118—"Advice to Those Visiting a Baby," by Christopher Morley from *The Baby Reader*, edited by Marie Winn, Simon and Schuster, New York, NY. Copyright © 1973 by Marie Winn.

p 120—"The Options," quoted from *Mother Care/Other Care* by Sandra Scarr, Basic Books, New York, NY. Copyright © 1984 by Basic Books, Inc. Reprinted by permission of Basic Books, Inc.

p 124—Kay Thompson, *Eloise*, Simon and Schuster. Copyright © 1955, 1983.

p 124—"The Children's Nurse and Her Duties," from *Harper's Bazaar*, September 1909. Copyright © 1909, The Hearst Corporation. Courtesy of *Harper's Bazaar*.

p 130—"Baby-Sitter to a Nation," excerpted from an article by Kenneth Englade in *Continental*, February 1988. Copyright © 1988.

p 140—"A Treatise of the Management of Female Complaints and of Children in Early Infancy," by Alexander Hamilton, M.D. Reprinted by permission of Rare Books and Manuscripts Division, The New York Public Library, Astor, Lenox and Tilden Foundations.

p 143—"The Experience of Touch," from "The Experience of Touch: Research Points to a Critical Role" by Daniel Goleman, *The New York Times*, February 2, 1988. Copyright © 1988 by The New York Times Company. Reprinted by permission.

p 144—Chart of Famous Women Who Breast-Fed Their Babies excerpted from *The Book of Lists #2* by Irving Wallace and David Wallechinsky, William Morrow & Company, Inc. Copyright © 1980.

p 146—"Warfare at the Supermarket," excerpted from "Life in the 30's," by Anna Quindlen, *The New York Times*, April 8, 1987. Copyright © 1987 by The New York Times Company. Reprinted by permission.

p 150—"How A Baby Becomes A Mummy," taken from *The Mechanical Baby*, by Daniel Beekman, Lawrence Hill Books. Copyright © 1977.

p 160—"Baby Talk," from the research of E.H. Lenneberg, *Biological Foundations of Language*, John Wiley & Sons, New York, NY. Copyright © 1967.

p 162—"Body Talk," adapted from Edward Tronick's *Small Talk*, Procter and Gamble. Copyright © 1987.

p 163—"Did He Have Postage?" Sheila and Joseph Perino excerpted from *Parenting the Gifted*, R.R. Bowker, New York, NY. Copyright © 1981.

p 164—"A New Image of Mom," by Dave Barry from *Dave Barry's Greatest Hits*, Crown Publishers, Inc. Copyright © 1988.

p 166—Language Chart from Hall & Skinner, *Somewhere to Turn*. Courtesy of Teachers College Press, Columbia University, New York, NY.

p 167—"Parents As Teachers," Sidney Ledson excerpted from *Raising Brighter Children*, Walker and Company, 1987. Copyright © 1987 by Sidney Ledson. Reprinted by permission of Walker and Company.

p 187—"Sing Along," adapted from D. Linda Kelley and Brian Sutton-Smith, "Infant Musical Productivity," in J. Craig Peery, et al., *Music and Child Development*, Springer-Verlag. Copyright © 1987. Reprinted by permission of Springer-Verlag.

p 190—"Arthur's Alphabet," Aunt Mavor's Toy Books, London: Routledge, Warne & Routledge, 1877, taken from *100 Nineteenth Century Rhyming Alphabets in English*, from the Library of Ruth M. Baldwin. Southern Illinois University Press, Carbondale and Edwardsville. Feffer & Simon, Inc., London and Amsterdam. Copyright © 1972 Southern Illinois University Press. Reprinted by permission of Southern Illinois University Press.

p 192—Quotations from Benjamin Spock, M.D., excerpted from *Baby and Child Care*, Pocket Books, 1976. Copyright © 1945, 1946, 1957, 1968, 1976 by Benjamin Spock, M.D. Reprinted by permission of Pocket Books, a division of Simon and Schuster, Inc. Excerpted also from *Raising Children in*

Difficult Times, W.W. Norton & Company, Inc. Copyright © 1974.

p 192—Quotations from William Sears, M.D., excerpted from *Creative Parenting: How to Use the Concept of Attachment Parenting to Raise Children Successfully from Birth to Adolescence*, Dodd Mead & Company. Copyright © 1987.

p 193—Quotations from Selma Fraiberg excerpted from *The Magic Years*. Copyright © 1959 Selma H. Fraiberg; copyright renewed.Reprinted with permission of Charles Scribner's Sons, an imprint of Macmillan Publishing Company.

p 194—Quotations from Burton L. White excerpted from *The First Three Years of Life*, The Revised Edition.

Copyright © 1985. Reprinted by permission of the publisher, Prentice Hall Press, New York.

p 194—Quotations from Penelope Leach excerpted from *Your Baby and Child: From Birth To Age Five*. Copyright © 1977, 1978 by Dorling Kindersley Ltd., London. Text Copyright © 1977, 1978 by Penelope Leach. Reprinted by permission of Alfred A. Knopf, Inc.

p 194—"Copy," by Richard Armour from *Small Beginnings: Things People Say About Babies* by Nanette Newman. Copyright © 1987 by Bryan Forbes Limited. Used by permission of Crown Publishers, Inc.

p 195—Quotations from Stanley Greenspan, M.D., and Nancy Thorndike

Greenspan excerpted from *First Feelings: Milestones in the Emotional Development of Your Baby and Child*. Copyright © 1985 by Stanley and Nancy Thorndike Greenspan. All rights reserved. Reprinted by permission of Viking Penguin Inc.

p 195—Quotations from T. Berry Brazelton, M.D., excerpted from *Doctor and Child*. Copyright © 1976 by T. Berry Brazelton. Reprinted by permission of Delacorte Press/Seymour Lawrence, | division of Bantam, Doubleday, Dell Publishing Group, Inc. Excerpted also from *To Listen to a Child, Understanding the Normal Problems of Growing Up*, Addison-Wesley Publishing Co. Copyright © 1984.

PICTURE CREDITS

pp. 8, 12 Barbara Campbell 13 Top: Peter Menzel—Stock, Boston; bottom: Sybil Shelton—Monkmeyer Press 14 Taurus Photo 15 Top: H. Armstrong Roberts; bottom: Shirley Zeiberg—Taurus Photo 16 Monkmeyer Press 17 Top: Erika Stone; bottom: Paul Conklin—Monkmeyer Press 18 Jean-Claude Lejeune—Stock, Boston 19 Erika Stone 22 Left: The Bettmann Archive; right: Franklin D. Roosevelt Library 23 Top: AP/Wide World Photos; bottom: Globe Photos 24 The Bettmann Archive 25 Left: The Bettmann Archive; right: AP/Wide World Photos 26 Top: Globe Photos; bottom: AP/Wide World Photos 27 The Bettmann Archive 33 Art Resource 44–45 From: *The Mode in Costume*, by R. Turner Wilcox, published by Charles Scribners' Sons © 1958 46 Courtesy Ethel Traphagen Leigh Memorial Research Library at the Traphagen School of Fashion 47 © Sevenarts Limited, London 52 Courtesy of Verdi 54 Top:

Nancy Durrell McKenna—Photo Researchers, Inc.; bottom: David Madison—Focus on Sports 55 Rameshwar Das—Monkmeyer Press 56 Top: Phil Roach—Photoreporters; bottom: Allan S. Adler—Photoreporters 57 Phil Roach—Photoreporters 58 Top: Courtesy Hallmark Cards, Inc.; bottom: Chester Higgins, Jr.—*The New York Times* 59 Michael Tweed—*The New York Times* 60–61 Illustrations by Ann Shirazi 62–65 The National Library of Medicine, Bethesda, Maryland 66–67 Anthony Accardi 71 Cartoon by Mort Gerberg 76–77 The Library of Congress 78 Courtesy Crane & Company 79 Bottom right: Andrea Lang; all others: Courtesy Crane & Company 83 Erika Stone 84 Top: The Bettmann Archive/BBC Hulton 86–87 Art Resource 88 The Jewish Museum, New York 89 The Jewish Encyclopedia, 1905 95 Courtesy Bonpoint, 1269 Madison Avenue, New York, NY 97

The Hancock Shaker Village, Inc. 99 Courtesy Laura Ashley, Inc. 100 Ann Hagen Griffiths—Omni-Photo Communications, Inc. 101 Burton Berinsky 102–103 The Bettmann Archive 106 The Library of Congress 107 David Strickler—Monkmeyer Press 108 Top: The Library of Congress; bottom: Stock, Boston 109 Burton Berinsky 110 Top: Shepard Coleman; bottom: H. Armstrong Roberts 113 Erika Stone 114 Shirley Zeiberg—Taurus Photo 115 Hunter Thomas 116–117 Marilyn M. Pfaltz—Taurus Photo 120–125 Erika Stone 126–127 The Bettmann Archive 128 Erika Stone 129 Top: Erika Stone; bottom: © 1952 *The New Yorker* magazine 130 Eve Arnold—Magnum 132 Drawing by Modell; © 1973 *The New Yorker* magazine 133 From: *Centuries of Childhood: A Social History of Family Life*, by Philippe Aries, published by Vintage Books,© 1962 136 World Book

Encyclopedia 137 Stephen Green-Armytage—The Stock Market 138 Stock, Boston 139–140 H. Armstrong Roberts 141 Joan Teasdale—The Stock Market 142 Doris Pinney—Monkmeyer Press 143 Erika Stone 144 From: *Dream Babies: Three Centuries of Good Advice on Child Care*, by Christina Hardyment, published by Harper & Row, © 1983 145 H. Armstrong Roberts 146 Cartoon by Mort Gerberg 147 The Library of Congress 149 Erika Stone 150 The Bettmann Archive 151 William Acheson—Courtesy Gymboree Corporation 154 Monkmeyer Press 155 Cartoon by Mort Gerberg 156 Erika Stone 157 George Goodwin—Monkmeyer Press 158 Top: H. Armstrong Roberts; bottom: Erika Stone 159 Suzie Fitzhugh—Stock, Boston 160 Cartoon by Mort Gerberg 161 Hugh Rogers—Monkmeyer Press 162 Stock, Boston 163 Top: Alan Cederstrom—Photo Resources; bottom: Harold Naideau—The Stock Market 165 H. Armstrong Roberts 166 Cartoon by Mort Gerberg 167 Courtesy Mueller, Jordan and Weiss 168 Cartoon by Mort Gerberg 169 Erika Stone 170 The Bettmann Archive 174–175 Schecter Lee—Esto Photographics 176 Goat on Wheels, Unknown Odd Fellows, Waterloo, Iowa; Leather, horn, cotton, silk, painted metal; 1890–1900; 53x36¾x62½ inches long; Collection of the Museum of American Folk Art; Gift of Thomas J. and Janyce E. McMenamin 177 Schecter Lee—Esto Photographics 178 Top: From: *Pageant of Toys*, by Mary Hillier, published by Taplinger Publishing Co., © 1965; bottom: Schecter Lee—Esto Photographics 179 Girl reaching for doll seated in Windsor armchair, Helene von Streker Nyce, Warren County, New Jersey; Scissor cut paper; 1904–1924; Image: 4⅜x3⅞ inches, Sheet: 5⅞x6⅛ inches; Collection of the Museum of American Folk Art; Gift of Andrew Nyce 180 Erika Stone 181 Top left: Child sliding down banister, within floral border, Helene von Streker Nyce; Collingswood, New Jersey; Scissor cut paper; 1905; 5⅞x5⅞ inches; Collection of the Museum of American Folk Art; bottom left: Boy on tricycle with girl reaching to unlock door, Helene von Streker Nyce, Warren County, New Jersey; Scissor cut paper; 1904–1924; Image: 4⅜x3⅞ inches, Sheet: 5⅞x6⅛ inches; Collection of the Museum of American Folk Art; Gift of Andrew Nyce; right: Erika Stone 188 Elizabeth Crews—Stock, Boston 189 Seated girl reading to her dolls, with iron and ironing table, Helene von Streker Nyce, Warren County, New Jersey; Scissor cut paper; 1904–1924; Image 3⅝x5½ inches, Sheet: 7 × 7⅞ inches; Collection of the Museum of American Folk Art; Gift of Andrew Nyce 192–197 Illustrations by Judy Clifford from her book on drawing your baby, forthcoming from Watson-Guptill Publications, Spring 1990 200 Culver Pictures 201 Top: The Bettmann Archive; bottom: Cartoon by Mort Gerberg 202 Stock, Boston 203 Jerry Howard—Stock, Boston 204 William Strode—Woodfin Camp & Associates 205 Left: Elihu Blotnick—Omni-Photo Communications, Inc; right: Culver Pictures, Inc. 206 Frank O. Braynard Collection 209 Peter Rosendale—United Airlines 213–217 Barbara Campbell 218 The Bettmann Archive 219 Barbara Campbell 223–231 Erika Stone 252 Michael Weisbrot—Stock, Boston

INDEX